HEMINGWAY

In Our Time

Edited by
Richard Astro and Jackson J. Benson
with an introduction by Jackson J. Benson

Corvallis:
Oregon State University Press

Library of Congress Cataloging in Publication Data

Hemingway in our time.

"Published record of a literary conference devoted
to a study of the work of Ernest Hemingway held at
Oregon State University on April 26-27, 1973."

Includes bibliographical references.

1. Hemingway, Ernest, 1899-1961—Addresses,
essays, lectures. I. Astro, Richard, ed.
II. Benson, Jackson J., ed.
PS3515.E37Z618   813'.5'2   73-18428
ISBN 0-87071-445-7
© 1974   Oregon State University Press

PREFACE

HEMINGWAY IN OUR TIME is the published record of a literary conference devoted to a study of the work of Ernest Hemingway held at Oregon State University on April 26-27, 1973. In most cases, the articles are printed here exactly as they were delivered at the Oregon State conference. On occasion, minor revisions have been made for the purpose of converting papers intended for oral delivery to essays for a reading audience.

Even a cursory look at university library holdings in American literature reveals the fact that there has been a recent explosion in Hemingway criticism. More than a dozen full-length critical and biographical studies have appeared in the last decade, and the scholarly journals continue to publish so many articles on various facets of the novelist's work that little of Hemingway's iceberg remains intact. Accordingly, the editors of this volume concluded that another book of Hemingway criticism was warranted only if it explored entirely new vistas, new points of view. The title *Hemingway in Our Time* dictated the book's contents; the essays focus on the novelist's literary reputation, on his late and posthumous works, and on his influence on contemporary fiction. Additionally, the selections in *Hemingway in Our Time* have been chosen because they are based on the premise that worthwhile literary criticism should motivate rather than undermine discussion. These essays raise provocative new theories, new perspectives; they raise as many issues as they answer in the hope of stimulating others to think and talk about Hemingway's work. The result is a volume with a new approach to Hemingway studies which will broaden rather than constrict future assessments of the Hemingway canon.

I would like to express my sincere thanks to President Robert MacVicar, Dean Stuart Knapp, and Dr. Robert Phillips of the Executive Office of Oregon State University, to the University Lectures and Convocations Committee, and to Dean Gordon Gilkey of the College of Liberal Arts and Dr. Walter Foreman, Chairman of the Department of English, without whose generous and unquestioning support there would be no book at all. I also want to express my deep sense of gratitude to my colleague and the co-director of the Oregon State conference, Dr. Jackson J. Benson of the California State University at San Diego. Special thanks are due Profs. Robert Frank and Willard Potts of Oregon State University and Glen Love of the University of Oregon who helped insure the success of the Oregon State conference, and to Peter Copek who drove. Thanks are also due my typist, Marilyn Barton, and Sharon Springer, Secretary of the Department of English. To Dr. J. Kenneth Munford, Thomas T. France, Shirley Hill, and Marilyn Holsinger, my thanks for making the publication process so painless. Finally, I want to thank my wife, Betty, who commented and criticized, read, proofread, and indexed. The success of the Oregon State conference and *Hemingway in Our Time* are in no small measure the result of her continuing support and encouragement.

RICHARD ASTRO
Corvallis, Oregon
April 30, 1973

CONTENTS

INTRODUCTION

I

A WRITER'S REPUTATION is gained, grows, and declines in mysterious ways—ways that sometimes seem to have little to do with a writer's talent or the merit of his work. To become a well-known and well-respected writer in our time is a feat which defies the odds of success even more blatantly than the young Midwestern girl who hitchhikes her way from the cornfields to Hollywood stardom, or the bushleaguer from Memphis who pitches his way into baseball's Hall of Fame.

There are two exercises I can think of which illustrate the odds involved, odds that those of us who are critics ought to be reminded of now and then as we sit above our decks of "Authors" cards and shuffle them. One exercise is to visit any large used bookstore. Go down aisle after aisle of fiction and look at the thousands of titles. The chances are good that you will not recognize one title in a hundred. I remember as an aspiring young poet, looking for bargains in Byron and Milton, staring at shelf after shelf of little thin volumes of poems (it seems to me in retrospect that there must have been fifty yards of floor to ceiling poetry). It staggers the sensibilities to try to add up the total of emotion and effort represented by those shelves taken altogether. There was even a struggle for many, I suppose, to raise enough money to buy a little self-respect from a vanity press. Only to end up as a forgotten twenty-cent volume that nobody will even spend a dime on.

Or, look at the lists of best-selling novels from the past. Even most of those which had their month, their year or even years of fame are lost now to public and critical memory. The best-sellers of decades past are now entombed on the dusty shelves of countless little county libraries. Trilby? What, in heaven's name, is that? A household word that has faded from memory as surely as Fibber Magee's closet. How many novelists from the last several decades have published three or four novels of genuine literary merit but have remained unnoticed, their names included, if at all, for a brief time in the footnotes of critical surveys and literary histories? What kind of hell is it for those who have sold their souls, not just to have tried and failed, but to have tried and succeeded—but not really?

By all odds Ernest Hemingway should have ended up a Robert Rourk, or a stringer here and there for the news services, free-lancing now and then for *True* and *Argosy*—a testy old bastard who in a mellow mood would raise a glass occasionally to the time in his youth when he did a little writing of his own in Paris. What made the difference? I think it was that he was so very typical of what we are, while being so extraordinary. Gertrude Stein called him a Rotarian at heart. And that is precisely the point. He brought a good deal of what is middle-class Americanism into literature without very many people recognizing what he had done. Like Faulkner's Benjy, the intellectuals smelled it but couldn't quite locate the source of their discomfort.

He was a stud, a big lumbering boy out of a high school in Middle America who believed in sport as a vehicle for manhood, who thought Indian girls were a fine way to learn about sex, who condemned anyone who didn't work hard and earn their way, and who made fun of artistic "types," Jews, homosexuals, and anyone who couldn't hold his liquor. The very Protestant intolerance and provincial Victorianism that had smothered his boys-will-be-boys high spirits in the Midwest, he took with him to Europe. He disapproved of nearly everyone, particularly of Midwestern boys who went East into the Ivy League and became effete snobs.

And out of all that disapproval came one of the great novels of the century. Little did Grace Hemingway realize when she complained about *The Sun Also Rises*, that she couldn't "make head nor tail of such crazy people," she was a lot closer than she would ever know to her own son's point of view. Mrs. Hemingway had become disgusted with her son because he was not, she thought, sufficiently conscientious and industrious. Hemingway was typical of the American male in that after he revolted against those expectations, he carried them with him as his own, applying them rigorously to himself and to everyone he met. He whipped himself with a stern will and pressed himself constantly with an unbounding determination. He took well to the coaching he received and practiced long hours. And in the end, he won the championship.

II

What was extraordinary about Hemingway, therefore, was not his energy, ambition, and Horatio Alger faith—a million Midwestern boys came off the farm and out of the small town with the same equipment—but with all his rigidity, he exercised an extraordinary capacity for learning, remembering, and adapting. And beyond those gifts, add the greatest gift of all: perhaps the best ear that has ever been brought to the creation of English prose. From Oak Park High School, to Kansas City, to Chicago, to Paris, one can detect a steady rhythm of growth in response to new, and often difficult, circumstances. He almost always despised the people he learned from (he never really liked established writers), but he had a writer's mind, a vacuum cleaner that swept his experience clean, picking up any little thing, technique, or possible subject that might be of use. His ethic of progress was largely the ethic of the American Dream; he played corporation chess with editors, reviewers, and his fellow artists and ended up Chairman of the Board. He was, when he had to be, Sherwood's rapt pupil, Gertrude's little boy, and Ezra's gifted barbarian. The target of his scorn was Robert Cohn, not James Gatz.

After several years of mailing manuscripts off to periodicals without success, Hemingway began, about the time he went to Paris, to work almost as hard cultivating those who could help him as on his writing. But the amazing thing, when one stops to think about it, was that this naive and narrow-minded rowdy could be immersed among some of the greatest literary talents of the time—Stein, Pound, Ford, Joyce, Fitzgerald—and not drown. He entered the scene unknown, unpublished, and nearly uneducated, and won some measure of respect or admiration from nearly all those around him, and won it with a few scraps of unpublished prose.

A second amazing thing was that his keen ear and appetite for material led him into habitual and extensive imitation and borrowing; yet, he eventually became one of the most individually distinctive voices in modern literature. Throughout the first decade of his apprenticeship, he continually parodied the work of others. He parodied Anderson and Eliot and Pound; he parodied Stein and Joyce and a dozen other lesser known writers. He imitated Lardner, O'Henry, de Maupassant, and the slick stories out of the magazines that rejected his early work. He borrowed from Ford and he borrowed from Eliot, and he borrowed from nearly every major novelist he ever read, from Fielding and Sterne, through Stendahl, to James and Joyce. Scholars haven't even scratched the surface of his borrowings and sources—to a great extent because he was able to assimilate them so thoroughly. Yet Ernest Hemingway never came out a second-rate version of somebody else. Even when he was terrible, he was terrible in his own way. He displayed an incredible strength of individual assertion along with his instinct for larceny, building on the work and ideas of others, but always breaking free to become himself. In the process, he was often callous, selfish, and ungrateful. He wasn't able to muster the grace necessary to acknowledge that he didn't do it all himself, by himself. But at the same time, a lesser talent with less determination to emerge with his own identity might well have been submerged by a sense of indebtedness and inferiority.

A third amazing thing was Hemingway's metamorphosis from a young man anxious to use writing as a means to success into an artist completely devoted to the processes and possibilities of writing as an art form. He began really as a failed commercial writer, in the sense that his initial interest was selling short stories to slick magazines. In Chicago, as Charles Fenton tells us, he was always very impatient with the talk about art; he was interested in what would sell. " 'Artist, art, artistic!' he would shout. 'Can't we ever hear the last of that stuff!' "[1] In 1920-21, he was not much more than a rough-hewn high school boy who had some idea he'd like to be something on the order of a Ring Lardner. Yet only a year or two later he was assiduously learning what he could from those masters he had met in Paris, reading the works that they had recommended, and spending hour after hour sharpening his style and technique with the care and insight that was to make him a master artist in his own right.

III

Having taken so much from others, it is only right that so many have, in turn, taken from him. Yet the cumulative debt is very difficult to measure. The influence that has been claimed for Hemingway varies from the broad extreme of all modern writing since the twenties, to the narrow bounds of Raymond Chandler and the dialogue for George Raft and Edward G. Robinson. (Chandler, by the way, was not influenced by Hemingway, but developed a style independently which has some superficial characteristics in common.) Many of the practices and techniques that we have attached to Hemingway did not, of course, originate with him, but it was largely through his work that their influence was broadcast. His brevity and readability have made him far more accessible than many of his sources, and it is safe to say that he has probably been the most read and reread—by professionals as well as by the general public—of the major writers of the century. In a sense, he has been a pivotal, dynamic figure who, rather like Rousseau in his age, gathered together materials from many sources, and be-

---

[1] *The Apprenticeship of Ernest Hemingway* (New York: The Viking Press, 1958), p. 102.

cause the time was right and because his presentation was vigorous and inspired, made his mark where others who might have been more original (Gertrude Stein comes to mind) failed.

My own view is that Hemingway's influence has been profound. I suspect that it has been largely through the impact of his work that we have altered radically our standards of style and our concepts of the writing process itself. My parents have told me that when they were in school, during the time when Hemingway's first books were appearing, their models were the nineteenth century essayists (I recall the names of Lamb and Hazlitt, although there may have been others). The ideal was the long, balanced, complex sentence, which should be moderated here and there with a simple or periodic sentence for variety. By the time I got to high school, the direction had changed considerably. No longer was the student rewarded for a fancy vocabulary and imaginative figures as a sign of precociousness. If a student's sentences were overly long or complex, he was graded down for lack of clarity and a failure to be succinct. "Get to the point!" "Get rid of the deadwood!" and "Write to express, not to impress" were the things that appeared on my papers.

If the change had been primarily one from a "formal" to a "colloquial" style, I doubt that it would have taken quite so long for the colloquial styles of such writers as Twain and Stephen Crane to have influenced our general stylistic preferences. Furthermore, I don't think that if the schoolteachers had felt that the change was essentially an "easing up of standards," a movement toward a less demanding type of writing, they would have carried it through. On the contrary, rather than easing up, this new style was presented as a bearing down, a type of writing which was pointed toward clarity and precision as a result of imposing a great discipline on oneself. The prescription was pure Hemingway, although I doubt that my teachers knew that (we were assigned *Ivanhoe, Tale of Two Cities,* and *The Magnificent Ambersons*—the last was our modern novel). But tastes had changed, and those who taught the teachers and wrote the handbooks might have realized that Hemingway had a hand in changing those tastes.

The doctrine as it was presented to me in high school and as a college freshman went like this: the writer must begin with a clear idea of what he wanted to say; he must strive to say it in the fewest words possible; he must eschew "fine writing" and write toward making his meaning perfectly clear—that is, he must be direct and economical ("Prose is architecture, not interior decoration, and the Baroque is over"); the writer must choose the right word, which was usually the more familiar or shorter word. Above all, one wrote well as a result not of inspiration, but of care, hard work, and extensive revision. A better word than "colloquial" might be "classical"—one achieved the classical style through the application of the Victorian virtues. That too was Hemingway.

By the time I got to college I came to realize that the best way to get along with one's English teachers was to suppress any enthusiasm one might have for literature or for life. The best stance was a measured understatement. Never let yourself out (Hemingway, of course, hid constantly), but be cool. A good definition of "cool" as we have used it for the last few decades, by the way, is "grace under pressure." School was a pressure situation, but you must never show your peers that you cared, and you only showed your teachers by getting your work in on time, something I never could quite manage. I remember distinctly any number of fellow students in my freshman and sophomore classes who were unwise enough to gush about something they had read and who were promptly led to the rock-throwing wall. The climate of education itself was stoic, Hemingwayesque; the worst sin of all was to be a Romantic.

I remember, after scraping up enough grade points to get into Stanford, taking a number of creative writing classes. Why I kept on taking them, I don't know. I mistakenly put them in a separate category. The rest of the curriculum was a charade that I was willing to endure for the sake of somehow improving my low standing with my parents and with the world in general. But creative writing was something I would do for myself. It was going to be secret, a bit mysterious, a way of getting around stern English teachers into the delight that books read for pleasure had given me.

But the creative writing professors had pretty much the same doctrine as my English teachers. I don't remember any of them praising Hemingway or recommending him, although I do remember one professor saying something about Hemingway revising a story as many as fifty times. Writing was obviously something that was not supposed to be much fun. I remember the emphasis here also was on plain writing and understatement. One should avoid long descriptions, surprise endings, and dialogue tags that went any further than "he said" or "she said." Always we were warned against telling things rather than dramatizing them. The Hemingway story had made its mark, but it wasn't the kind of story I had been reading and that I wanted to write. I remember that I wanted to write about imaginary people and places (I was really a reader, not a writer), and the teachers kept insisting that I write from "experience." To write in a plain mode disappointed me, to have to dramatize everything took away all my rhetorical strategies, and to have to write from experience defeated me, since I thought I had none. Hemingway did me in.

IV

Even fifteen or twenty years ago when I first looked into Hemingway criticism, I recall complaints about its proliferation. What those complaints added up to, I suspect, was a protest against spending so much publication space on a writer who didn't really merit such attention. But the flood of criticism which rose in the late fifties and early sixties has been but an overfilled Doughboy compared to the high tides of recent years. Anyone who has any stock in what William White and Julian Smith have called—with what I hope is a certain amount of self-conscious irony—the "Hemingway industry," must ask himself, what does it all mean? And many of us will have to consider whether, as Philip Young has indicated in his essay in this volume, it isn't time to row quickly to shore and seek out another country.

I have my own theories as to why Hemingway has become one of the top half-dozen most analyzed and interpreted authors in all of American literature. First, however, I should point out that all this critical activity is not happening in a vacuum, in a sealed glass dome where a perpetual motion machine is fueled by the kinetic energy of the publish or perish system. One of the canards that has been passed from essay to essay in recent years holds that Hemingway is passé, that he is not read by young people any more. I don't know that there ever was a Hemingway fad, in the same way there have been Kerouac, Salinger, Tolkien, and Hesse fads. Hemingway's claim has been a more fundamental and persistent one. He is simply there, at the center; if you read at all, you will find him; but you won't rush out into the streets claiming a discovery. If personal testimony will do, Hemingway seminars fill and overflow while other seminars, which seem more currently fashionable, may languish. Evidence of a more general nature can be found in the fact that his major works are still selling at near best-seller levels. I am convinced that Hemingway's novels and short stories have never had a larger audience among a college generation.

The main reason that Hemingway will continue to be read and discussed lies in the nature of the work itself. Simply stated, his position is in a closer alignment with our felt positions than that of any other modern writer. I said a moment ago that the thrust of his style and the method behind that style is Classical. I think that his fundamental position in regard to the world is Classical also. Hemingway deals essentially with contained space. His style, imagery, descriptive patterning, and narrative strategy all relate directly to the task of carving out a defensible position from which the forces of chaos can be excluded and within which the power of justice and virtue can be established and sustained.

In a chaotic world with competing claims, slippery values, and omnipresent pressure and fear, this contained space, which has its inner as well as outer dimensions, is an island of cool.

As long as that island can maintain its independence, then meaningful life can exist. The enemies are many, but by and large they are those who would violate the selfhood of others. Among the most dangerous of these are the individuals or groups who may not intend to destroy us and who hide behind or justify their destruction on the basis of "love" or other conventional virtues. These include parents, wives, and husbands at one end of the scale and movements and governments at the other end.

There are many labels one can apply to such a vision with a certain amount of accuracy. First, we are dealing with what might be called "civilized" in the Classical sense—self-discipline and true community within the barbarian wasteland. We are also dealing with art and the role of the artist, for art is the imposition of humane order on inner space. We might think also of "existential," in that each of us is required to create his own authentic life within a wilderness of decayed institutions and values. One might also add "paranoia." Unlike the author's own fears near the end of his life, however, these fears are justified—society everywhere *is* in conspiracy against the manhood of every one of its members.

The appeal to youth in all of this is, I think, obvious. Yet the application is not to the young alone. The social anthropologists tell us that in few other cultures do so many individuals have the task of "making" themselves. It is to this problem of growing up, a problem not confined to the young, that Hemingway speaks so eloquently. The task of establishing one's manhood is, of course, an archetypal theme in literature, but I don't think that it was from literature that this theme found its way into the center of Hemingway's consciousness. Rather, I think it came from what I have called here his "typicalness," out of his Midwestern, middle-class Americanism, out of the forceful Victorianism of his parents, and out of the frontier values and skills (somewhat decadently preserved in the Midwestern "sports frontier" of Northern Michigan) passed on to him by his father.

Hemingway's movement toward individuality made up the substance of both his life and his work. Life and work became a tandem opportunity for self-dramatization. One could not really have the one without the other, yet it was the strength of that self-assertion which alienated him constantly from those around him. In other words, those things—the intolerance, the overcompetitiveness, and rigid discipline—we have come to dislike him for were part and parcel of the means by which he achieved greatness. If from his heritage he grew to become what critics recently have described as a kind of monster, his work drew from the same native roots to form some of the most powerful fables of modern consciousness. His existentialism, if one wishes to call it that, came from American rather than European sources, out of the tradition that produced *The Confidence Man,* "Bartleby the Scrivener," "Benito Cereno," "Ethan Brand," and "The Minister's Black Veil." It is very much the doctrine set forth in Emerson's "Self-Reliance":

> Check this lying hospitality and lying affection. Live no longer to the expectation of these deceived and deceiving people with whom we converse. Say to them, O father, O mother, O brother, O friend, I have lived with you after appearances hitherto. Henceforward I am the truth's. Be it known unto you that henceforward I obey no law less than the eternal law. I will have no convenants but proximities . . . I appeal from your customs. I must be myself.

Beyond the appropriateness of the work itself, I think that the recent flood of Hemingway criticism has much to do with the provocations posed by the narrow-mindedness, the antagonism, and even the sheer stupidity of much early Hemingway criticism. I have a hunch that graduate students in English are often possessed of an inordinate sense of poetic justice, perhaps gained by too much early reading of Sir Walter Scott. But then, who wouldn't become incensed, determined to write about wrongs, after reading the sagas of the Dumb Ox, the Hairy-Chested Breast Beater, and the Simple-Minded, Sentimental Narcissist? In the fifties, graduate schools often turned strongly toward the New Criticism and the close reading of texts, so that on the one hand students read about Hemingway's work, and on the other, they read the work itself, closely, and the two simply didn't match. They found contrary to the clichés (they came early and stayed late) that Hemingway's work was very often rich, complex, and thought-provoking, and so they set out on a crusade. And the students of those students have followed after, reading closely, explicating, and protesting.

And exclaiming. I think that a large measure of the motivation for writing about Hemingway's work has been surprise. Even though one doesn't totally accept any longer the legends of his stark simplicities, his narrowness, his crude, obsessive delight in violence, one is still surprised that he wrote so very well. In my own graduate school experience I took a seminar on Twain and James in which the professor proposed that for scholars there were two kinds of authors: on the one hand, that author, like James, whose work is so richly endowed with interconnected ideas and evolving techniques that from any point of departure, one is led on and on endlessly to further study. And on the other, that author, like Twain, whose work, regardless of the brilliance of any particular performance, seems to start and stop, every line of inquiry leading rather quickly to a dead end. Twain scholars may well be able to refute this as a specific observation, but I think there is some truth in the existence of two such general categories. The final amazing thing about Hemingway is that he has turned out, in this sense, to be more like James than Twain. Among scholars of literature generally, Hemingway has been grossly underrated. He is still underrated. But as long as he continues to surprise us, we will continue to read him, teach him, and write about him.

JACKSON J. BENSON
California State University
San Diego, California

PHILIP YOUNG

POSTHUMOUS HEMINGWAY, AND NICHOLAS ADAMS

YOU ARE PROBABLY not going to believe this, though it is perfectly true. In 1946, newly home from the war, I told my professor—a distinguished scholar/critic who in a fine book had
published as knowledgeably and extensively on Hemingway
as anyone—that I proposed to write my term paper on Nick
Adams. This idea met with such resounding silence—i.e., Approval Withheld—that I filed it away and did something else.
Why was that? Perhaps you have guessed. If I had said Harold
Krebs, another soldier home, my mentor would have known
who(m) I was talking about. Alfred Kazin, whose *On Native
Grounds* was the *other* bible for the likes of me in those days,
also discusses Krebs but never Nick.

Well, that's how far we've come—to the point where I for
one would be willing to argue that this Adams is the most
important single character in Hemingway. But not here, though
the task at hand is not easier labor. I have already delivered
myself of Nick twice, full-term. The first time was in 1948, in
that aborted term paper, eventually published in 1952 as the
first chapter of a book; the second was in a long introduction
to the collection called *The Nick Adams Stories*, which was not
printed in that volume but elsewhere, exactly twenty years later.
Even Hemingway conceived this narrative but once.

Block That Metaphor, and to the topic at hand, which is
Nick again—but only a couple of aspects of him and his book,
and those in the larger context of the effect all the posthumous
publication has had on Hemingway's reputation, which hits

13

me as the biggest question before us, and leads me finally to the problem of the recent surge of academic interest in this writer. What I purpose, then, is to render some quick judgments on each of the posthumous books (four, as I count), file a special bulletin on the initial reception of *The Nick Adams Stories* (a small detail of the large picture), submit some unrecorded facts about the "editing" of that book, and, last—since I don't think the volumes issued since 1961 have done much one way or the other for Hemingway so far—consider what they have done for us.

It is a good time to be assessing the posthumous achievement, because it is doubtful that there is anything left to publish that would change our minds one bit about the measurable stature of our man. One didn't have leisure to read all the unpublished manuscript that is in the bank vault. But there was time to form snap judgments that have not yet been upset about the manuscripts that remain unpublished. And this takes us briefly into the realm of an unstated topic, subsidiary but related to ours: the Posthumous Non-Publication of Ernest Hemingway. It appears to me that—unknown to him as to us— our writer was not a very good judge of how well or ill he was writing, day to day, over some long periods of time. He had better judgment than to try to publish his abortive efforts (as a rule) when he was more or less done. But it is hard to detect any lack of enthusiasm in his efforts as he persisted month after month after year in the production of things that simply were not working out. There are three very bulky manuscripts that did not: *The Dangerous Summer*, parts of which were published during the author's lifetime in the late *Life*, inspiring no appetite in the public for the whole corpus; the long "African Book," selections from which appeared in *Life's* healthy younger sibling, *Sports Illustrated*, with the same negative result; and an endless tedious novel, *Garden of Eden*, which has unsurprisingly not even been sampled in print. Hemingway had, apparently, whatever it takes to con oneself into thinking one is going good when one is not; and this is why all his life, off and on, he could continue to write poems which would have convinced most of us that we had no special talent for verse. This is also why he could claim that "At Sea," the last section of *Islands in the Stream,* was "impervious to criticism," like Beethoven's last quartets or something.

If the picture is unlikely to change, then, what are we to make now of the overall result of posthumous publication? Or, to put the question most simply, should the books have been published at all? One, *A Moveable Feast?* Absolutely. Two, *By-Line: Ernest Hemingway?* Surely. Three, *Islands in the Stream?* Probably but not certainly. Four, *The Nick Adams Stories?* Mostly. My overall judgment, then, is affirmative—with reservations. Let's consider it in a little detail, with eventual focus on the last title.

A Moveable Feast is the easiest book to handle—that is if you roughly agree with me that it is a minor masterpiece, a small jewel, flawed ever so slightly here by sentimentality, and just a little there by malice, but glittering none the less, and cut to last. But, according to this appraiser, Hemingway left behind little if anything else of quite that quality. There are some marvelous if even more minor things in *By-Line: Ernest Hemingway,* which are comparable to fiction. But the book *is* journalism, which is not the same thing as literature, and there is an ominous drift to it in which the reporter begins by interviewing certain notables and ends interviewing himself, by then among the foremost of them. The four previously uncollected *Stories of the Spanish Civil War* reveal a similar tendency: fiction stained with autobiography, and distorted by it.

In *Islands in the Stream* this current became a tide and provided much the biggest disappointment, since we knew the author had pinned such hopes on this novel and made such claims for it. In the first place it is not a "novel" at all, but three related novellas which the author had optimistically planned to weld into one. Of these, "Bimini" seems much the best, "Cuba" much the worst, while "At Sea" rather describes itself—neither here nor there, an adventure story without excitement. Of course we must take into account the fact that Hemingway was not really done with this book. He had not much revised it, save for the last section, and he had not even begun trying to work the parts together into a whole. But worse than that: in relating all the experience the book deals with he had never, it seems to me, discovered its meaning. Indeed the central fact about his protagonist Hudson (patently Hemingway himself) is his stoicism, and there is no reason provided for that position. Not, anyway, beyond a desperation shot at a reason—the deaths of his three sons, which seem utterly manufactured, on two separate occasions—to substitute for what is not understood. (Another way of putting this is that Hudson's despair is Hemingway's, but John, Patrick, and Gregory Hemingway are alive and fairly well and living all over the place.)

Increasingly, as his career moved toward its close, and beginning with *Across the River and Into the Trees* in 1950, Hemingway was less and less inclined to turn himself into a protagonist who is anything more than or much different from Hemingway, self-centered as a tornado. It was when he put on a mask that de-personalized, or re-personalized, that the autobiographical method worked for him, and that is partly why it was so exciting to discover in that bank vault two unknown pieces of fiction involving Nick Adams—the first-written, "Summer People," and the last, "The Last Good Country." Now it is true that that is not quite the same taciturn, rather *im*personal and understated Nick we have long known. Far more fleshed out as a character, if no more impressive still far more "alive," he is more like his creator than when he was more of a sketch. But I do not think Hemingway has spoiled him any, or hurt him much—just that in rounding him out he has changed him some, by filling in some blanks.

I've already expressed in print my qualified pleasure in these two new stories, and turn to a topic I've not discussed before, though I believe myself to be the world's expert in it. This is the critical reception of *The Nick Adams Stories* to date, which bears directly on our concern with the posthumous publication and its effect on the writer's reputation; I conscientiously researched the matter for this very occasion. Doubtless you have noticed that reception of the book has been what is called mixed; doubtful that you realize just *how* mixed. Consider the range of these differences of opinion, taken from the book reviews. (I quote literally, and almost constantly.)

The book is "dazzling"; it "stands with Hemingway's finest work"; "enormously exciting"; a "treasure." Or it is "a waste of time and money," a "sign of indiscriminate greed"—"Young and Scribner's should withdraw it." (That last is Quentin Anderson, and Mark Schorer agrees: the whole thing was "misguided.") The idea of the book's chronological organization is a "marvelous revelation" of "surprising importance"; it is "nonsense." The book is a good idea if you read *Newsweek;* if you read *Time* it's a bad one. The *National Observer* called it "a damn shame," and another newspaper said it's a "good edition, *The Nick Carter Stories.*"

As for the two new pieces, exactly ditto. "Summer People" is "perfectly splendid"; it "ranks with his best"; or it is "pretty thin," "pretty flat." "The Last Good Country" is "mawkish," "puerile," "banal"; it is a "lovely, serene idyl." It's a "tremendous narrative," and "a plot that ran out of gas." On the six other new bits of Nick fiction, the jury is also hung; every single piece was praised or knocked by someone ("More is less," said one disgruntled scholar.) Likewise Young—who "fancies himself a Hemingway authority" on the one hand and is peerless among them on the other. (Also a "truly creative editor," a "garbage collector," and a "grave robber.") As for his little Preface, it is "pithy," "worthless," and "essentially meaningless." It should be longer—has "an airy lack of apparatus"—or its wisdom lies in "holding back." (For a change of pace, three asides: one, the Preface was scarcely "worthless" to such reviewers as took virtually their entire copy from it; two, there are more adventurous reviewers about the land who cannot read on a level of comprehension that we regularly demand of our freshmen; three, it is remarkably little fun to read 107 reviews of a book, 106 of which one would not have been pleased to have written himself. The exception ought to get a medal: it is by Louis D. Rubin, Jr. of the University of North Carolina in the *Washington Sunday Star* for April 23, 1972; we'll return to it.)

Chaos, then, there was. But consensus, or at least majority, too, without the mention of which the record is utterly distorted. If tabulation and arithmetic serve, the results are quite changed. Favorable responses to the book outnumbered the unfavorable by a ratio of 5.7 to 1. "Summer People" is approved more often than not by a margin of 2.3 to 1, and "The Last Good Country" by 6 to 1. Doubtless the data need further adjustment; I've a sad hunch that the brighter reviewers tended toward hostility, while the dumber ones were inclined to accept what the Preface (and the jacket copy) told them. But I have no plans for testing the taste and intelligence of the 107; I don't agree with the friend who wrote of Nick "more is less," but maybe "enough" is already "too much."

Anyway, how much does "initial reception"—these reviews —matter in the long run? How this book makes out in books and journals to come matters more, and how it fares in a place we often forget to consider matters most: in classrooms all over the country, where I predict the real market awaits the paperback (Bantam, in March of '73, I'm told, to be followed by one from Scribner's).

Enough of that, too. But where will one find a better opportunity than this to clear up some misconceptions that prevail about the book and its "editor"? The book had no editor in the usual sense. I edited nothing, but proposed the volume, selected and arranged the published stories, inserted the two new ones, and wrote that little Preface, which was all that Scribner's wanted. The reviewers who praised or blamed one for "holding back" might as well know that a full-scale introduction was provided, but turned out to be not at all what Scribner's wanted (it was printed in *Novel*, Fall, 1972). At that point I was paid for my efforts and done with the book, and I hereby assign to those who accused me of greed my total royalties, which are zilch.

One important result of that truncated Preface was predictable and predicted: the objection that two stories seem badly misplaced in the book, and without a word of explanation. "The End of Something" and "The Three-Day Blow" are

put after the war, and the trouble is that as he appears in them
Nick seems far less a veteran of the war than a pre-war ado-
lescent. The overriding point here is that there *is* no completely
satisfactory way to resolve this dilemma; putting the stories
before the war raises its own problems. The reasoning that pre-
vailed was that in this pair of stories Hemingway was as always
seeing himself as Nick, and that because the stories deal directly with events that occurred and people he knew in the
post-war summer of 1919 he was seeing Nick at that time too.
What people forget is that for almost half of that summer
Hemingway was himself both a veteran and a teenager. I for
one perfectly believe Marcelline Hemingway (Sanford) when
she wrote that a full year later, as her brother approached his
twenty-first birthday, he seemed more like a kid of sixteen.
That's why Nick does; the stories bear her out. In his review,
Louis Rubin was quick to see the point and get its import: "the
persistence of [boyish] qualities in the 'mature' Hemingway of
the post-war years gives us a different picture from the customary stereotype of the youthful Hemingway being changed
overnight into the tough cynical, winner take nothing adult
by the horrors of war. . . ." Hemingway had a lot of youthful
fun in that last summer up in Michigan, and he turned some of
it (and some guilt as well) into three Nick Adams stories, the
third being "Summer People," his farewell to the place.

The other thing about one's role in the book that should be
set straight is that of the eight new pieces in it I proposed to
print only the two already mentioned. To these I would have
gone along with adding "The Indians Moved Away" (which I
believe Hemingway once planned to publish as "They Never
Came Back"), and perhaps what is now called "On Writing"
(with the flagrant anachronisms and irrelevance removed, and
in an appendix). When it comes to the other snippets, I'd agree
that more is less. And when it comes to "Three Shots," which
the author rejected as a false start to a story he then proceeded
with differently, the justification for inclusion is invisible. (The
fact he didn't throw it away means nothing; he didn't throw
anything away.) And there we have it. The book might have

been better, but if I didn't think it was worth having I wouldn't have proposed it, or would subsequently have bowed out of it.

Which brings us to the central question: has publication of the four posthumous books enhanced or weakened Hemingway's stature? My first answer would have to be Neither or Both; the plusses and minusses just about cancel each other in my mind, leaving him about where he was when he died. It occurs to me, however, that it may not be always thus. If we judge a writer by his best work, and if we judge him the better the more there is of it, then there is more good work in print now than there was in 1960. The lesser stuff should fade in memory as we fail to reread it, and the better won't, so that in time his stature may seem a little greater than it was. At any rate that's my second thought.

But are we mindful that this is not quite the whole question? The rest of it is: what has this publication done for Hemingway's readers? To that one the answer is simple: they have benefited. We have things to read that we are happy to have, and we can skip the rest. We also *know* more about the object of such remarkable interest—strengths and weaknesses both—as both man and writer, if in this case you can separate the two.

The last thing we might consider, hoping not to get too cynical about it, is what has it done for us?—his students, scholars, critics, whatever. Obviously we have more to work on than we did before, and I have some thoughts about this, on which I'll close. What I'm getting at is that just about the time when I thought there wasn't much left to be done with this writer, I was made a fool of and the Hemingway Industry went into production. Shortly thereafter, according to a 1969 count by one of his bibliographers, William White, Hemingway became—with Hawthorne, Melville, James, and Faulkner—one of the Five Most Written About American Authors. In the way of scholarly/critical attention (for reasons that are not entirely clear to me) our man has now passed Poe, Emerson, Whitman, and Mark Twain, all of whom have of course been around to be written about a lot longer. And one can bear witness: during the single week in which I was busiest with this paper, I received one new Hemingway book (Grebstein's, which looks good), got word of a brief postponement of a second (essays collected by Waldhorn, our Reader's Guide), was asked for "permissions" in the scheduling of a third (on the Critical Reputation), and, doubtless in view of the competition, was notified that two long-scheduled books had been cancelled. On top of that I had a lettter from a man who wanted to do one consisting entirely of interviews with me. That's six Hemingway books, or non-books, in six days, not counting this one. And all of this is to say nothing of the gradual emergence—largely from without the academy—of a Hemingway *cult:* witness recent books on his first wife, Hadley, on the originals for the characters in *The Sun Also Rises,* and so on.

This business of radically increased production might be fun to pursue for a moment, though it's a game with terrifying implications—like playing with population explosion figures. Working from Lewis Leary's two bibliographies called *Articles on American Literature* and counting roughly, it appears that between 1930 and 1950 Hemingway items averaged circa five per year; there were no books. Between 1950 and 1967, where Leary quits, there were approximately twenty-seven articles per year, and many books. Working from the MLA bibliographies for 1968, 1969, and 1970, there were an average of 78 items per year, including books. With a little more arithmetic and a lot more nerve, it would be possible to play the rest of this game, which is called extrapolation.

As we all know, however, this phenomenon has scarcely taken place in a vacuum, but in the immediate context of a publication explosion. To have any real meaning our figures have to be fitted into the larger picture of increased production on practically all fronts. As it happens, however, this doesn't change the picture much. Applying a rough yardstick (namely a yardstick) to the most recent *MLA International Bibliography* (1970), you can take measurements for what might be the Top Ten American writers in terms of the number of titles devoted to them. Here is how that comes out: (1) Whitman: 30 inches, (2) Faulkner: 24 inches, (3) Melville: 22½ inches, (4 and 5—tie) Hawthorne and Hemingway: 20 inches, (6) Twain: 18½ inches, (7) James: 18 inches, (8) Poe: 17 inches, (9) Thoreau: 13 inches, (10) Emerson: 11 inches.[1]

Just as this explosion has not taken place in a vacuum, so (as already remarked of the cult) it has not been confined to the journals. Has the likelihood ever occurred to you—a crude but telling point—that Hemingway is making far more money dead than he ever did alive? In 1972 there were six paperbacks that sold over 150,000 copies in American *bookstores,* and he wrote three of them.[2] Meanwhile *Islands in the Stream* was selling 900,000 copies in the drugstores. But let us end where we began and are safest, in the academy.

Perhaps I don't get around enough, but I don't recall ever having seen any kind of discussion of what happens when a writer becomes the subject of such intense professional activity. It's a paradoxical piece of business. Since the number of things that can be said on any subject would seem finally to be finite, it stands to reason that the more that's written on a man the less there is left to write. But, and here's the rub, the reverse is also true: the more that's written on a man, the more there is to write. This is because the more that's written on a man the more important he is deemed to be, and the more important he is deemed to be the narrower or more trivial are the areas considered worthy of investigation. Thus we have the probability that a short decade ago editors of journals would have returned without reading "When Hemingway's Mother Came to Call," "Nick Adams, Prince of Abissinia [sic]," "Hemingway's Praise of Dick Sisler in *The Old Man and the Sea,*" or "Carelessness

---

[1] Nothing amazing there, but pursuing this a little farther turns up some small surprises. For example, if you think of Eliot as an American writer, as I do and the *Bibliography* does not, then he's in second place: 26 inches. For others, Stephen Crane ties with Emerson at 11, James Branch Cabell (wow) beats them both with 12, Emily Dickinson (sob) measures only 6½, and is thus beat by Ralph Ellison and Robert Frost, 7, Steinbeck and Stevens, 8, and Fitzgerald, 9½.

[2] *The Sun Also Rises, A Farewell to Arms,* and *The Old Man and the Sea.* The other three titles were *The Foxfire Book, The Great Gatsby,* and *The Stranger.* (*New York Times,* February 11, 1973, Section 7, Part II.)

and the Cincinnati Reds" in the same work. But all of these items are now in print. And if you think that means we are getting close to the bottom of the barrel then you're forgetting that when an industry churns into full production the bottom of the barrel is awfully hard to locate. Articles beget articles, the machinery feeds on itself; areas are opened for debate, "discoveries" are made that lead to new discoveries, new arguments are advanced that then need to be disputed; the more you have the more you get until at some unpredictable point the machinery begins to wear out, and production is minimal again.

Well, as long as the Publish/Perish thing remains in force, which is as far as I can see, what I'm saying is that it's a good thing we've now got a larger territory to operate in, and some new material. I say "we," but the fact of the matter is that I personally have come to the point where the word Hemingway, usually accompanied by some physical or tonal nod in this direction, produces a discomfort which registers somewhere between acute shame and nausea. I am getting out, as of now. Of course this makes the third time I've announced that decision. What happened before is that something would turn up that was too hard to turn down. Which of us, if handed the keys to those enormous safe-deposit boxes, would have said "No thanks, I'm through with all that"? Of course nothing of that sort can happen again, but you never know what will. See you around.

GEORGE WICKES

SKETCHES OF THE AUTHOR'S LIFE
IN PARIS IN THE TWENTIES

THE TITLE OF MY PAPER, with its intimations of a portrait of the artist as a young man, is of course the subtitle of the book that was posthumously christened *A Moveable Feast*. Actually "the Paris sketches," as Hemingway referred to them, are sketchy indeed, providing neither a full portrait nor an adequate account of those five formative years that made him the writer he was. Nevertheless these sketches, written during the closing years of his life, must be regarded as a kind of literary testament, the dying man's final summing up of accounts, the last official word he would pass on to posterity about his life and work. They tell us much—more than he intended, I would say—about the kind of man he was and about his all-consuming ambition to be the best writer of his time. But they are very astutely written and must be read judiciously. My purpose is to consider—with a healthy measure of skepticism—what Hemingway put into his last book and what he left out, to examine how he selected certain episodes and sketched certain individuals from his apprentice years and to try to explain why.

Throughout this process I shall have to deal with the ticklish business of distinguishing fact from fiction. Let me announce at the outset that I have always thought *A Moveable Feast* belonged to the realm of fiction as well as autobiography. And add that I find it natural rather than reprehensible that a writer of fiction should fictionalize his memoirs somewhat. Particularly a writer like Hemingway whose fiction has always been so close to autobiography. Therefore, from the time I

25

first reviewed the book[1] until now I have always found it necessary to keep in mind that prefatory word of caution:

> If the reader prefers, this book may be regarded as fiction.
> But there is always the chance that such a book of fiction may
> throw some light on what has been written as fact.

To begin with an obvious example: in *A Moveable Feast* Hemingway frequently portrays himself as the starving young artist—well, not exactly starving but very poor and often hungry for the sake of art.[2] But consider the sketch most explicitly devoted to this theme, the one entitled "Hunger Was Good Discipline." Complaining that fiction doesn't pay and that he must skip lunch, the author carefully charts his way through streets where he can avoid the sight and smell of food to Sylvia Beach's bookshop. There he finds a windfall from his German publisher and immediately proceeds to one of his favorite restaurants, the nearby Brasserie Lipp, where he consumes the equivalent of three hearty meals and washes them down with a liter and a half of the beer that made Lipp's famous. Then he walks to his favorite café, orders a coffee, and begins writing "Big Two-Hearted River." The moral of the tale is not so much that hunger sharpens the writer's perceptions as that it is easier to write well on a full stomach. But so persuasive is Hemingway's storytelling that we readily swallow a sentimental cliché that is older than the hills of Bohemia.

---

[1] George Wickes, "Ernest Hemingway Pays His Debts," *Shenandoah* (Winter 1965), pp. 46-54.

[2] How poor Hemingway actually was in Paris is open to question. The internal evidence of *A Moveable Feast* does not suggest poverty, for he traveled frequently and indulged his taste for sports, not to mention good food and drink. He states there that two could travel in Europe on $5 a day, so that even after he stopped earning money as a journalist, he and his wife could live on the income from her trust fund, which originally amounted to $2,000 or $3,000 and eventually dwindled to almost half that amount. See Carlos Baker, *Ernest Hemingway, A Life Story* (New York: Charles Scribner's Sons, 1969), pp. 78, 124.

His yarn about hunting pigeons in the Luxembourg Gardens, sounds like the kind of tall tale Papa would tell gullible admirers. See A. E. Hotchner, *Papa Hemingway* (New York: Random House, 1966), p. 45.

As autobiography *A Moveable Feast* leaves much to be desired, not only because it is fictionalized but because it is so fragmentary, omitting more than it reveals. Obviously Hemingway knew what he was doing. Witness his explanation of his technique of omission which he illustrates with a startling revelation about one of his earliest stories:

> It was a very simple story called "Out of Season" and I had omitted the real end of it which was that the old man hanged himself. This was omitted on my new theory that you could omit anything if you knew that you omitted and the omitted part would strengthen the story and make people feel something more than they understood.

To my knowledge no one ever guessed that "Out of Season" was supposed to end in suicide. But anyone can see that the unwritten plot of *A Moveable Feast* is a success story culminating in the publication of *The Sun Also Rises*. And the implicit theme is innocence before the fall. And the sequel is, I suppose, "The Snows of Kilimanjaro" with the writer now ten years older, disgusted with himself for having debauched his talent and for not having written, among other things, *A Moveable Feast*.

"The Snows of Kilimanjaro" is a useful reminder that Hemingway was always preoccupied with his career as a writer and commented frequently on writers and writing, although he liked to pretend otherwise. In the *Paris Review* interview, for instance, he bridled at many literary questions and at one point gruffly declared: "This backyard literary gossip while washing out the dirty clothes of thirty-five years ago is disgusting and boring to me."[3] Yet, even when writing about bullfighting, big-game hunting, and deep-sea fishing he managed to introduce literary comment, not a little of it gossip. In *Death in the Afternoon* he made a number of gratuitous asides at the expense of fellow writers; in *Green Hills of Africa* he inter-

---

[3] *Writers at Work, Second Series*, introduced by Van Wyck Brooks (New York, 1963), p. 227. The interview, by George Plimpton, was conducted over several years during the mid-fifties and appeared after Hemingway had begun writing *A Moveable Feast*.

viewed himself at length on the subject of writers and writing;
and in several of the articles he wrote from the Caribbean for
Esquire in the mid-thirties he introduced further comments on
writing. Even in his fiction we find the Hemingway hero taking
sideswipes at Hemingway's fellow writers, the most notorious
being the remark about "poor Scott Fitzgerald" in "The Snows
of Kilimanjaro" and a less conspicuous instance occurring in
Robert Jordan's free association in *For Whom the Bell Tolls:*
"A rose is a rose is an onion . . . An onion is an onion . . . a stein
is a rock is a boulder is a pebble." The callous attack on Sherwood Anderson in *The Torrents of Spring,* far from being an
isolated and deplorable instance, is fairly typical of Hemingway's treatment of his fellow writers. And *A Moveable Feast*
is simply his final summation after most of them were safely
dead.

Of course no one would make the mistake of taking *The
Torrents of Spring* seriously. *A Moveable Feast* is another matter
entirely, subtly compounded of nine parts fact to one part fiction,
so compellingly and convincingly wrought that any reader is
ready to suspend disbelief. Sometimes there is hardly any
fiction—but then there is likely to be all the more craft. Take
the three sketches of Scott Fitzgerald, for example, which
obviously presented Hemingway with his most serious challenge, for Fitzgerald was both his major rival in the twenties and
a legendary personage familiar to the common reader. Hemingway's portrait is so masterful that Arnold Gingrich, who came
prepared to find fault, pronounced it the best "ever done in
print, for as I read there Scott stood alive again, at his inimitably
exasperating best and worst. It simply *is* Scott to the last breath
and the least bat of an eyelash."[4]

So far as I can tell, Hemingway hardly fictionalized the
first two Fitzgerald sketches. The first, which is the longest and
the most accomplished in the book, begins when the author
meets Fitzgerald in the Dingo bar, observes with clinical de-

---

[4] Arnold Gingrich, "Scott, Ernest and Whoever," *Esquire* (December 1966), p. 188.

tachment how he is progressively affected by alcohol and concludes with a marvelously comic narrative as they drive Fitzgerald's car from Lyons to Paris. All of this, needless to say, reflects more glory on the author than on Fitzgerald, but all of it may very well be true: it is no secret that Fitzgerald was chemically unable to hold his liquor, and that memorable journey from Lyons to Paris is history. I don't know whether Hemingway first met Fitzgerald in the Dingo, but by placing him in that setting with its "worthless characters," two of them evidently the originals of Brett Ashley and Mike Campbell, he ingeniously casts Fitzgerald for a role in *The Sun Also Rises*. One disingenuous sentence is particularly telling:

> I was very curious to see him and I had been working very hard all day and it seemed quite wonderful that here should be Scott Fitzgerald and the Great Dunc Chaplin whom I had never heard of but who was now my friend.

Dunc Chaplin, who had been "famous" as a baseball player at Princeton, may remind us that another Princeton athlete, Robert Cohn, appeared at the beginning of *The Sun Also Rises*, just as the author who had been working hard all day may remind us that Jake Barnes was the only ant among grasshoppers in that novel. It seems reasonable to conclude that Fitzgerald must have spent his day dissipating.

Hemingway's full-length portrait of Fitzgerald is a remarkable display of his extraordinary powers of observation and ability to render what he observed. It is not, however, totally objective.

> Scott was a man then who looked like a boy with a face between handsome and pretty. He had very fair wavy hair, a high forehead, excited and friendly eyes and a delicate long-lipped Irish mouth that, on a girl, would have been the mouth of a beauty. His chin was well built and he had good ears and a handsome, almost beautiful, unmarked nose.

That unmarked nose Hemingway apparently regarded as a flaw that he would gladly have corrected. And later he went out of his way to intimate again that there was something effeminate or at least girlish about Fitzgerald, who was excited about drinking wine from a bottle "as a girl might be excited by going swimming for the first time without a bathing suit."

The second Fitzgerald sketch describes his disorderly life and places the blame largely on Zelda. Again Hemingway's intense scrutiny is brought to bear, characterizing her and dramatizing the situation in one compressed paragraph.

> Zelda had hawk's eyes and a thin mouth and deep-south manners and accent. Watching her face you could see her mind leave the table and go to the night's party and return with her eyes blank as a cat's and then pleased, and the pleasure would show along the thin line of her lips, and then be gone. Scott was being the good cheerful host and Zelda looked at him and she smiled happily with her eyes and her mouth too as he drank the wine. I learned to know that smile very well. It meant she knew Scott would not be able to write.

In the same controlled, restrained, seemingly objective manner Hemingway follows the story to its inevitable denouement.

It is the third Fitzgerald sketch that raises the most doubts and eyebrows. I don't propose to go into the matter of measurements, which is hard to document—the dialogue even more than the measurements—but there is one clear fabrication in that sketch that can be exposed, and that the unkindest cut of all when Hemingway quotes Georges, the chief barman at the Ritz, as saying he cannot remember Scott Fitzgerald. Quite probably this dialogue dates from December 1956 or January 1957 when Hemingway stayed at the Ritz and discovered there the old notebooks from the twenties on which *A Moveable Feast* is based.[5] It so happens that in February of 1957 a French student preparing a thesis on Fitzgerald interviewed the same

---

[5] See Mary Hemingway, "The Making of the Book: A Chronicle and a Memoir," *New York Times Book Review* (May 10, 1964), pp. 26-27. See also Valerie Danby-Smith, "Reminiscence of Hemingway," *Saturday Review* (May 9, 1964), pp. 30-31, 57. The latter article re-

Georges and recorded her conversation with him. He told her
that the barman in the twenties had been a great friend of Fitzgerald's. "The actual head-barman, Georges," her thesis reports,
"was then bellboy. He remembers Scott rather well."[6] Once
again we find a precedent in fiction. Hemingway used exactly
the same tactic in *The Sun Also Rises* to denigrate Robert Cohn
in the opening paragraph which begins:

> Robert Cohn was once middleweight boxing champion of Princeton.

and ends:

> I never met any one of his class who remembered him. They did
> not even remember that he was middleweight boxing champion.

It would be churlish as well as tiresome to go all through
A Moveable Feast picking nits in this fashion. Sufficient to say
that the book appears to be just about as slightly fictionalized
as *The Sun Also Rises*,[7] but with one all-important difference:
that it is presented in the guise of memoirs written with scrupu-
lous precision. However it might be worthwhile to point out
some of Hemingway's major sins of omission in his memoirs,
not only to fill out those sketches of the author's apprenticeship
but to throw some light on his motives in committing those sins
against the memory of his former friends. To return once more
to the case of Scott Fitzgerald: what is omitted entirely is Hemingway's very considerable debt. Some critics consider this a
literary debt. I am not altogether convinced that Hemingway
was directly influenced by Fitzgerald's work, but undeniably

---

ports that Hemingway stayed at the Ritz again in 1959, but it is hardly
likely that Georges had suffered from amnesia in the interim.

  [6] Françoise Féret, "F. Scott Fitzgerald in Paris," unpublished thesis
submitted to the Sorbonne for the *Diplôme d'Etudes Supérieures* in 1957,
p. 39.

  [7] See Donald Ogden Stewart, "Recollections of Fitzgerald and Hemingway," *Fitzgerald/Hemingway 1971*, pp. 177-188. Stewart, who figures
as a character and who witnessed the events on which the novel was
based, sums it up as "nothing but a report on what happened. There's
no creation, no imagination. This is journalism."

Fitzgerald did much to promote Hemingway's career at a time when Fitzgerald was the brilliant young star and Hemingway virtually unpublished and unsung beyond the slopes of Montparnasse. He was also indebted to Fitzgerald's critical acumen, notably in cutting *The Sun Also Rises* to that wonderful offhand opening I have just quoted and in the process leaving Hemingway with makings of the sketch of Ford Madox Ford he eventually used in *A Moveable Feast.*[8] Since none of this gets mentioned in that book—on the contrary the author creates the impression that he would not let Fitzgerald tamper with his first novel—we can only conclude that Hemingway could bear indebtedness no more than rivalry. "The truth was," to paraphrase *The Great Gatsby* slightly, "that Ernest Hemingway of Paris, France, sprang from his Platonic conception of himself."

During his Paris years he was indebted to quite a few writers. Some of them are overlooked entirely or mentioned only in passing, most conspicuously Robert McAlmon, who paid for Hemingway's first trip to Spain and published his first two books. Others are singled out only to be disparaged, such as Ernest Walsh, the editor of *This Quarter*, who paid tribute to Hemingway in a poem and a review in that little magazine and who published two of Hemingway's early stories. Only two friends emerge unscathed—Sylvia Beach, who was everybody's fairy godmother and who depicted Hemingway as a nice young man in *Shakespeare and Company*, and Evan Shipman, an exceedingly minor poet with no ambitions of any kind.

By now McAlmon, Walsh, and Shipman have been buried in the footnotes of literary history, and there is no great need to exhume them. But four major writers lived in Paris in Hemingway's time, and all of them figure in *A Moveable Feast*. Joyce appears a number of times but only as part of the

---

[8] See Philip Young and Charles W. Mann, "Fitzgerald's *Sun Also Rises:* Notes and Comments," and Fitzgerald's letter to Hemingway recommending cuts in the novel, *Fitzgerald/Hemingway Annual 1970*, pp. 1-13.

fabulous local color, an awesome figure to be venerated, too sacred to be the subject of a satirical sketch. The three others—Gertrude Stein, Ezra Pound, and Ford Madox Ford—were not only more vulnerable but played far more influential roles in the author's apprenticeship. Unquestionably these were Hemingway's three most important mentors during those Paris years that were his higher education. Hence in *A Moveable Feast* each of them must be disposed of somehow, and Hemingway is too astute to use the same method each time.

Ford is the easiest, a notorious mythomaniac with all kinds of foibles that Hemingway deftly exposes through a comical bit of dialogue. Gertrude Stein might have been satirized just as easily, but Hemingway has a real grudge against her, so he attacks her quite viciously, not once but three times. Evidently she represented as great a threat as Fitzgerald, for she occupies as prominent a position in the front of the book as he does toward the back. Granted, the scheme of the book is basically chronological, and he knew her early and Fitzgerald later, but the symmetrical structure is calculated here as in all of Hemingway's books, and clearly Gertrude Stein's role is meant to balance Fitzgerald's.

This leaves Ezra Pound, who is usually regarded as one of the sympathetic characters in *A Moveable Feast*—the loyal, selfless, and tireless champion of struggling artists. But for all the praise of Pound, the portrait Hemingway presents is satirical, emphasizing Pound's eccentricities and buffoonish traits, his bassoon, his ineptitude as a boxer, his errors in judgment, his crackpot economic theories, and by implication his equally ridiculous scheme to rescue T. S. Eliot from a bank. More revealing than anything else in the Pound sketch is Hemingway's gratuitous derision of Eliot—revealing not so much Pound's absurdity as Hemingway's animosity.

After all why should Hemingway drag Eliot across the channel and into *A Moveable Feast?* Obviously there was something about Eliot that gnawed at him, for he had gone out of his way to attack him several times before.[9] One may speculate about the reasons behind Hemingway's apparently unmotivated resentment of Eliot, beginning with the profound temperamental differences between them. The most plausible explanations, it seems to me, are once again professional jealousy and indebtedness.[10] Hemingway was not likely to cheer magnanimously with Pound when the success of *The Waste Land* established Eliot as the leading spokesman for the postwar genera-

---

[9] In the *transatlantic review* (October 1924) he had offered to put Eliot through a sausage grinder. Two titles dating from the same year are, I believe, jibes at Eliot: "The Lady Poets with the Foot Notes" and "Mr. and Mrs. Elliot," a story about a poet from Harvard who writes long poems with ease yet cannot beget a child. And in *Death in the Afternoon* (New York: Charles Scribner's Sons, 1932, p. 139) he expresses contempt for "the children of decorous cohabitation . . . . with their quaint pamphlets gone to bust and into foot-notes all their lust," explaining that the line is taken from Andrew Marvell: "I learned how to do that by reading T. S. Eliot."

[10] Eliot received the *Dial* award for *The Waste Land* in 1922. In *A Moveable Feast* Hemingway not only mentions the *Dial* award in writing about Eliot but brings it up again in his sketch of Ernest Walsh, this time citing the "huge sum" involved and explaining that two people "could live comfortably and well in Europe on five dollars a day and could travel." The two people he has in mind are obviously himself and his wife. Clearly Hemingway coveted the award and felt—justifiably— that he should have won it, not in 1922 but certainly by 1925 or 1926. And to add insult to oversight the *Dial* never published Hemingway, although Pound had sent in some of his earliest writings and Hemingway himself had later submitted a story that was rejected. Naturally, then, the *Dial* represented for him the most supercilious Brahminical literary establishment, and just as naturally. I would guess, Eliot, another Harvard snob, became guilty by association.

Besides, Hemingway owed a literary debt to Eliot. I am not thinking now of Hemingway's use of the objective correlative (which I believe he was more likely to have adopted from Flaubert than from Eliot's critical essay on *Hamlet*), nor even of the parallels between *The Waste Land* and *The Sun Also Rises*, but of even more specific borrowings. Hemingway doesn't seem to have been much of a reader of poetry, not at any rate of the Elizabethans and Jacobeans, but scraps of their poetry or allusions to them do appear in his works. Most if not all of these were first borrowed by Eliot. Hemingway may have loathed every line of *The Waste Land*, but he appears to have studied it with profit.

tion, nor was he likely to appreciate Eliot's insidious and all-pervasive influence, especially if he found it creeping into his own work.

Hemingway's debt to Pound was no secret and thus easier to acknowledge. Pound was his impresario, editor, and tutor. He went over Hemingway's early writings and indoctrinated him with the discipline of Flaubert and *le mot juste*, with the imagist principles of economy and precision. A recent article makes a convincing case that Hemingway's views on the writer's craft, his high critical standards, and his respect for nineteenth century French authors came from Pound,[11] and *A Moveable Feast* confirms this view.

Ultimately Flaubert was everybody's true Penelope, although originally Pound is supposed to have had Ford Madox Ford in mind. Certainly Hemingway must have heard more about Flaubert from this garrulous source, along with a good deal of rambling reminiscence about writers he admired, like Crane, Conrad, and James, and some astute theorizing about craftsmanship. Hemingway considered Ford a poseur[12] and quarreled with him over the editing of the *transatlantic review,* but a young writer from the Middle West could learn much about writing from such an experienced man of letters, not to mention other kinds of expertise he might have picked up from such a cosmopolitan *bon vivant*. Hemingway's favorite restaurant in *A Moveable Feast* was Ford's discovery, as was his favorite café about which he feels so territorial, the Closerie des Lilas.[13] I have long suspected that Hemingway also learned

---

[11] Harold M. Hurwitz, "Hemingway's Tutor, Ezra Pound," *Modern Fiction Studies* (Winter 1971-72), pp. 469-482.

[12] Arthur Mizener suggests that Ford was well aware of Hemingway's opinion and was putting him on, performing a parody of the British snobbery that Hemingway expected of him. See Mizener, *The Saddest Story: A Biography of Ford Madox Ford* (New York: 1971), p. 208. Anyone who has read *Parade's End* will recognize the affinity between Ford and his incredibly Tory protagonist. Still, if Mizener's interpretation is correct, Hemingway too was good at the game of parody; here his dialogue seems to me faultless.

[13] See Mizener, p. 327.

from Ford's writing and have only recently come upon the evidence. There are passages in *A Farewell to Arms* and in some of Hemingway's war stories that are reminiscent in style and method of passages in the great war novel which Ford was writing at the time he and Hemingway were most closely associated. What I have but recently learned is that the only known typescript of *No More Parades*, with many corrections in Ford's hand, has turned up among the Hemingway manuscripts.[14]

Hemingway must also have read Ford's book of literary reminiscence, *It Was the Nightingale*, and noted Ford's introductory announcement that he was writing this book as he would fiction: "I have tried then to write a novel drawing my material from my own literary age." Hemingway learned still more—much more—about fictionalizing memoirs from Gertrude Stein's *Autobiography of Alice B. Toklas*, whose very title suggests a spoof and whose gossipy anecdotes were meant to entertain, not to be taken as documentary truth. Yet, as Hemingway realized, biographers will cite such legendary works as evidence;[15] Hemingway himself repeats one of the legends from the *Autobiography*—the one about the death of Apollinaire on Armistice Day—and apparently believes it.

By now we should have learned to distrust what writers say in their memoirs, particularly when they have scores to settle. Like Gertrude Stein, Hemingway was writing legends for posterity; only he was determined to endow his legend with a great air of authenticity. For a more reliable account of their relationship in the twenties it is necessary to go back to contemporary documents such as the letters he wrote her at the time. These show him in the role of a humble and willing pupil, echoing her lessons and seeking advice—even on bullfighting, which they discussed before his first trip to Pamplona. One

---

[14] Philip Young and Charles W. Mann, *The Hemingway Manuscripts: An Inventory* (University Park: Penn. State Univ. Press, 1969), p. 122.

[15] For a fuller discussion of this point see Chapters 3 on *The Autobiography of Alice B. Toklas*) and 9 (on Hemingway) of George Wickes, *Americans in Paris* (New York: Doubleday, 1969). For the use of *A Moveable Feast* as documentary evidence see Carlos Baker's biography, *passim*.

letter in particular has often been quoted, in which Hemingway
reports on a long story "where I'm trying to do the country like
Cézanne" and exclaims:

> . . . but isn't writing a hard job though?
> It used to be easy before I met you. I certainly was bad,
> gosh, I'm awfully bad now but it's a different kind of bad.[16]

In his later years and in *A Moveable Feast* Hemingway made
much of writing like Cézanne, as though he had invented the
idea. Actually it came from Gertrude Stein, who always said
she had learned about writing from a Cézanne that she acquired
in 1905 when she was writing *Three Lives*. In *A Moveable Feast*
Hemingway repeats another claim he often made in his later
years, that Gertrude Stein had learned to write conversation
from him. But as early as *Three Lives* she demonstrated a remarkable ear in recording the spoken language, and in *The
Autobiography of Alice B. Toklas* she was not writing dialogue
in the Hemingway sense at all, but repartee and epigrams.

Hemingway's debt to her on the other hand was the greatest of all and the hardest to dismiss; hence his sketches of her
require the most artful dodging. The first, promisingly entitled
"Miss Stein Instructs," says nothing of her lessons in writing;
her subject matter, strangely enough, is homosexuality. The
second exposes the personal bias behind her literary judgments
(strikingly similar to the author's own) and criticizes her remark about the lost generation (which, after all, *he* immor-
talized) in an astonishingly emotional, irrational, and finally
condescending diatribe. While shedding crocodile tears over
a totally fictitious wounded French "boy," who conveniently
serves as a reminder of the author's ambulance service, he con-
demns Gertrude Stein's "lost-generation talk and all the dirty,
easy labels," conveniently overlooking her wartime service to

---

[16] Donald Gallup, ed., *The Flowers of Friendship: Letters Written to
Gertrude Stein* (New York; Knopf, 1953), pp. 164-165. Only a sampling
of Hemingway's letters to Gertrude Stein appears in that volume; the
others are located in the Gertrude Stein Collection at Yale. Carlos Baker
identifies the story in question as "Big Two-Hearted River" (Baker,
p. 132).

just such French boys, not to mention the underlying sympathy for them which prompted her remark about the lost generation in the first place. But then Hemingway can be expected to ignore her explanation of that remark, even though it makes more sense than his.[17]

His third sketch of Gertrude Stein, "A Strange Enough Ending," is not merely strange but preposterous, if I understand correctly, indicating that his motive for breaking off the friendship was her lesbianism, which after all was hardly news after three or four years' acquaintance. This ending is just as discreditable as his third sketch of Fitzgerald—discreditable to the author—and reminds us of Gertrude Stein's quip in *The Autobiography of Alice B. Toklas* that Hemingway was "ninety percent Rotarian."

From start to finish *A Moveable Feast* manifests his distrust and scorn, not only of homosexuals and wastrels but of all kinds of nonconformists and bohemians, including writers. His values throughout are those of the Protestant ethic, he feels entitled to material rewards for his hard work, and his poverty is virtuous only because of the Horatio Alger ending to his success story. Above all he wants to be a self-made man, and in order to spring from his own Platonic conception of himself, he must destroy all the writers who helped make him. So inevitably his "Sketches of the Author's Life in Paris in the Twenties" are sketchy and fictional. But to the biographer what he omitted and fictionalized is often more revealing than what he wrote.

---

[17] "Gertrude claimed no personal part in the coining of the immensely durable epithet and, in fact, doubted that she had uttered it. If, as people said, the phrase was her invention, the idea must have been the result of a talk she once had with M. Pernollet, the hotelkeeper in Belley, where she was later to take up summer residence. It was M. Pernollet's conviction that every man becomes civilized between the ages of eighteen and twenty-five. If the civilizing experience does not occur within that period, the individual has lost his chance. And that is what had happened to those who went to the war. Missing their opportunity, they had become "une génération perdue." John Malcolm Brinnin, *The Third Rose: Gertrude Stein and Her World* (Boston: Little, Brown and Co., 1959), p. 233.

Joseph M. DeFalco

HEMINGWAY'S ISLANDS AND STREAMS: MINOR TACTICS FOR HEAVY PRESSURE

THE EARLY REVIEWS of Ernest Hemingway's *Islands in the Stream* were unanimous almost in their assessment of the work as a rather cheap and consciously contrived affair that marked the disintegration of Hemingway's power as an artist. Irving Howe thought the work lacked "vision or coherence" and that it was a rehash of the shopworn "cult of manliness." Edmund Wilson attacked the book on a milder note but agreed with those who saw a strong autobiographical element dominating the narrative. Malcolm Cowley felt the central character did not achieve the mythic dimensions of the best of the Hemingway characters because he was a reflection merely of a "mask or persona that Hemingway adopted in his relations with the world." Those reviewers who did see virtue in the book pointed to particularly vivid descriptions or to the intensity of the action depicted in portions of the third section. What these and other reviews reflect is a widespread tendency to read Hemingway's fiction as autobiography and to judge his work by standards alien to fiction.[1]

---

[1] Irving Howe, "Great Man Going Down," *Harper's*, Oct. 1970, pp. 120-125; Edmund Wilson, "An Effort at Self-Revelation," *The New Yorker*, 2 Jan. 1971, pp. 59-62; Malcolm Cowley, "A Double Life, Half Told," *The Atlantic Monthly*, Dec. 1970, pp. 105-106, 108. For a thorough digest of the early reviews, see William R. Anderson, Jr., "*Islands in the Stream*—The Initial Reception," in *Hemingway/Fitzgerald Annual 1971*, ed. Matthew J. Bruccoli and C. E. Frazer Clark, Jr. (Washington, D. C.: NCR Microcard Editions, 1971), pp. 326-332.

The bitterness and despair of Thomas Hudson in *Islands in the Stream* may or may not reflect a kindred feeling in Hemingway at certain moments in his life. Attending to the imaginative structure of the work, however, reveals that Hemingway's artistic vision mediates Hudson's bleakness and that an authorial judgment of a different order informs the work. Although the novel may not be a finished product, the theme is not a replay of old, gloomy naturalistic views. In fact, Thomas Hudson's universe is the same one in which Santiago dwells in *The Old Man and the Sea*. If we identify with Santiago's tragic grandeur more readily than with the pathos of Thomas Hudson, perhaps it is our own sentimentalism that leads us to choose the less painful alternative. Colonel Cantwell in *Across the River and Into the Trees* shares this universe as well, for all three novels reflect a major shift to the affirmative mode in the realism of Hemingway's later fiction.

The clearest indication of Hemingway's changing viewpoint came when he adopted the Gulf Stream as a major metaphor and abandoned his long-favored use of the bullfight. The experiment of *Green Hills of Africa* suggests that he was seeking new and fresh ways of rendering reality in his work. Big game hunting furnished him with the materials he needed to formulate his patterns of imagery and establish a metaphorical dimension in his work, but it did not yield much that was new. It raised the same kinds of questions and demanded similar responses, e.g., the need of a code and the supremacy of skill over luck. The vastness of Africa and its various "countrys" did open vistas of thought, and in one of the more valuable meditations in the work Hemingway establishes the Gulf Stream as a metaphorical equivalent of past, present, and future reality: "This Gulf Stream you are living with, knowing, learning about, and loving, has moved, as it moves, since before man . . . and those that have always lived in it are permanent and of value, because that stream will flow, as it has flowed."[2] In *To Have and Have*

----

[2] *Green Hills of Africa:* Scribner Library Edition (New York: Charles Scribner's Sons, 1935), p. 149.

Not the stream image is one of the controlling figures in the narrative. As imaged by the tanker in the last paragraph, "hugging the reef as she made to the westward to keep from wasting fuel against the stream,"[3] life goes on in spite of Harry's travail.

Perhaps the need to find meaningful metaphors and images to express themes of human solidarity and brotherhood led Hemingway away from the sophisticated rituals of the bullring to the pastoral primitiveness of the Gulf Stream. Whatever the impetus, the world of these middle novels is one where the Harry Morgans and the Robert Jordans can and do engage the forces of a reality they can perceive. Man's willed actions have meaning here in a way they do not for a compromised Jake Barnes or a despairing Frederic Henry. Jordan's world in *For Whom the Bell Tolls* does not have a literal affinity to the Gulf Stream setting of Morgan's world, but the reading directions provided by the "No man is an *island*" epigraph point to strong thematic similarities. There is no qualitative difference between Harry's realization that "a man alone ain't got no bloody fucking chance" and Jordan's "you can do nothing for yourself but perhaps you can do something for another."[4] Each reflects the view that there are forces which prey upon man and that his only hope is to band together.

Although the solution projected through these novels is a significant advance toward an affirmation of the worth of human endeavor, there is about that solution a taint of the maverick-and-the-herd oversimplification. The estrangement between man and forces he cannot understand remains. Individual dignity and worth are subsumed under Donne's rubic "*Mankinde.*" With the advantage of hindsight that Hemingway gives us through the example of Santiago, we know that these values concern the self and that the self must have dimensions of no less magnitude than those of the forces with which it contends.

---

[3] *To Have and Have Not:* Scribner Library Edition (New York: Charles Scribner's Sons, 1937), p. 262.

[4] *To Have and Have Not,* p. 225; *For Whom the Bell Tolls:* Scribner Library Edition (New York: Charles Scribner's Sons, 1940), p. 466.

Across the River and into the Trees represents the initial step toward a resolution of the dilemma inherent in the view of the essential duality of the universe. The nature of that dilemma is articulated early in the novel by the protagonist, Colonel Cantwell: "I ought to write the manual of minor tactics for the heavy pressure platoon."[5] Cantwell is musing over the medical deception he has practiced in order to remain in the service, but Hemingway is engaging larger issues through the military metaphor. The aging Cantwell is rootless, physically battered, and psychologically beleaguered, and his vicious self-irony serves to buffer the certain knowledge that he will die soon. As the novel proceeds through an extended series of memory rounds, it becomes apparent that Cantwell is undergoing an intense self-analysis. What he is seeking from the past is some sort of principle of life by which he has lived that will negate the implications of the military metaphor. Phrased in another way, the metaphor is almost a capsule definition of literary naturalism: life is an endless war against inscrutable forces, and individual effort is nothing more than a temporary evasion of the inevitable.

Cantwell's quest for a valid strategy of life has another dimension that reveals the extent to which Hemingway had modified his own view of reality by the time he wrote *Across the River*. As the narrative is structured, the orientation is both introspective and retrospective. In a fashion reminiscent of Conrad, Hemingway employs the memory rounds in such a way that they surpass the ordinary expositional function of flashback. Here they serve not only to acquaint us with past action in a dramatic way but also to yoke that past with an ongoing reality. The result is that through dramatic simultaneity, past and present reality become a new reality. The instrument that effects this paradox is Renata's love for Cantwell. Reflecting upon her love, Cantwell calls it "a great miracle."[6] This is more

---

[5] *Across the River and Into the Trees* (New York: Charles Scribner's Sons, 1950), p. 9.

[6] *Across the River*, p. 288.

than a recognition that the forces that wound may bless as well. Renata's love is doubly miraculous for having transformed Cantwell's meaningless past into a coherent, meaningful life of dignity without despair. Love, then, has the capacity to invade the seemingly inviolate past and alter it.

Hemingway had not discovered a new metaphysical principle in the power of love, but he had made a significant discovery in the psychology of man. Colonel Cantwell found a temporary respite among the islets of Venice in time-present, but he cannot escape the processes of biology. The synecdochical hunting scenes which envelop most of the narrative reveal both the limitation these processes impose upon man and the possibility of reconciliation with them. Cantwell's dispute with the figurative eternal boatman in the initial scenes of the novel and the pacific accord between himself and the boatman in the closing scenes mirror what has taken place in the intervening narrative. The many comparisons of Cantwell's heart with machinery suggest that biological processes are mechanistic, but the power of love to transform reality enlarges considerably the psychic or spiritual space available within those processes.

In *The Old Man and the Sea*, Santiago inhabits that same space. Hemingway invests the character with such a vigor of will, however, that ongoing reality tends to encompass not only all of the past but also all of indeterminate time. Santiago seems larger than life because he is as large as Hemingway's conception of man's possibilities. External forces cannot strangulate man's efforts in this new view, for the source from which these forces derive their power and the source from which man derives his power are the same. Hemingway suggests as much early in the narrative when he describes Santiago's eyes: "Everything about him was old except his eyes and they were the same color as the sea and were cheerful and undefeated."[7] The sea throughout the work functions as a symbol of the generative power of the universe which manifests itself in ongoing

---

[7] *The Old Man and the Sea*: Scribner Library Edition (New York: Charles Scribner's Sons, 1952), p. 10.

reality. Linking Santiago's eyes with the sea points to the extra-ordinary capacity with which he is endowed. As Hemingway completes the physical description of Santiago he completes the trope and effectually reconciles the seemingly dichotomous forces within reality. The thin, gaunt, blotched Santiago, we are told, has scars "as old as erosions in a fishless desert."[8] The meaning Hemingway urges through the trope is that the plight of the flesh is of the same order as the fate of external nature in geological time. Neither form can resist change, but physical change is an effect of process not the dynamic of process. As mirrored by Santiago's eyes, that dynamic element is associated with the impulses of the generative sea. This is the power within him that Hemingway describes as "undefeated."

Santiago's actions define this impulse in man as the will. In Santiago the will is indomitable, but Hemingway does not over-simplify or sentimentalize the implications of this premise. Santiago is an idealization of the capacities of Everyman, not a representation of Everyman as he functions in the world. The other fishermen do not choose to go "far out" into the Gulf Stream; they remain content to fish within sight of the island. They trust to "luck," but their way can be the way of terror and desperation. Their desire for security forces them to subject themselves to the contingencies of the flux in natural processes. As always for Hemingway, those processes are brute, nonrational, and without purpose. Santiago is a self-realized man. By willingly and consciously choosing he avoids the folly of such a surrender and molds his own reality.

The Christ motif that operates throughout the work illustrates further Hemingway's celebration of the realized will. Although the many references to crucifixion seem to suggest that the way of the flesh is "The Way of the Cross," we should not conclude that Hemingway is reiterating the already postulated thesis that existence entails pain and suffering. More importantly, I think, he employs the pattern of Christ in order to give dramatic emphasis to the theme of the indestructability of

---

[8] *The Old Man and the Sea*, p. 10.

the will. The formula Hemingway employs relies upon traditional views. Christ is the Word made flesh. To incarnate the Word is to incarnate an abstraction. The logical inference is that if man adheres to the pattern in its entirety he can will and create his own reality. Santiago's voyage into the Gulf Stream in these terms affirms the ability of man to contend with the inchoate stuff of ongoing reality, to dominate that stuff, and, finally, give it shape and direction that has meaning and worth. Man cannot avoid pain and suffering in this view, but he can exert his will to the extent of achieving a God-like dignity.

Thomas Hudson's final words in *Islands in the Stream* are, "I think I understand Willie."[9] The implications of those words go beyond the immediate context, for they reveal Hudson's basic flaw in all three sections of the work. Put simply, that flaw is his inability to comprehend the nature of reality. As much as Santiago is an idealization of Everyman, so Hudson is a realistic presentation of the way most men respond to the bewildering flux which is reality. Before Hudson can utter those final words, however, he must undergo a journey of pain and suffering. Once again Hemingway employs the motif of "The Way of the Cross" in order to achieve his thematic purpose. The island and stream imagery provides a metaphorical substructure for that motif as it catalogues the various states of mind through which Hudson passes.

As we find Hudson in the Bimini section, he is a fallen Adam who has constructed for himself a loveless Eden. Perched just above that part of the ocean which is the Gulf Stream, Hudson's house images his belief that it is possible to divorce himself from the stream of existence with impunity. Hudson conceives of his sanctuary as an emotional haven. As he has survived various emotional traumas, so too the house has survived three hurricanes. For him it is like a ship: "Placed there to ride out storms, it was built into the island as though it were a part of it."[10] The delusive smugness of these attitudes is sug-

---

[9] *Islands in the Stream* (New York: Charles Scribner's Sons, 1970), p. 466.
[10] *Islands*, p. 4.

gested further in his habits of mind. Throughout he practices a process of selected remembrance by suppressing the painful memories of the past and dwelling on pleasant memories only. Aside from the fact that pleasant memories become fewer as the novel progresses, these revisionist tactics plainly distort reality. Denial of the past is not a reconciliation, and what follows is a disfunction of the will and a concomitant emotional sterility.

Hudson's Eden contains within its conception the seeds of its own downfall. Predicated on the avoidance of a painful past on the one hand and the anticipation of a lonely futurity on the other, its existence depends upon the preservation of a static present. The impracticability of such a scheme is dramatized by Hemingway. Instanced by the arrival of the corrupt rich in their yachts, Hudson's illusion of order is shattered by near-anarchy and moral chaos. The nightmarish celebration of the Queen's birthday mocks the object it pretends to venerate. The assault upon the Commissioner's house and the failure of the Constable to intervene suggest that there are no restraints in this self-created sanctuary. The whole affair concludes with a fight between Rodger and a man from one of the yachts.

Throughout the chaos of the celebration Hudson's role remains one of passive detachment. His almost feminine reluctance to involve in any action is signified by his repetitious and conciliatory, "Take it easy." Frank Hart's sarcasm reflects both the virtue and the limitation of the role when he calls Hudson a "Christer." Rodger illuminates the role further, for in many ways he is a reflector of Hudson's inadequacies and possibilities. He too has loved and lost and is in full flight from life. After the fight, he recognizes his own deficiencies as a symptom of an inner violence that he cannot control. Hudson's havens are not possible for him because he is still engaged in the struggle. Rodger demonstrates his ability to actively contend with reality during David's crucial encounter with the broadbill fish later in the narrative. Even Eddy with all of his drinking reveals his capacity to contend with danger in the shark episode. In both instances Hudson fails to muster the necessary inner strength of will to engage the forces he has avoided for so long. After the incident with the fish, Rodger underscores this failure and points to the lesson it takes Hudson the length of the novel to learn when he tells Hudson that they have been "irresponsible."

Both Hudson and Rodger see David's encounter with the broadbill as a crucifixion. Hudson thinks of David afterward as a "well-loved mystery," and David describes his feelings in terms of a mystical experience. "Nobody knows how I feel," he tells them, and thus signifies the uniqueness of the experience. More meaningfully, he recalls the union of identities: "when I was tiredest I couldn't tell which was him and which was me." The formula of crucifixion is completed with an allusion to the doctrine of love: "I loved him so much when I saw him coming up that I couldn't stand it."[11] Only Rodger understands the tragic consequences their "gamble" with David could have had if David were not as strong as they thought. Thinking of it in terms of his own view of life Hudson believes that it is necessary to suffer and overcome in order to face further and deeper suffering. As a consequence, it is Rodger and David who achieve love in the mutuality of their effort to land the fish. The words that Rodger speaks to David after the fish escapes are words that reflect their kinship and common humanity. Hudson, on the other hand, "never knew what it was that Rodger had said."[12] This is the self-alienated and naysaying Hudson who responds to Mr. Bobby's questioning of his relationship to Rodger: "We're no kin."[13]

Sanctuaries are no more possible for Thomas Hudson to maintain than were the idyllic interludes of Jake Barnes and Frederic Henry. Hudson's personal retreat cannot arrest the flux, and the death of his two sons revealed in the denouement of the Bimini section suggests the futility of such evasions. Hemingway does not dramatize the total impact upon Hudson

---

[11] *Islands*, pp. 140, 142, 143.
[12] *Islands*, p. 143.
[13] *Islands*, p. 155.

during the passage of time between the Bimini and Cuba sections, but in the brief glimpse we get there is a foreshadowing of his almost total disintegration later when he receives the news of Tom's death. Here he responds with a feeble reaffirmation of the doctrine of detachment: "You should not have loved them so damn much in the first place."[14] The oppressiveness of the emotional hurt is more than evident, however, and his attempt to convince himself that he has adjusted is so steeped in irony that it mocks his earlier "separate peace" notion: "You see, he said to himself, there's nothing to it."[15]

Hudson's drinking at the Floridita bar in the Cuba section represents another attempt to create an "island" that will give him a safe place away from the dangers of time and contingency. Since he no longer believes in such sanctuaries, it is more a quest for that suicidal oblivion Rodger had rejected after his experience with David. The folly of his earlier attempt to repress unpleasant memories reveals itself fully in this context. With the death of all three sons all memory is painful. In effect he has delivered himself into the hands of death, for it is his inability to reconcile himself with death that has allowed it to transform happy memories into pain. Even ongoing reality offers no solace for Hudson. Literally and metaphorically, reality has altered its landscape from the surface serenity of Bimini to the war-enveloped Cuba. All the totally estranged Hudson can do is hope for momentary escapes into oblivion through the aesthetic of alcohol.

Hudson's retreat from consciousness and headlong flight into oblivion emphasizes his lapse into total despair. The loss of his sons and his inability to paint any longer mark the end of his powers to create. The stultifying effect of the catastrophies is an extension of his own conviction that escape from reality is possible. When he disengaged himself from that reality, he failed to understand the inevitability of the forces which operate in a willy-nilly way. What Hemingway reveals in the final

---

[14] *Islands*, p. 199.
[15] *Islands*, p. 200.

section of the novel echoes what he had revealed through Santiago. If man does not exert his own will and define himself then the forces of reality will define him. Hudson's egocentricity blinds him from understanding anything except his own loss. The result is that he is almost totally dehumanized by his grief. Only his commitment to duty suggests that at least the vestiges of will remain.

Through most of the "At Sea" section, Hemingway presents Hudson as a passionless Ahab who must see his enemy in order to define him. Like Ahab's enemy, Hudson's enemy, too, has its metaphorical dimensions. For Hudson the enemy is the dynamic of reality which he conceives of as death. The difference between the pair is that Ahab's quest is conscious and obsessive, while Hudson's rests limply upon the mechanism of duty and orders and does not originate from intense inner drives. Hudson's pursuit of the German sailors lack the romantic aura of Ahab's pursuit of the whale, but it does reveal Hemingway's concern with man's interrelationship with forces that emit the stuff of life and death in an undifferentiated way.

What becomes evident in Hemingway's resolution of the almost insolvable predicament in which he has placed Hudson is the principle of reciprocity that operates in the nature of things. This is not an Emersonian divine ordinance, but a principle of reality. Santiago catches a giant marlin because he seeks something of permanence and value in life. Since Hudson considers life a "death house," the end result of his quest must be death. Hemingway introduces that motif through Tom's mother when she refers to the world as a "house of death" after she learns of Tom's death. Hudson picks up the strain later in the narrative when he reflects upon the coming confrontation with the Germans: "It is my duty and I want to get them and I will. But I have a sort of fellow death-house feeling about them. Do people in the death house hate each other? I don't believe they do unless they are insane."[16]

---

[16] *Islands,* p. 376.

Although his orientation is still toward death, Hudson voices a significant insight into one dimension of reality when he sees that there is some common bond among men. The insight follows a highly suggestive passage in which the dying German sailor is pressed by Hudson to give information about the rest of the submarine crew. Hemingway consciously presents the scene in a symbolic way, for the place is *Cayo Cruz*, Cross Key, the interpreter's name is Peters, and the sailor's description suggests a mystical function: "His hair was long and uncombed and in the late afternoon light, with the sun almost down, he looked like a saint."[17] Later, after the sailor dies, Hudson marks a cross on his chart to indicate the place of burial. The oracular pronouncements of the transfigured Christ-like sailor suggest that at the point of death he speaks of death in a knowing way. Earlier Hudson had been "very happy" after he removed the bullets from the massacred Bahamians because it was the first tangible evidence of the enemy he acquired. He looks at them as a miner would look at "four nuggets in his pan," for he can define them and the weapon from which they came. Viewing death as a mechanistic force tends to verify his preconceived notions. When the sailor tells Hudson that "nothing is important" and that "it doesn't hurt anymore," he reveals the futility of Hudson's quest. The conception of death as an awesome force of a nature totally different from that of man is denied by the embodiment of that force in the figure of the gangrenous sailor. Death is the fulfillment of the flesh simply, and it is nothing more than a cessation.

Although Hudson does not fully understand the message of the sailor, he does begin to reflect upon the past and his own self-flagellation. That he moves toward a reconciliation is evident in his ability to accept finally the reality of the past. Thinking of Tom as a young boy, he recognizes that the pain will remain but that happy memories will effect a balance. "The time of innocence," he recalls, were all happy times. Eventually he

---

[17] *Islands*, p. 362.

brings himself to admit that "death is what is really final,"[18] and with that admission he accepts the fact of Tom's death for the first time.

Hudson's understanding of death does not complete his quest, and Hemingway gives him two more revelations within the last few pages of the narrative. Having come to terms with death, he now thinks of painting the sea "better than anyone." In "Bimini" he had painted the face of the stream and men who engaged that stream. Now that he has engaged that sea directly, he finds the capacity to reduplicate the generative functions of the sea and create something of worth. The final negation of the death-house motif comes through Willie, however, for Hudson's understanding that man's ability to realize his will through his work does not free him from what amounts to a solipsistic predicament. After Hudson had ceased to care about himself earlier, Ara had warned him that his irresponsibility would endanger the boat. The larger context of that warning was Rodger's earlier indictment of Hudson on the same charge. Willie's revelation that he loves Hudson provides a positive and affirming counter to a death-house kind of brotherhood. Although Willie's final charge that Hudson never understood love remains in tension with Hudson's "I think I understand," Hemingway's meaning is clear. Love is a transforming agency that can change all things, and it forms the common bond of humanity. Rodger discovered this earlier through David, but it took three chance bullets and many guides along the way before Hudson could understand.

---

[18] *Islands*, pp. 448, 449.

DELBERT E. WYLDER

INTERNAL TREACHERY IN THE LAST PUBLISHED SHORT STORIES OF ERNEST HEMINGWAY

> *A lone woman is troubled with such dreams and such thoughts that she's afraid of herself sometimes.*
>
> Faith Brown in
> Hawthorne's "Young Goodman Brown"

RAY B. WEST saw in *For Whom the Bell Tolls* a failure on Hemingway's part to fuse his Donne-like mysticism with his naturalistic materials, resulting in a failure in sensibility. He indirectly accused Hemingway of imposing his ideology upon the material rather than letting it grow out of that material. At the end of the essay, West suggested that "His present limitations would incline me to prefer that his future work would be done in the field of the short story, but these are limitations no greater than have been overcome by other artists."[1] In fact, however, Hemingway published very little in the way of short stories after writing *For Whom the Bell Tolls,* and those stories that were published have received very little critical attention. Typical examples are "Two Tales of Darkness" published in *The Atlantic* in 1957. I would agree with Julian Smith, who calls them "The true capstone to his career . . ."[2] The stories are that capstone because they provide a more perfect fusion with his long development of a romantic sensibility, and they

[1] Ray B. West, Jr., "Ernest Hemingway: The Failure of Sensibility, *Forms of Modern Fiction,* ed., William Van O'Connor (Minneapolis: University of Minnesota Press, 1948), p. 101. Originally published in *The Sewanee Review,* 1945.

[2] Julian Smith, "Eyeless in Wyoming, Blind in Venice: Hemingway's Last Stories," *Connecticut Review* 4 (April 1971), pp. 9-15.

provide us as readers with his most concise symbolic statement of the concept of internal treachery, a concept that he had been discovering throughout his career.

As early as 1944, Malcolm Cowley, in writing his introduction to the Viking Portable *Hemingway*, pointed out that, although Hemingway wrote in a naturalistic style that linked him with Dreiser and London, when you go back to his work, "you perceive his kinship with a wholly different group of novelists, let us say with Poe and Hawthorne and Melville: the haunted and nocturnal writers, the men who dealt in images that were symbols of an inner world."[3] The haunted quality of that world becomes more perceivable in these two stories, contrasting tales but artfully juxtaposed for an effective dualistic commentary on "blindness." Taken together, they seem to suggest a statement about "the blind being able to see," and its reversal (almost a double *dicho*), "the seeing being able to blind." The first story is a statement of cruelty and horror in the tradition of Hawthorne and Joseph Conrad; the second story is an equally horrific statement about love and compassion. In both stories, Hemingway explores the depths of human experience.

Like Shirley Jackson's "The Lottery," Hemingway's "A Man of the World" is a story of the scapegoat. In Hemingway's story, there are two scapegoats, however. One of them is Blindy, once known as Blackie. In his younger years, he was involved in a no-holds-barred fight with a man named Willie Sawyer. Willie gouged out both of Blackie's eyes and bit them off. In his turn, Blackie bit off Willie's nose. Hemingway chooses to tell this story with its oedipal overtones indirectly through the narrator Thomas Hudson, and provides as a setting a world in which there are few obvious distinctions.

The narrator, as Julian Smith has already pointed out, plays an extremely important role in the story. His commentary at the beginning of the story is as seemingly ambiguous as the nar-

---

[3] Malcolm Cowley, "Nightmare and Ritual in Hemingway" in *Hemingway: A Collection of Critical Essays*, ed., Robert P. Weeks (Englewood Cliffs, N.J., Prentice-Hall, 1962), p. 40. Originally published as the introduction to the Viking Portable *Hemingway*.

rator's description of the two roads in Robert Frost's "The Road Not Taken."

> Everybody knew him and they called him Blindy which is a good name for a blind man in that part of the country, and the name of the saloon that he threw his trade to was The Pilot. Right next to it was another saloon, also with gambling and a dining room, that was called the Index. Both of these were the names of mountains and they were both good saloons with old-days bars and the gambling was about the same in one as in the other except you ate better in The Pilot, although you got a better sizzling steak at The Index.[4]

Part of the ambiguity of Frost's "The Road Not Taken" results from the irony of the title, for the poem at first seems to be centered on the road "taken." The poem is about both roads or, more accurately, about all the roads that might have been taken except for man's limitations. In Hemingway's tale, the emphasis seems to be on the repugnant and symbolically castrated Blindy, but the symbolically emasculated Willie's presence looms in horror precisely because he is not there. Tom, the narrator, has a difficult time just looking at Blindy. As the story of the fight is indirectly narrated by the bartender, Willie seems to have been the winner of the fight, but it is clear that the violence has left Willie a hollow man. Tom tells us that Blindy says he put his hands on Willie's face and warned him that "on a cold night like this he'd ought to bundle up so the whole inside of his face wouldn't catch cold."

There is one major distinction between the saloons in Jessup, and Thomas Hudson believes that this is important to Blindy. The distinction is that, in The Index, the slot machines are scattered, but in The Pilot the machines are ordered along the left-hand wall, and this gives Blindy better control over the machines. Furthermore, although we are not told this directly, Blindy has control over the management and the clientele. Blindy exists through the guilt of others. He has become an

---

[4] Ernest Hemingway, "Two Tales of Darkness," *The Atlantic Monthly*, 200:5 (November 1957), pp. 64-68. All future references to the stories are from this source.

institution associated with luck. When someone wins money on one of the coin machines, Blindy gets a coin as a percentage of the take—a tithing, so to speak. But Blindy has even better methods of control in either The Pilot or The Index, in The Flats or in Jessup. His strong odor and his repugnant appearance drive people away from the machines when he stands too close to them. This is negative control, in a sense, but most important and on the positive side, he is able to control people through constantly reminding them of their guilt.

The narrator, then, makes the important statement about distinctions, but even more important is Thomas Hudson's own role in the story. After cataloging the "cadging" activities of Blindy, the narrator is ready to remove to The Index because The Pilot "had been nice until Blindy had come in." But the bartender, Frank, wisely chooses this moment to offer a drink on the house to Tom and a young stranger who has paid off some quarters to Blindy. When the stranger asks how Blindy lost his sight, Tom disclaims any knowledge. He knows, however, for both the bartender and Blindy point out that Tom had been there on the night of the fight. Tom refuses to tell the story of violence, and the bartender tells it. When the young stranger dressed in city clothes asks what Blindy did to the other man, Blindy will not tell. "You'll recognize him any time you see him. I'll let it come as a surprise." The narrator interrupts, "You don't want to see him."

It should be made clear that although Tom cannot tell the story of violence and brutality to the young stranger at the bar, he tells it to the reader as narrator of the story, even though indirectly through the words of the bartender. The rest of the story he narrates with little comment.

In its totality, the story has suggestions of a Hawthorne-like story, but with a dualism that is prevalent in the later Hemingway. Willie Sawyer is the anti-hero who, like Young Goodman Brown, has isolated himself from the world. As Blindy says, "You know that Willie Sawyer will never be a man of the world." Disillusion has been too much for Willie. Blindy, even though symbolically castrated, has a new name which he insists on being called. The disillusion from the violence and evil that Blacky helped bring to himself, and from which he has gained his human scars, has not shaken him. On the contrary, he makes his presence felt even more strongly. The odious, repugnant, repulsive man is still both the undefeated hero and the scapegoat and still in operation after knowing what he has done and what has been done to him.

Tom gives adequate warning to the young stranger not to seek out the other victim of violence. The young man will not want to see Willie. It will be too much of a shock. Nor does Tom want to tell him the story of the fight. It is too much. The gouging and maiming are bad enough for the participants, but the community of men is also involved. They watched it. Tom, the narrator, had been there. And it was one of the watchers, Hollis Sands, who lent his own violent propensities to the fight. Hollis was the one who first shouted "Bite it off." Now the community pays its penance by a token percentage from the slot machines, and the myth is perpetuated by the bartender. But the narrator is the sensitive artist, and he must relate the horror, but twice removed from it, much as Joseph Conrad might have done. Through his indirect method of telling and his attempt to prevent the stranger from confronting the horror of Willie, the narrator, as artist, demonstrates his awareness of the necessity for restraint.

The analysis of Hemingway's "The Killers" in Cleanth Brooks and Robert Penn Warren's *Understanding Fiction* made the point that the reaction to the "evil" by all the characters in the story adds to the depth of the story. Julian Smith makes the same point about "A Man of the World," although I would disagree strongly with the inclusion of "indifference" as one of the reactions. The young stranger reacts with reluctant charity when Blindy claims his reward, and then with curiosity about the nature of Blindy. Frank, the bartender, tells the story of the fight, almost glorying in the details because he is consciously unaware of the implications in the story, and then extends charity to Blindy by giving him a drink on the house and, though he will not go out of his way to take him home, will let him sleep in the back room. Thomas Hudson also orders a drink, though he mistakenly orders it for Blackie. Then Blindy reminds Tom that he isn't Blackie (or blackness) but Blindy. "Blindy's the name, Tom. I earned that name. You seen me earn it." Then, at the end of the story, the man with the new name for evil accepts his final drink of the story. "His hand reached out and found the glass and he raised it accurately to the three of us." He thus toasts the innocent stranger, the man who accepts evil without an awareness of his own involvement, and the narrator who has tried to hide his own involvement but whose inner torment will lead him to tell the story. Blindy can toast these men, but he has nothing but contempt for Willie Sawyer, who has isolated himself from the rest of the world. "Probably alone by himself. That Willie Sawyer he don't know how to have any fun at all."

Blackie-Blindy is, of course, the scapegoat who represents the violence and evil within us all. "A Man of the World" is a story about the nature of evil. It is even more a story about the nature of man, and of that internal treachery that must be restrained. Hemingway has given us the sensitive narrator, and we thus become aware through him, for Tom becomes part of the story and adds the deepest dimension to it. We are aware of his sense of guilt through his need to tell the story of the fight. Tom must have been caught up in the violence much as Robin is caught up in the punishment of his scapegoat uncle in Hawthorne's "My Kinsman, Major Molineaux." We know that the narrator cannot recount directly, just as Marlowe cannot tell Kurtz's fiancee everything that happened in the jungle. Repulsive as the story is, there is a deeper horror beneath.

There is unspoken horror, too, in the second tale, concerned also with the writer and his sensibility. From a casual reading, it appears to be exactly what Carlos Baker called it, "a sentimental episode about an American gone blind in Venice, an idea probably suggested by Ernest's bout with erysipelas in 1949."[5] It is in some ways a more simple tale than "A Man of

---

[5] Carlos Baker, *Ernest Hemingway: A Life Story* (New York: Charles Scribner's Sons, 1969), p. 534.

the World," but even the narrative perspective is more subtle than it looks. There is a third-person narrator hidden deftly behind the central intelligence—a man named Philip. Philip is a writer, blinded and injured about the head. He and his wife, or the woman who is living with him and has lived with him for a long time, are sensitive people, unlike Blindy of the companion tale. Blindy obviously relished his role as scapegoat to the community, and his story is one of selfishness as he assumes the guilt of mankind and uses it. "Get a Seeing-Eyed Dog," however, is concerned with people who love one another, yet face all the insecurities involved in human relationships. It is the undercurrent of psychological horror that is the dominant force in the story because even love and sacrifice can be treacherous.

The tale seems to be simply enough told. "And what did we do then?" the writer asks the woman at the beginning, suggesting the major problem for both of them. That problem is "What do we do now?" Unfortunately for the characters but artistically sound, the ending of the story indicates that nothing can be done now. Their love is too complex to allow for an adequate solution.

The early dialogue seems inconsequential as the man tries to remember events preceding his accident. What he does remember and reports to his wife does not become meaningful until the writer poses the problem to himself. His wife has assumed a self-sacrificing martyrdom as his nurse, although she recognizes that she is not good at this role. His concern is that the assumption of this role will destroy her and thus their relationship, for "She has been good and she was not built to be good. I mean this sort of good. I mean good every day and dull good." It is only at this point almost one-fourth of the way through the tale that the opening descriptions of what he *does* remember become meaningful to the reader.

He has remembered two scenes. The first is a scene in which the writer remembers native women with pots on their heads, and geese being herded by a herdsman, making endless trips back and forth to the water. As he remembers it, this was an endless domestic routine. "I remember how slowly they all went and they were always going down and coming up." This is the first description, and it is suggestive of the present roles of the man and the woman. Like the women, Philip's wife makes trips up and down the stairs to bring him food and drink. He travels the same path on numerous occasions as he is led down the stairs by the physical guide of his wife and the banister. The goose, after all, is like the swan in being a masculine phallic symbol. And these tamed geese, like the writer, are fixed in a dull routine.

The major problem of the writer is that he is intelligent enough to know that this type of routine is destroying his wife. She is becoming a "seeing-eye" dog, one which has had its "dogness" trained out of it for service to the blind. He loves his wife and does not wish to destroy her, and suggests that she leave for a trip to London and Paris so that she can revivify herself by some excitement. At the same time, he is unconsciously afraid of the results of such a trip. The second scene he remembers is something his wife suggests.

> "Do you remember when the big dhow came in and careened on the low tide?"
> "Yes," he answers, "I remember her and the crew coming ashore in her boats and coming up the path from the beach, and the geese were afraid of them and so were the women."

Both the geese and the women were afraid of the excitement intruding itself into their routine and private world. The image of the masculine forces also point up the writer's symbolic impotence, which is not so much physical as mental. He is, of course, no longer the man he was. He has been blinded, and injured about the head. They have now retreated to a geographical area with which he is very familiar so that he can adapt himself to the feeling, rather than the seeing, world.

He is adapting very well, in fact. He is sensitive to the dark world. He can tell the difference from her tread whether she carries something up the stairs or is empty-handed, he is learning to enjoy the sound of tourists talking, he is able to remember the particular place they live well enough that he can picture the only place along the river that cannot be crossed with the tide out. But he is also insecure in the darkness, an insecurity heightened by his sensitivity. The insecurity is evidenced when he reaches out his hand "a little too soon" for the drink she has brought him, not "accurately" as Blindy had operated in the first story. Then he saves the drink until she is almost finished. As she drinks, he asks her about the birds. She tells about the big birds, the gulls and terns that are caught by the wind when they get up into the air. This, too, seems to remind him too much of the free life, and he asks, "Aren't there any shore birds?" Her answer is that there are only a few, and that they are working on a part of the flats that is only there during this bad season. It is then that he asks if she thinks it will ever be spring again. She answers, "I don't know. It certainly doesn't look like it."

He suggests that she leave for a trip. He tells her that when she comes back "it would have to be spring by then and you could tell me about everything." He evidently knows that there is nothing she can do by his side that will not be self-destructive. Even writing, which he needs now more than ever, is a skill which involves her cooperation on a subservient level. His excitement is apparent as he describes how he can see the words in his mind, and he can picture the place they live. "We couldn't have come to a better place *for me*." (my emphasis) Her role, however, is technical, and one for which she is not really suited. "If you take your time with the tape recorder you can get the words right," he tells her.

He also tells her that it is the "intelligent" thing for her to leave. In order to convince her of the wisdom of such a move, he tries to make clear his concept of seeing. At one point they talk about the tourists, and she remarks that some of the tourists are nice, that "the nicest ones . . . go out to Torcello." He agrees, says he hasn't thought of it, and then makes a comment about "seeing" one of their favorite places. "There's really nothing for them to see unless they are a little bit nice." They must, then, have some niceness or sensitivity to see the beauty. He is quite concerned about making this woman understand the

difference from the usual concept of seeing, and to understand
that he has this sensitivity.

When she talks about the lion she had evidently shot on a
safari one time in the past, she says, "I can't wait till we see
him." He replies that he can't either, and she immediately
apologizes. But he was being honest, and he could have seen
the lion in his memory. His attempt to describe the possibility
of his resumption of writing is also in terms of "seeing" and
"hearing" the words. He remembers the place where they are
staying and says it is "palpable." That is, it can be made evident
through a process other than sight. It is "touchable" through
memory. He tries to make a case for the dark, but she thinks
he is being noble. He mentions that they do wonderful things
in the dark. Her answer emphasizes the difficulty in their position. "And we did wonderful things in the daytime too." Because she is a "seeing-eyed" animal, she can only think of his
reactions from the point of view of loss. His attempts to make
her understand otherwise are exaggerated, and she thus rejects
them as an attempt at martyrdom. Her own martyrdom he
understands, and thus tries to communicate indirectly his fears.

He tries again to make a distinction.

> "Anyway, I don't want you just to be a seeing-eyed dog."
> "I'm not and you know it. Anyway it's seeing eye not seeing-
> eyed."
> "I knew that," he told her.

He did, of course. He is worried both that she will be a
"seeing-eye" dog and not be able to stand the boredom, but
even more that she will remain only a "seeing-eyed dog." His
grave concern is that she will allow her sightfulness and her
own love for him to trap her into the destruction of her personality and thus their relationship. If she fails to recognize
that he must touch her face to see as a blind man sees, without feeling sorry for his loss of sight, then they will be destroyed. Through their love for one another, their lives have
become more complex. There is no easy or even adequate way
out, because love is difficult.

They are both selfish in certain ways. Yet they both want to help one another. His desire is to send her away so that it might be possible for spring to come again. "You might be mad about me when you came back," he says, although he is frightened by the prospect of her loss. Yet, he is willing to sacrifice his momentary well-being for her happiness and their future happiness. She thinks that the weather indicates that spring will never come again, but she is willing to sacrifice herself for love of him. "I just don't want to be sent away." And she especially does not want to be sent away for her own good.

It is also clear from her question "What would you do nights?" that she is in some way aware of his unconscious sexual fears. She knows what her loss would mean to him, and she is willing to sacrifice herself. He tries to control his fear that he might lose her to the excitement of the external world. He thinks, "I must not be so stupid about it. She feels so lovely and I love her so much and have done her so much damage and I must learn to take good care of her in every way I can. If I think of her and of her only, everything will be all right." He too is willing to make the sacrifice of self, even though everything he says to her indicates his dependence. When he tries to answer the question of what he will do nights, he suggests that he will be able to sleep. But it is his insecurity about her that will keep him awake, and she knows it. "I don't want you to sleep with any lousy pillow," she says. Trying to reply humorously, he brings out his own fears about selecting someone to sleep with. "I won't. Not *any* lousy pillow." Selective promiscuity for him will be restricted to a choice in pillows. For her, in the external world, that would not be the case. She has told him that he is getting strong. He has contradicted this by suggesting that he *is* strong. When they leave their room to go downstairs to sit in front of the fire, he will tell her what happy "kittens" they are. But the virile vision of the sailors haunts them both, as it frightened the geese and the women— the geese because they have been tamed, the women because they are human. Like Faith, in Hawthorne's story, she is afraid of herself. There is a further contrast between ways of life in these two early descriptions of which both are unconsciously aware. In the placid and routine life of geese and women, there was safety. Nothing disturbed them, not even flies or mosquitoes. The day the sailors came, however, was "the day we caught so many fish but had to come in because it was so rough." It was a productive day, in other words, or a fertile one, but the elements were too violent and disruptive. The calm, however, has its own dangers, and they are destroying one another in their self-sacrifice.

The first "Tale" was centered around violence. The second is centered around love and compassion. The human relationships are far more complicated in the second tale. There is far more poignancy in the gradual destruction of two people who understand one another too well to reach one another because they love. In this situation, there are no simple answers. The blind writer asks himself what he can do, and the answer is, "There's nothing you can do."

The "Two Tales of Darkness" make contrasting statements about darkness. Their importance, however, for this study is not in what they have to say, but in the way that Hemingway tells the tales. When Hemingway finished *For Whom the Bell Tolls,* it was the end of something. It was the end of his work in the conventional short story form. The Tales, simply and disarmingly told, are highly complex stories packed into extremely short form. Although they are both based on human events, they are basically allegories of violence and charity, love and selfishness, and they demonstrate Hemingway's capacity to enter into that haunting internal world where our own treachery creates the life around us. They are as haunted as the works of Poe and Hawthorne and Melville, and they deal with some of the same materials with which those great Romantics dealt.

Upon reflection, Ray B. West's concern with *For Whom the Bell Tolls* was warranted, at least to some degree. Hemingway, at that point, was obviously a mixture of the naturalist and the romantic. Hemingway's last published tales, however, are the most complex of all his short stories, and the most concise, being told with a compression that is almost poetic. They indicate that Hemingway, in his late years, had managed to blend perfectly his use of naturalistic detail with his romantic sensibility in order to explore the greater depths of human experience.

Gerry Brenner

TO HAVE AND HAVE NOT AS CLASSICAL TRAGEDY: RECONSIDERING HEMINGWAY'S NEGLECTED NOVEL

PROBABLY THE ONLY thriving critical dispute over *To Have and Have Not* is whether it is worse than *Across the River and Into the Trees,* both novels competing for the nadir of Hemingway's career. Its reputation, however, is caused by our customary disinclination to read it—and other Hemingway works as well—from perspectives other than psychobiographical or new critical ones. After all, what other perspective gives reliable access to someone whose writing—so goes the myth—swells largely out of the context of lived experience? To puncture the oversimplification of that myth and so to reveal the limiting value of both psychobiographical and new critical approaches, I would advance a generic approach. In brief, testifying to what I regard as Hemingway's basic artistic commitment, fictional experiment, several of his novels studiously imitate traditional literary modes or works. While *For Whom the Bell Tolls,* as I have argued elsewhere, is fashioned upon the formula of the epic[1] and *Across the River and Into the Trees* upon the features of Dante's *Divine Comedy,* *To Have and Have Not* is fashioned upon the model of classical tragedy.

I am grateful to the University of Montana Foundation for a grant which enabled me to write this essay.

[1] Gerry Brenner, "Epic Machinery in Hemingway's *For Whom the Bell Tolls,*" MFS 16, No. 4 (Winter 1970-71), pp. 491-504.

"No matter how a man alone ain't got no bloody fucking chance."[2] These words, Harry Morgan's last, comprise his "anagnorisis." They formulate that utterance classically required of any tragic hero, his recognition, and so establish the genre by which the measure of this novel must be taken: tragedy. Hemingway may not generate a Shakespearean or Sophoclean "catharsis," due partly to his creation of a questionable hero, someone whose actions seem too saturated with villainy for us to discern in them tragic qualities. But the last thing we expect from Hemingway's "realistic" canon is a tragic protagonist; our unpreparedness, then, thwarts any purging of our emotions of pity and fear. Inclined to regard the words spoken over Harry's dead body as merely ironic, we overlook the diction pointedly attending to that quality found in every tragic hero, suffering:

> "He didn't suffer at all, Mrs. Morgan," the doctor said. Marie did not seem to hear him.
> "Oh, Christ," she said, and began to cry again. "Look at his goddamned face." (p. 256)

Customarily cited as signaling Hemingway's thematic shift from individualism to brotherhood,[3] *To Have and Have Not* more markedly signals an artistic shift from the autonomous form of his previous fictions to the prescriptive form of tragedy. Notwithstanding the novel's harshly criticized structural flaws

---

[2] *To Have and Have Not* (New York: Charles Scribner's Sons, 1937), p. 225; subsequent parenthetical references are to the paperback edition. Representative of the disdain Harry's last words have elicited are discussions by Philip Young, *Ernest Hemingway: A Reconsideration* (New York: Harcourt, Brace & World, 1966), pp. 99-100; Jackson J. Benson, *Hemingway: The Writer's Art of Self-Defense* (Minneapolis: Univ. of Minnesota Press, 1969), p. 151; and Delmore Schwartz, "Ernest Hemingway's Literary Situation," *Southern Review* (Spring 1938), reprinted in *Ernest Hemingway: The Man and His Work*, ed. John K. M. McCaffery (New York: World Publishing Co., 1950), pp. 108-109.

[3] See, for example, W. M. Frohock, "Violence and Discipline," *Southern Review* (1947), reprinted in McCaffery, p. 256.

and its interrupted gestation,[4] both its apparent problems and its considerable achievement are clarified by viewing it as tragedy, whether centering upon its species, its protagonist, or its dramatic structure.

To speculate upon its species: it easily shares features of "common" tragedy. Fittingly, its hero, Harry Morgan, is concerned with a most rudimentary human problem, economic survival in a society which offers him the debasing options of starving, digging sewer for relief wages, operating a filling station with one arm, or seeking money by unlawful means. A "Conch," his place in the social order is by definition among its "dregs," its "sediment," its "leftovers." Proud and properly resentful of such status, Harry struggles to slip no lower. Neither pirate scouting adventure, thane exercising ambition, nor prince meditating metaphysics, his endeavors, however adventuresome on the surface, are appropriately domestic, pragmatically devoted only to providing for his family without injuring his self-esteem.[5] Commonplace though he is in this regard, he fulfills Arthur Miller's definition of the "flaw" shared by all tragic heroes, that "inherent unwillingness to remain passive in the face of what he conceives to be a challenge to his dignity, his image of his rightful status."[6] To follow Miller again, the catastrophe which ends Harry's life suitably asserts his dignity because his "destruction in the attempt [to evaluate himself justly (i.e., as more than the negligible means to other's ends)] posits a wrong or an evil in his environment." Hemingway emphasizes Harry's commonness by his death wound, whose location in the stomach focuses upon Harry's major concern: " 'my kids ain't going to have their bellies hurt' " and " 'my family is going to eat as long as anybody eats' " (p. 96). Inasmuch as the novel dramatizes several forms of "starvation"—social,

---

[4] Carlos Baker, *Hemingway: The Writer as Artist* (Princeton: Princeton Univ. Press, 1952), pp. 203-205.

[5] William James Ryan, "Uses of Irony in *To Have and Have Not*," *MFS* 14, No. 3 (Autumn 1968), p. 330.

[6] Arthur Miller, "Tragedy and the Common Man," *New York Times*, 27 Feb. 1949, Sec. 2, p. 1.

sexual, political, and psychological—one might read Harry's death by stomach wound as the common denominator of those hungers.

Several of the novel's features also resemble Renaissance tragedy, particularly that variation of Revenge Tragedy which specializes in murder, mutilation, and morbid excitement as means to effect revenge and retribution, the "tragedy of blood." An inheritance from Senecan Tragedy, one of the traits of this species, the blood-and-lust motif of sensational scenes and unnatural crimes, seems amply present. Both Harry's actions and the supposedly digressive episodes on the Gordons, the vets, and the yachters, center upon adultery, perversion, brutality, and sadomasochism. Moreover, revenge motivates much of the novel's action. Harry's murder of Sing, the go-between for Chinese seeking illegal entry into the States, is usually regarded an unmotivated, cold-blooded act.[7] Yet such labeling overlooks Hemingway's careful preparations for it. The novel not only begins with Harry watching the Chicago-style gunning-down of three Cubans who have both solicited him to ferry them to the States and threatened him with the fate of *lengua largas,* betrayers. But it also indicates the political motivation of their death, the Cubans regarded as traitors, a fact established during their conversation with Harry: " 'Afterwards, when things are changed, it [your having served us now] would mean a good deal to you' " (p. 4). To this milieu of revenge Hemingway adds Johnson's departure from Havana before paying the eight hundred twenty-five dollars he owes Harry for carelessly lost tackle and three weeks of chartered fishing. By the time Sing propositions Harry and declares he may land the Chinese wherever he wants, the odor of double-cross is pervasive. To prevent treachery to himself or subsequent Chinese, Harry, with no little justification, murders Sing. Further, though not championing the Chinese, Harry cannot help identifying with them since their naive trust mir-

---

[7] Richard B. Hovey, *Hemingway: The Inward Terrain* (Seattle: Univ. of Washington Press, 1968), p. 134.

rors his earlier relationship to Johnson. Finally, knowing Sing's deceitfulness, Harry's murder of him can be seen as a compensatory act of revenge, Sing serving as Johnson's scapegoat.

Sadistic as it appears, Harry's later killing of the four Cuban revolutionaries also fits a revenge motif. Even before Harry manages to knock overboard Roberto's submachine gun, Roberto has insinuated his intent to kill him gratuitously, thereby making Harry's act one of self-defense. Moreover, the loss of Harry's arm and boat, directly caused by Cuban officials who had previously ignored Harry's post-Prohibition rum-running operation, gives him some claim to avenge a recent wrong. And still alive in Harry's mind may also be the sense that their betrayal traces back to and makes good the threats against him as a *lengua larga* (p. 49). To the complexity of his motive must be added the desire to avenge Albert's, if not Bee-Lips', death. Like a Jacobean hero, Harry must grapple "with the question of how virtuous action can be taken in an evil world when that action itself must be devious, politic, or tainted with evil."[8] Part of the novel's pity may be that it lacks a Tudor-Jacobean audience.

The novel also meets Aristotle's formula of classical tragedy.[9] Harry possesses the "stature" required of the tragic hero by virtue of his superiority to the novel's other characters. People turn to him when they need something done well: Eddy and Frankie, Johnson and Sing, Albert and Bee-Lips, the Cuban trio at the novel's beginning and the quartet at its end. Satiric butt though she is, even Mrs. Laughton instinctively responds to his stature, calling him "wonderful," "Ghengis Khan," her

---

[8] Robert Ornstein, *The Moral Vision of Jacobean Tragedy* (Madison: Univ. of Wisconsin Press, 1960), p. 23.

[9] The following discussion draws upon Gerald F. Else's brilliant translation and commentary, *Aristotle's Poetics: The Argument* (Cambridge, Mass.: Harvard Univ. Press, 1963); parenthetical references are to this edition. For a fine, brief discussion of Else's major points about tragedy, especially "catharsis," see Lois M. Welch, "Catharsis, Structural Purification, and Else's Aristotle," *Bucknell Review* 19, No. 3 (Winter 1971), pp. 31-50.

"dream man" (pp. 130, 136, 149). "Not a paragon of virtue and justice," Harry is nevertheless King of the *Conchs*, the boat upon which he dies even being named *Queen Conch*. The "nobility" of Harry's actions is questionable only if one ignores its analogue to everyman's struggle for survival. And the tragedy's "magnitude" partly resides in its compass, literally sweeping not an Aegean, but a Gulf archipelago, from Cuba to the Florida Keys. Harry's *hamartia*, "an ignorance or mistake as to certain details" [i.e., that he had slain his assailant] is appropriately "a 'big' mistake, one pregnant with disaster for the hero" (Else, p. 383). His *hamartia* both dramatizes his "overweening pride" that he alone can handle the four Cuban revolutionaries and brings about the "peripety," the sudden reversal of fortune necessary to his ultimate downfall. Moreover, this *hubris*, his self-sufficiency, is precisely what his *anagnorisis*, quoted earlier, acknowledges. *Proairesis* is also in order. Harry thinks fatalistically about transporting the Cubans: "I don't want to fool with it but what choice have I got? They don't give you any choice now" (p. 105). Nevertheless he chooses to transport them, conscious of the potential calamity of his voluntary decision. The novel's "catastrophe" occasions our pity and fear, fear because Harry "is like the rest of us" (Else, p. 365), his struggle for economic wherewithal replicating ours, pity because Harry "suffers undeservedly" (Else, p. 370). Certainly he should suffer as recompense for murdering the Cubans; yet the slow agony of his twenty-four-hour death exceeds justice. More significantly, he has done nothing to deserve the promise of being shot by the Cubans and his acceptance of the inevitable confrontation both necessitates his firing upon them first and exculpates his "motive from polluted intent" (Else, p. 447). Given the circumstances, then, because Harry's act is not morally repugnant we pity his undeserved suffering.

Despite the structural problem of the inclusion of the Gordons, the vets, and the decadent yachters, the novel otherwise complies with the Aristotelean dictum of "unity." Not episodic, its plot is "complete and a whole" (Else, p. 282), seen in the seasonal sectioning (Spring, Fall, Winter) which suggests completeness despite its omission of Summer, a season whose bounty is properly deleted from the novel's bleak landscape. Moreover, the novel's events possess the "logical sequence, continuity" (Else, p. 297) required of tragedy. For as Johnson's doublecross "causes" Harry's Chinese cargo and murder of Sing, the economic depression "causes" his rumrunning, and the loss of arm and boat—the means for normal employment—"causes" his dangerous exploit of transporting the Cuban revolutionaries for a mere two hundred dollars. The consistency of these four variations upon the "single action" of Harry's occupation as transporter underscores the novel's unified action, as does the circular repetition of transporting Cubans at the novel's beginning and its end. Even the novel's numerous, unexpected events—the sudden deaths of the first Cubans and Sing, the abrupt defection of Johnson, the unanticipated gunfire Harry and Wesley receive from Cuban authorities, the swift reconfiscation of Harry's boat, and the unforeseen bullet from Harry's assailant—all these further accord with Aristotle's inductive conclusion that a tragedy's events "happen contrary to our expectation" and "possess the quality of surprise" (Else, p. 323). Finally, Hemingway rejects the dramatic mode required of tragedy. Yet the dramatic monologues by Harry, Albert, and Marie approximate both dramatic methods and choric effects. Hesitantly one might argue that the digressive chapters provide choric commentary upon the environment within which Harry must fulfill his destiny. More confidently one might offer a choric argument in trying to account for Hemingway's decision to end the novel in Marie Morgan's consciousness: "The chorus," Aristotle says, "should be considered as one of the persons in the drama; should be a part of the whole, and a sharer in the action. . . ."[10] Moreover

---

[10] *Aristotle's Politics and Poetics*, trans. Benjamin Jowett and Thomas Twinning (New York: Viking Press, 1957), p. 246; I drop Else here only because Jowett's more traditional translation conveys the meaning Hemingway would probably have used—if he used Aristotle at all.

her thoughts provide a fitting *kommos,* the "lamentation" with which a classical tragedy often concludes.

Admittedly, species-seeking may be academic. For as readers or spectators of a literary work termed tragedy, our concern is not with its obedience to a prescribed formula but with its ability to generate those emotions accruable only to tragedy. Nevertheless, those emotions occur only when a hero performs an act which, paradoxically, both "runs counter to man's deepest moral instincts" and yet is "purified" because its motive is not morally repugnant (Else, pp. 420, 439). Further, to prevent the term tragedy from becoming either reduced to an intellectual paradigm, used to define any pathetic situation, or employed honorifically,[11] requires attending to the quality of life invested in the hero. Despite assessments of him as an amoral tough,[12] Harry Morgan repeatedly displays those qualities prerequisite to dubbing a hero tragic: dividedness and intelligence.[13]

The three-episode sequence of Part One—the solicitation by Cubans, the defection of Johnson, and the murder of Sing—charts Harry's rapid alternation from law-abiding charter-boat fisherman to ruthless murderer. This switch might well be regarded either as too swift for credibility or as evidence of Harry's basic villainy. Yet the switch outlines Harry's dividedness, rooted in both a strong sense of decency and moral right as well as an inclination to let circumstances lure him into lawless acts. Indicative of this division is the information Hemingway provides of Harry's former activities: while he can boast of precisely how many cases of rum his boat will hold and so hint of experience as a rum-runner, he also reveals he has been

---

[11] For perhaps the best discussion of tragedy and its illegitimate pretenders, see Robert B. Heilman's "Tragedy and Melodrama: Speculations on Generic Form," *TQ* 8, No. 2 (Summer 1960), pp. 36-50; or his *Tragedy and Melodrama: Versions of Experience* (Seattle: Univ. of Washington Press, 1968), pp. 3-31.

[12] For example, see Robert W. Lewis, Jr., *Hemingway on Love* (Austin: Univ. of Texas Press, 1965), p. 121.

[13] Heilman, *Versions,* pp. 227-251.

a policeman in Miami. And though greed seems to prompt his decision to smuggle a dozen Chinese into the States, his earlier refusal to smuggle in three Cubans for considerably more money undermines that notion. Admittedly he appears to relish the death of Sing: "He was flopping and bouncing worse than any dolphin on a gaff. . . . I got him forward onto his knees and had both thumbs well in behind his talk-box, and I bent the whole thing back until she cracked. Don't think you can't hear it crack, either" (pp. 53-54). Yet since he mentions his former employment "on the police force up in Miami" (p. 44) while preparing for this episode, one might surmise that Harry's sense of justice and moral responsibility surfaces in the situation. For his murder is fit reparation for Sing's indirect murder of countless Chinese, the betrayal of whom has provided him for two years with, as Harry observes, the means to wear ". . . a white suit with a silk shirt and black tie and one of those hundred-and-twenty-five-dollar Panama hats" (p. 30). Moreover, Harry's betrayal of Sing, through congruent with the treachery surrounding him, is at odds with his basic trustworthiness, revealed by deaf Frankie's loyalty to him, by the Cubans' choice of him to ferry them to the mainland, and ironically, by Sing. Not only is Sing surprised at Harry's willingness to smuggle his compatriots: "Now what are the circumstances that would—that have made you consider . . ." (p. 31); but he also knows Harry's reputation well enough to trust him with a two-hundred-dollar down payment. When Harry asks " 'Suppose I went off with the two hundred,' " Sing replies " 'But I know you wouldn't do such a thing, captain' " (p. 34). Sing's unpreparedness for Harry's murder of him confirms Harry's judgment, "Maybe he just trusted me" (p. 60) and testifies that both traitors and criminals respect Harry's moral responsibility.

Emphasizing his dividedness, the several episodes of Part One converge upon Harry's dilemma of whether to kill Eddy, witness to Sing's death. Tempted additionally by his assumption that Eddy is not on the crew list and so will cause complications with Customs officers when he reaches Key West, nevertheless Harry dislikes "doing something you'd be sorry for afterwards" (p. 60). No inveterate killer, Harry has already dismissed the notion of massacring the dozen Chinese: "Now I tell you it would take a hell of a mean man to butcher a bunch of Chinks like that" (p. 57). He even ignores the impulse to silence the Chinaman who keeps calling him "'Goddam crook'" (p. 58). Nor is his compunction diluted by heavy drinking on the return to Key West. Waver though he does, Harry's interior debate makes unlikely a homicidal intent, even had Eddy not been saved by the presence of his name on the crew list after all.

The sensationalism of Harry's impulse for masculine action and lawless self-expression in Part One projects the distorted mug-shot most readers see. Yet Hemingway delineates a balanced and complex portrait, the remainder of the novel dramatizing Harry's equally strong obligation to domestic security and moral decency. Like Jack Brennan's finely counterpointed fisticuffs and tightfistedness in "Fifty Grand," Harry's violent actions play against his middle-class values, his domestic pleasure, for instance, upon his return to Key West at the end of Part One: "That night I was sitting in the living room smoking a cigar and drinking a whiskey and water and listening to Gracie Allen on the radio. The girls had gone to the show and sitting there I felt sleepy and I felt good" (p. 64). The motive common to all his hazardous endeavors, to provide for his family, may appear a sleazy rationalization allowing him to indulge his penchant for violence.[14] Yet both the novel's setting during the Depression and the frequency of Harry's financial anxieties authenticate his motive. Thinking of the dangers of transporting the Cuban revolutionaries, he mulls "I could stay here now and I'd be out of it. But what the hell would they eat on? Where's the money coming from to keep Marie and the girls? I've got no boat, no cash, I got no education" (p. 147). The narrative silence regarding Harry's motive for smuggling rum in Part Two's fiasco seems again to feed

---

[14] Hovey, p. 135; Lewis, p. 117.

a view of him as merely an outlaw by nature. But since this is a post-Prohibition run, Harry's venture is robbed of both a large profit and any criminal thrill of thwarting the law. Captain Willie Adams correctly defines his motive, dismissing the charge that Harry is a "lawbreaker" and retorting—however awkwardly—"He's got a family and he's got to eat and feed them" (p. 81). A homebody, before Harry leaves his house for the last time, "He sat at the table and looked at the piano, the sideboard and the radio, the picture of September Morn, and the pictures of the cupids holding bows behind their heads, the shiny, real-oak table and the shiny real-oak chairs and the curtains on the windows and he thought, What chance have I to enjoy my home?" (p. 127). And lying in the cockpit mortally wounded, Harry's monogamous morality reflects, "I wonder what she'll do? I wonder what Marie will do? Maybe they'll pay her the rewards. . . . I wish I could do something about Marie. Plenty money on this boat. I don't even know how much. Anybody be O.K. with that money" (p. 174). This passage also indicates Harry's basic considerateness. Regarding the driver who will taxi the Cubans to the boat, he tells Bee-Lips " 'Get one hasn't any kids' " (p. 134). And when he comes home "he did not turn on the light but took off his shoes in the hall and went up the bare stairs in his stocking feet" (p. 112). Just as Harry sympathetically tolerates Wesley's whining, he rejects Albert's help, silently attempting to shield him from its foreseeable danger: " 'I'm sorry, Albert, I can't use you,' Harry said. *He had thought it out that far already*" (p. 122; italics added).

While Harry's contradictory values are consonant with the novel's paradoxical title and vouch for his dividedness, they also evidence the intelligence required of a tragic hero. To convey his intelligence may well have prompted Hemingway to begin the novel with Harry's dramatic monologue, articulateness a corollary of intelligence. "You know how it is there early in the morning in Havana" he begins the novel, demonstrating his doubleness as a man of words and man of action. His role as narrator of Part One is particularly crucial to its moral ambiguity and accounts for the sparseness of his moral reflectiveness. When Eddy asks " 'What did you have against [Sing]?' " Harry answers " 'Nothing' " and adds that he killed him " 'to keep from killing twelve other chinks' " (p. 55). Ruthless as both statements sound, Harry is recounting this exchange, as the idiom makes clear, to a chum. Hence, either he modestly mutes his real motive, or sees little point in revealing it to a rummy, or knows better than to bore a friendly listener with the niceties of Jamesian moral desiderata. Neither vainglorious nor defensive, Harry is justly proud of the exploit by which he both recoups his loss and serves justice, and he knows well his listener's interest in the "what" of the adventure rather than its "why." Buttressing his intelligence is his inferable reason for turning away the Cuban trio at the novel's beginning. His fear of having U.S. Customs officials seize his boat is legitimate. But equally important is his desire to avoid the crossfire of the Cuban political warfare. Being unruffled by the fates of both the trio and *lengua largas* indicates their commonness and the wisdom of his refusal to charter the Cubans.

Radically dissimilar to Hemingway's usual hero, who doesn't want to think, Harry enjoys thinking about the problems of landing a marlin, unloading sacked liquor with one arm, doublecrossing Sing, deciding Eddy's fate, and planning for the contingencies of his last exploit:

> Suppose they figure about me and Albert. Did any of them look like sailors? Did any of them seem like they were sailors? Let me think? Maybe. The pleasant one, maybe. Possibly him, that young one. I have to find out about that because if they figure on doing without Albert or me from the start there's no way. Sooner or later they will figure on us. But in the Gulf you got time. And I'm figuring all the time. I've got to think right all the time. I can't make a mistake. Not a mistake. Not once. Well, I got something to think about now all right. Something to do and something to think about besides wondering what the hell's going to happen. (pp. 106-107)

Despite its outcome, Harry's shrewdness fully surfaces in this last episode. Wary of its dangers, he conceals from the

Cubans his knowledge of Spanish, hides his submachine gun, bumps Roberto's gun overboard, and ingratiates himself with Emilio to better surprise him. When he realizes the murderousness of the foursome, the narrator observes that Harry "had abandoned anger, hatred and any dignity as luxuries, now, and had started to plan" (p. 159). Interestingly, by concealing from friends his knowledge of the specific job, pretending to be chartering just another fishing party until commandeered by the Cubans, Harry causes the sheriff and Coast Guard retrievers to regard him a victim. Imperative to tragedy, however, Harry victimizes himself,[15] by guilefully nudging overboard Roberto's machine gun, thereby inflaming his resolve to kill Harry, and by beginning the fatal shooting. Most important, he makes that error in judgment expected of all intelligent tragic heroes, ignorantly assuming his assailant, the shoulder-wounded Cuban, to be dead. Linked to his earlier mistakes—trusting Johnson, anticipating no difficulties running rum, and overlooking the visibility of his stolen boat from a tall truck—this error contributes the inevitability of his tragic death.

As it ought, Harry's recognition best reveals his intelligence and dividedness. Indeed socio-political matter seems to clutter the novel. Yet the backdrop of war vets and Cuban revolutionaries, of Marxist portraits and Depression-era Weltanschauung exists neither to assist facile cataloguing of another social protest novel nor to render Harry's concluding line a remorseful exhortation to join ranks with one's downtrodden brothers. Instead the backdrop objectifies Harry's dilemma. While his impulses seek individual freedom and independent action, his sense of family duty acknowledges the imperative of being his brother's keeper, the exact dilemma on which the novel's social problems pivot. Hence, loner though he would like to be, his dependence upon such "dregs" as deaf Freddie, rummy Eddy, whining Wesley, and wife-nagged Albert pre-

---

[15] For a view of Harry as victim, see Baker, p. 213.

pares for his early acknowledgment that loners are doomed: "I got to have somebody I can depend on. If we make it I'll see he gets a share. But I can't tell him or he wouldn't go into it and I got to have somebody by me. It would be better alone, anything is better alone but I don't think I can handle it alone. It would be much better alone" (p. 105). Though critical of social conditions, he denies the label of "radical" (p. 97) and wisely refuses to endorse social or political involvement. As he sees, while existing social structures baldly strip Cuban, *conch*, and vet of dignity, yet the revolutionists' pragmatic rationale— " 'the end is worth the means' " (p. 166)—is equally destructive: "What the hell do I care about his revolution. F—— his revolution. To help the working man he robs a bank and kills a fellow works with him and then kills that poor damned Albert that never did any harm. That's a working man he kills. He never thinks of that. With a family" (p. 168). In contrast Harry does think of Albert, their relationship clarifying Harry's conflict, to be beholden to no man and yet his need of him. Given their discussion of family obligations (pp. 95-96), Harry's rejection of Albert's help expresses both desire for independent action and concern for Albert as family provider. And when he still later reverses this decision, he does so not as an act of betrayal, but, preparatory to his last words, as an admission that as Albert needs money, he himself needs help, that he alone may not be able to cope with the hazardous voyage. Those fears confirmed by subsequent events, Harry understands the obsolete and fatal luxury of autonomy, aptly comparing it to " 'trying to pass cars on the top of hills. On that road in Cuba. On any road. Anywhere' " (p. 225). Moreover, Hemingway understands the artistic need to make ambiguous Harry's final illumination: " 'No matter how a man alone ain't got no bloody fucking chance.' " Harry's repetition of "man" nine times before this utterance would seem to italicize properly its universal truth. Yet while the imperative of brotherhood lies at its core, the degree of involvement is unspecified. Nor does it guarantee that because individualism has no "chance," collective effort will—as the dead bodies of the four Cubans indicate. Finally, the rich imprecision of "chance" leaves open what "a man alone" will lack the opportunity to do: eke out a living? reform social inequities? express meaningfully his individuality?

Significant though Harry's stomach wound is to our recognition of his representative economic struggle, the loss of his right arm is equally significant. It is a synecdoche of those personal and—as the novel's maimed world insists—social handicaps all men must live with, handicaps which necessitate interdependency. Further, the loss of a right arm, long a symbol of assistance, reliability, and dependence, is a Hardyesque reprimand by the gods for Harry's flagrant individualism, making compulsory his dependence upon others. Yet only by literally achieving his desire, to operate single-handedly, does Harry recognize both the limits of single-handedness and man's need of the assistance of either literal or figurative right arms.

Politically unsophisticated as his rude environment requires, Harry's illegal activities are nevertheless an individual protest against the social injustices of every age. As Lear and Oedipus flout communal dictates, Harry's lawlessness similarly expresses his need to obtain the means necessary for a measure of security, autonomy, and dignity. Ultimately, Harry is the avatar of the Cuban revolutionaries, the downtrodden *conchs*, the betrayed Chinese, and even the dispossessed vets—of all societies' "leftovers" whose frustrated sense of injustice incites them to violence or illegal action. Yet Harry's failure to recognize this muffles the novel's tragic resonance. Tragic pleasure, says Aristotle, best emanates from a horrible act performed by a hero initially ignorant of the kinship between himself and his victim (Else, pp. 413-415). Harry's massacre of the Cubans is justified as an act of self-defense, to be sure. Yet both the terror and the pity of the act would have been heightened had Harry realized his resemblance to the Cubans: that their claim to social justice is his, that their ethic (illegal means to achieve noble ends) is also his, that they are, in effect, his brothers. Though he recognizes the imperative of brotherhood, he gives no indication that he has unwittingly committed fratricide.

One matter yet remains: those digressions. To be bold about it, of all Hemingway's novels, this is structurally the tightest. Its discrete episodes are fully developed, its sequence easy to recall, and its outline transparent, even to an eye not apprised of its generic roots. Appropriate to tragedy, it obeys the formula of "dramatic structure," dividing readily into the seven components of the classical Freytag pyramid.[16] It has an Introduction, an Exciting Force that generates the Rising Action, a Crisis or Turning Point, a Tragic Force that precipitates the Falling Action and, of course, the Catastrophe. (Lest one be inclined to regard such a stock structure alien to Hemingway's artistry, one only need recall the work following this, the play *The Fifth Column*.) The scene in the Perla cafe with the solicitous Cubans provides the tragedy's *Introduction*, a "setting" whose world is in the throes of social warfare; distrust, treachery, and violence also establish quickly the novel's "tone" or "mood." Johnson's defection comprises the *Exciting Force*. His doublecross defines the "conflict of opposing interests" between the haves and have-nots, the trustworthy and deceitful, the brotherly and egocentric, the law-breakers and law-abiders. The episode also "sets in motion the *Rising Action*," Harry's murder of Sing, for as the witches' prophecy stirs Macbeth into scheming for kingship, Johnson's betrayal motivates Harry's scheme to recover his losses and avenge himself on doublecrossers. True to the pyramid, Harry returns to Key West "in the ascendency." Part Two is the *Crisis* or *Turning Point*, "the point at which the opposing forces that create the conflict interlock in the decisive action on which the plot will turn." Harry's fate as rum-runner clarifies his personal conflict against collective forces, a conflict duplicated in Captain Willie's

---

[16] For a discussion of this conventional formula, I use William Flint Thrall, Addison Hibbard, and C. Hugh Holman, *A Handbook to Literature*, rev. ed. (New York: Odyssey Press, 1960), pp. 156-158 et passim. Oddly, Robin H. Farquhar's "Dramatic Structure in the Novels of Ernest Hemingway," *MFS* 14, No. 3 (Autumn 1968), pp. 271-282, overlooks this novel for ones whose employment of "dramatic structure" is much more arguable and considerably more opaque.

verbal tussle with Harrison, "one of the three most important
men in the United States today" (p. 80), and in his defense
of Harry as family provider against Harrison's charge of "lawbreaker." Prohibition over, Harry anticipates no danger in
transporting liquor. Yet "interlocking" with the Cuban government on the one hand, he loses his arm, and with the U. S.
government on the other, he loses his boat. Inasmuch as the
rest of the novel observes Harry's efforts to wrest a living
without his boat or arm, this episode's "decisive action" locates
the "incident wherein the situation in which the protagonist
finds himself is sure either to improve or grow worse." Not to
be confused with the "climax" ("the point of highest interest
at which the reader makes his greatest emotional response"),
this Turning Point results in events "which produce climatic
effects without themselves being of compelling interest." That
is, Hemingway selectively ignores the three events of "compelling interest" in Part Two—the escape from the Cuban
harbor, the confiscation of the boat, and Harry's amputation—
centering instead on the single event that contains them. The
Tragic Force, the single event "closely related to the crisis"
occurs when Customs officers reconfiscate Harry's boat. The
event also "starts the *Falling Action*," Harry precipitously re-
solving to rent Freddy's boat and to carry the Cubans across.
"A moment of final suspense," Harry's stomach wound answers
to the Falling Action, that event "which delays the *Catastrophe*," "seems to offer a way of escape for the hero," and
"often is attended by some lowering of interest since new forces
must be introduced."

Central to understanding the novel's structure are the
ancillary functions of Falling Action since they account for the
apparently disintegrating focus on Harry. Hemingway appears
to have sensed the need to magnify Harry's world in order to
"stress the activity of the forces opposing the hero." Hence
into the novel he brings characters representative of those
forces, self-indulgent rich and violent poor, perverse ego-
centrics and self-deceiving incompetents. A grotesque version
of Harry's conflict, the episode in Freddy's bar portrays the

vets as creatures who have submitted to society's dehumanizing forces. Thus their sense of brotherhood entails enslavement to a collective drudgery which accrues no more dignity than the anarchy of their sadomasochistic expression of individuality. No Steinbeck melodrama of sympathizable strikers, however, Hemingway keeps tragedy's proper focus by dramatizing the vets' self-victimization. Equally grotesque foils are the well-to-do, catalogued on their yachts. Exhibits of a social system that perpetrates such self-indulgence, they elicit scornful pity because they too lack the intelligence or courage to seek a dignified mode of life. That they mimic Harry's conflict is evidenced in Hemingway's juxtaposition of the perverse brotherliness of Johnson and Carpenter's homosexuality and the destructive individualism of the sixty-year-old grain broker, or again in Hemingway's juxtaposition of the domestic security of Frances' family, the frivolous thirst for adventure of the Estonians, and the narcissism of Dorothy Hollis. Further stressing "the activity of the forces opposing the hero," Hemingway places in the center of these vignettes the family whose security comes from selling a three-cent liquid for a dollar a pint, both an analogue of Harry's rum-running and an indictment of governmental double standards.

One other trait of Falling Action helps explain the novel's structure: "Relief scenes are often resorted to during the Falling Action, partly to provide emotional relaxation for the audience." Mrs. Tracy's farcical remorse for Albert is surely such a "relief scene." Though it lacks tragedy's proper dignity, its comedy is no less fitting than the scenes of Lear's fool, Hamlet's gravedigger, or Macbeth's gatekeeper. And despite her fradulent grief, she parodies the lament Harry deserves and receives in Marie's novel-ending soliloquy. A finer relief scene is the brief Chapter 20. Its matter-of-fact description of the damaged *Queen Conch,* drifting in the Gulf Stream, nicely modulates to a catalogue of the various fish feeding upon "the ropy, carmine clots and threads that trailed in the water from the lowest splintered holes" (p. 179). Only then does it turn to the phantasmagoria of Harry's muted agony.

Avoid them though I would prefer, the "relief scenes" demanding justification are those with Richard Gordon. Artistically indefensible, however, they seem to acknowledge Hemingway's diffidence regarding the adequacy both of the novel's broad social and moral context and of Harry's appeal. Consequently they reveal his attempt to convey and unify that context by creating a character whose distorted resemblance to Harry will paradoxically clarify the novel's issues. Hence Hemingway parallels Gordon's social protest novel and Harry's protesting illegalities, Gordon's impotence with Helene Bradley and Harry's unsuccessful one-armed struggle with the Cubans, Gordon's misreading of Marie and Harry's misjudgment of Johnson, Gordon's rejection of MacWalsey's fraternal help and Harry's strident self-sufficiency, Gordon's rapid disintegration and Harry's demise. Nevertheless, the bald contrast between a pathetic and a tragic character either augments excessively Harry's stature or, as the novel's reputation sadly confirms, detracts from its many excellencies. Only rationalization could regard this "flaw" as authorial tip-off of the novel's use of tragedy's formula.

Looked at harshly, the novel's obedience to ancient paradigms of tragedy and dramatic structure seems to argue the derivative quality of Hemingway's imagination, caught here in perhaps an epigonic act. Yet every writer who seriously courts the Tragic Muse defers to her preestablished criteria, whose difficulty is acknowledged by the dearth of modern tragedies. It is to Hemingway's credit that he silently accepts the self-imposed challenge to compose a tragedy. Equally commendable is his artistic integrity, his refusal to justify his novel and to castigate disparaging critics by declaring it to be a classical tragedy. The measure of his achievement, however, is another matter. That Harry Morgan's tragic lineaments have been mistakenly interpreted as villainous ones testifies to Hemingway's skillful creation of him. Yet whether his dividedness and intelligence are sufficient to raise him to a level comparable with even Macbeth, his closest cousin in tragedy, cannot be determined by critical fiat. The best one can hope for is to give substance to an otherwise cryptic statement in Hemingway's Nobel Prize acceptance "speech": "Things may not be immediately discernible in what a man writes, and in this sometimes he is fortunate; but eventually they are quite clear and by these and the degree of alchemy that he possesses he will endure or be forgotten."[17]

---

[17] Baker, p. 339.

PETER L. HAYS

HEMINGWAY AND FITZGERALD

THERE ARE TWO dominant tones throughout Ernest Hemingway's *A Moveable Feast:* the nostalgic and the patronizing. The first is easily explained: it is the tone of a man in his fifties recalling his youth, the city he spent youth's best years in, and the time in which he did some of his first and very best writing. The second tone, especially apparent in his treatment of older, established writers like Ford Madox Ford, Gertrude Stein, T. S. Eliot, and Scott Fitzgerald is harder to deal with. They may have been personally unlikable, though Hemingway says that only of Ford, not of the rest; he had not even met Eliot. What they do have in common is that they all helped his career, giving him journal space for publication (as Ernest Walsh, who is also satirically portrayed in *A Moveable Feast,* did at 1,000 francs per story), teaching him, giving him ideas, writing letters to publishers on his behalf. The patronizing attitude might be explained as the reminiscences of a Nobel Prize winner looking back on those who had more fame than he did before he did, but who had not lasted as long or as well, but the smug, superior tone seems out of place from the point of view of a largely unpublished twenty-three, twenty-four, or twenty-five year old. It could be that Hemingway in his fifties was still jealous of the fame others had won before him, whereas he can be more gentle in his portraiture of Sylvia Beach, Evan Shipman, or Pascin—who neither then nor now are threats to his fame—or to Ezra Pound, whose country certified him insane, and whom, therefore, Hemingway could afford to treat magnanimously. But beyond still-rankling

87

jealousy, Hemingway's tone could very well be based on ingratitude for help received and, characteristically, never graciously acknowledged. What he learned from Gertrude Stein has often been discussed, one small borrowing from Ford I have written about elsewhere,[1] and the full extent of his indebtedness to Eliot would take a separate paper; I want to examine here his dependence on Fitzgerald in *The Sun Also Rises*.

Hemingway describes his experience of reading *The Great Gatsby* in the "Scott Fitzgerald" chapter of *A Moveable Feast* (pp. 149-176),[2] and Carlos Baker's biography of Hemingway dates that experience as occurring in May of 1925,[3] before Hemingway began to write *The Sun Also Rises*, even before that June's trip to Pamplona that provided the characters and some of the tensions, as well as Hemingway's most recent re-exposure to the setting for the novel and to bullfighting. In June of the following year, 1926, Hemingway showed Fitzgerald the carbon copy of the novel's manuscript, and Fitzgerald recommended deletions, an editorial judgment Hemingway assented to, as is attested to by both his letter to Maxwell Perkins to omit the first three galleys, and the existing manuscript, examined by Philip Young and Charles W. Mann, which is fifteen pages longer than the novel as we know it.[4] Thus we know that Fitzgerald decidedly influenced the

---

[1] Peter L. Hays, "'Soldier's Home' and Ford Madox Ford," *Hemingway Notes* I (Fall 1971), pp. 21-22.

[2] Unless otherwise noted, all quotations from Hemingway's and Fitzgerald's published works are from the standard Scribner's editions.

[3] Carlos Baker, *Ernest Hemingway: A Life Story* (New York: Charles Scribner's Sons, 1969), pp. 146, 587; Baker's evidence is a letter by Hemingway to Maxwell Perkins, dated June 5, 1925, praising Fitzgerald's novel. Hereafter in the notes, Baker's biography will be referred to by its subtitle, *A Life Story*.

[4] *A Life Story*, pp. 170, 592.

Philip Young and Charles W. Mann, *The Hemingway Manuscripts: An Inventory* (University Park: Penn. State Univ. Press, 1969), p. 28.

Philip Young and Charles W. Mann, "Fitzgerald's *Sun Also Rises:* Notes and Comment," *Fitzgerald/Hemingway Annual* (1970), pp. 1-13.

present shape of the novel, and I submit that there are other influences as well.

First of all, both novels are told in the first person, after the events, by a narrator who is a veteran of World War I and who is involved in the incidents he is recounting,[5] and both interrupt their stories to remind us that they are authors recounting the past: Jake protests that he hasn't portrayed Cohn accurately and so adds an additional paragraph of characterization (*SAR*, p. 45); Nick protects against his own dramatic condensation of events and pauses to fill in details (*GG*, pp. 56-57). Both men are middle-class lookers-on at the sexual promiscuity of others, some of whom are upper class, and—to different extents because of their own degrees of involvement and habits of making judgments—both express or imply their envy or embarrassment at the behavior they observe. Both narrators are also closer to the romantics they criticize, Gatsby and Cohn, than they would like to believe: we see it in Nick's coming East to make his fortune, as Gatsby had, and in his fantasies with unknown women (*GG*, pp. 57-58); we see it in Jake's wanting to go away with Brett as he had before, even though he knows it will be no good (*SAR*, p. 26).

Secondly, both authors have obviously been influenced by T. S. Eliot's *The Waste Land* (1922). In *Gatsby*, Fitzgerald has used the valley of ashes as an obvious waste land, even using that term on page 24. Hemingway links Jake through his sexual incapacity and his predilection for angling with the Fisher King, as many critics have noted.[6] In both novels, as in Eliot's poem, water's life-giving properties are used ironically

[5] Cf. A. E. Elmore, "Nick Carraway's Self-Introduction," *Fitzgerald/Hemingway Annual* (1971), p. 138: "Nick's failure in love is associated, as is Jake's, with his experience in the War."

[6] To cite only some of the earliest: Malcolm Cowley, ed., *Hemingway* (New York: Viking, 1944), p. xxi.

Philip Young, *Ernest Hemingway* (New York: Holt, Rinehart and Winston, 1952), p. 60.

Carlos Baker, *Hemingway: The Writer As Artist* (Princeton: Princeton University Press, 1963), p. 90.

to accentuate the absence of fertility or spiritual peace. It rains when Daisy and Jay Gatsby are reunited in Nick's cottage; it is late spring and Daisy, like Eliot's hyacinth girl with her hair wet and her eyes shining, holds out a promise of fertility and new life to Jay; but instead Daisy brings death to Myrtle Wilson, and, through Myrtle's husband, "death by water" to Gatsby. In the last chapter of *The Great Gatsby*, during "The Burial of the Dead," we have rain again, but no resurrection for Gatsby. Thus Gatsby has been seen, by myth critics, as a failed fertility god;[7] while Jake, of course, is sexually incapable, infertile. Both novels follow the cycle of seasons briefly, moving from spring to late summer, early fall. There is a possible spiritual rebirth for Nick who turns his back on the corrupt East, but his newfound moral identity as he returns to the midwest, after the death of his alter-ego, and his baptism in the rain, may be as meretricious as the new identity assumed by James Gatz on the waters of Little Girl Bay when he joined the entourage of Dan Cody, who, like Eliot's ancient Phoenicians, traded in metals. In *The Sun Also Rises* Jake finds temporary wholeness by the waters of the Irati River with Bill and Harris and in the bay of San Sebastian—only to come back to Brett and despair each time. Throughout *The Sun Also Rises*, characters seek relief from heat and dust and pain with a bath of refreshing water (pp. 97, 159, 227, 234-5, etc.), but it provides no permanent renewal, and at one crucial instance there isn't even water: "I could not find the bathroom. After a while I found it. There was a deep stone tub. I turned on the taps and the water would not run" (p. 195). Similarly, in *The Great Gatsby*, Daisy suggests that the central characters escape New York's heat by bathing (p. 126). And both novels, like the poem, recount quests, a series of sexual encounters, parties composed of people (several of whom are oddly named) from various social and economic strata, determined to dispel ennui, but failing. All three works also detail a search for meaning

---

[7] For example, Douglas Taylor, "*The Great Gatsby*: Style and Myth," *University of Kansas City Review*, XX (Autumn 1953), pp. 30-37.

in modern life, not only by the narrators, but in the novels, also by the foils and antagonists, Robert Cohn, Jay Gatsby, and even Tom Buchanan. Let me at this point pause and admit that arguing about influences of Eliot's poem in 1922 on Fitzgerald's novel in 1925, and of both on Hemingway's novel in 1926 could simply be cases of *post hoc, ergo propter hoc* if we did not know, as we do, that Fitzgerald had read and admired Eliot,[8] and that Hemingway had read both Eliot and Fitzgerald. Pound loaned Hemingway a copy of *The Waste Land* in 1923. Although Hemingway made his opinion of Eliot known in the notorious *transatlantic review* eulogy for Joseph Conrad, October 1924, and in the equally notorious "Mr. and Mrs. Elliot,"[9] Hemingway was not above borrowing the title of "In Another Country" from Eliot's "Portrait of a Lady" or borrowing the idea of the Fisher King. He even admits in *Death in the Afternoon* (p. 139) that Eliot taught him to use quotations, and we see him using poetic quotations from Marlowe and Marvell on page 75 of *The Sun Also Rises* and page 154 of *A Farewell to Arms*, quotations he most likely encountered for the first time in Eliot's "Portrait of a Lady" and *The Waste Land*. So we can be sure that Hemingway had read both *The Waste Land* and *The Great Gatsby* and that his splenetic attitude toward Eliot and patronizing one toward Fitzgerald—whatever else they consist of—may partake of Hemingway's notorious ingratitude

---

[8] Robert Shulman, "Myth, Mr. Eliot, and the Comic Novel," *Modern Fiction Studies*, XII (Winter 1966-67), pp. 395-399. Cf. Daniel G. Siegel, "T. S. Eliot's Copy of *Gatsby*," *Fitzgerald/Hemingway Annual* (1971), p. 292.

[9] Although the manuscript of the story reveals it to have been originally titled "Mr. and Mrs. Smith" (*The Hemingway Manuscripts*, p. 49, and *A Life Story*, pp. 133, 585), and Baker deduces from subsequent correspondence that the Smith involved was poet Chard Powers Smith, it would seem that Hemingway changed the characters' names less to avoid a law suit by Smith than to mock by implication another poet, T. S. Eliot. Cf. Jackson J. Benson, *Hemingway: The Writer's Art of Self-Defense* (Minneapolis: Univ. of Minnesota Press, 1969), p. 66: "'Mr. and Mrs. Elliot' . . . can be seen as a gross attack on T. S. Eliot."

toward mentors like Sherwood Anderson and Gertrude Stein. But could not the similarities in the novels be coincidental, the not unknown instance of individuals coming to similar conclusions at roughly the same time? Other writers of the period attacked false standards, false values, a hypocritical society. Others experimented in form, used myth. Is there proof of influence? Except for Hemingway's deletion of fifteen pages to cut what Fitzgerald objected to and his attempt to cover up that help in A Moveable Feast,[10] I don't know of any, but in addition to the similarities already cited, consider these.

Some minor points first. Hemingway mentions in A Moveable Feast (p. 154) that Fitzgerald showed him Gilbert Seldes' review in The Dial of The Great Gatsby, a review that contains the sentence that "Fitzgerald regard[s] a tiny section of life and report[s] it with irony and pity . . ."[11]—a phrase that echoes in the scene where Bill Gorton sings to Jake about "Irony and Pity. . . . They're mad about it in New York" (SAR, p. 114), a scene with little direct relevance to The Sun Also Rises except for the general application of the two terms Bill celebrates. Fitzgerald's novel moves through a series of parties, from the reception for Nick at the Buchanans', to Tom's and Myrtle's "love nest," the gauche carnivals at Gatsby's, the tea at Nick's, the final excursion into New York to the Plaza Hotel, and back to the quiet wake in the Buchanans' kitchen; Hemingway's novel, originally titled Fiesta, and still printed as such in England, also traces parties from the bal musette and Zelli's in Paris, to San Sebastian, Pamplona, Burguete, and back to Pamplona. Also both novels use a Jew to represent an

---

[10] In A Moveable Feast, Hemingway wrote: "Scott did not see it [the SAR ms.] until after the completed rewritten and cut manuscript had been sent to Scribners at the end of April. . . . I did not want his help while I was rewriting" (pp. 184-185), implying that Fitzgerald could not have influenced SAR because the book was in type before Hemingway let him read the manuscript. While this is literally true, it denies the effect Fitzgerald had, as discovered by Young, Mann, and Baker.

[11] Gilbert Seldes, "Spring Flight," The Dial (August 1925), p. 162.

extreme position under attack: Wolfsheim is Fitzgerald's ultimate, immoral businessman; where young Jimmie Gatz's list of
General Resolves, patterned after Franklin's Poor Richard and
Horatio Alger's homilies, includes "study needed inventions"
(*GG*, p. 174), Meyer Wolfsheim studies opportunities, like
handsome young "Oggsford" men and the chance to fix the
World Series. Like James J. Hill, to whom Henry Gatz ironically compares his dead son, Wolfsheim is a capitalist and a
serendipidist, a robber baron. Together, Wolfsheim, Gatsby,
and Buchanan represent everything for which Carraway and
Fitzgerald had scorn: accumulation of wealth and its disburse-
ment with no regard, not only to the law, but to the feelings
of others. Robert Cohn, of course, is Hemingway's ultimate
romantic, a grown man who lives by a prep-school code, believes in W. H. Hudson's *The Purple Land* as an accurate
picture of South America and Mencken's accounts of Paris
rather than form his own, and believes that a weekend with a
woman is the same as love. In spite of the crumbling of worlds
and institutions and Jake's desperate efforts to learn something
as he went along, to learn to live in the world and thus discover what life is all about (*SAR*, p. 148), Cohn refuses to
learn anything from those he associates with or from his experiences. When he departs from Pamplona, he may, as Mike
says, be less likely to knock people about (*SAR*, p. 203), but
we have no reason to believe that his faith in romantic ideals
has been seriously diminished.

Beyond these, however, three parallels seem most important to me. First, both authors use sports as a metaphor for
the lives of the characters in each. Tom Buchanan seeks vainly
the control over life and other men that he had exercised on
the football field—the same control over a part of his existence
that Pedro Romero displays. That brief period of glory, however, is gone for Tom—as it is gone, analogously, for Gatsby—
and so Tom expresses his need to dominate by literally pushing
Nick around, figuratively doing the same to Wilson, and
voicing the superiority of Nordics over all others, and the old
rich over the *nouveau riche*. For Tom, as for Jordan, life is a

game with rules for the other players. If others can't play, it's just as well, for the game was only meant for the glorification of the Tom Buchanans and Jordan Bakers; if others do play and get hurt, or killed, that's a little sad but certainly not tragic, as long as the Buchanans and Bakers are not the ones hurt.

Significantly, the sports mentioned in *The Great Gatsby*, golf, riding, hydroplaning, tennis, footfall, polo, and swimming in one's pool were, in the 1920's and with the exception of football, exclusively the activities of the well-to-do. For the most part, though accidents and injuries might occur, the emphasis in these sports was not on the spilling of blood. And, with the exception of hydroplaning, all were or could be team sports. In contrast, the sports in *The Sun Also Rises*, except tennis, football, and bicycle racing, were individual endeavors: boxing, fishing, bullfighting. And in contrast to the games of life in *The Great Gatsby*, these feature blood rather prominently, with fishing and bullfighting even ending in the deaths of animals or man. The financial differences in the sports are, of course, related to the social levels of the characters involved, just as the team aspect of those in *The Great Gatsby* better suits Fitzgerald's indictment of the corruption inherent within the very structure and rules of our society. Hemingway, on the other hand, sees the individual as alone in the world, pitted against other men, as in boxing, or pitted against the forces of impersonal or hostile nature. Only through personal artistry can the individual control himself and his reactions to experience, just as the bullfighter shapes the actions and reactions of the bull, controlling not only himself but, to some extent, his destiny. Thus for both authors, life is a game by which the players are measured: Tom is cruel, a cheat; Gatsby is admirable, though the rules he plays by, like Cohn's, are juvenile; Romero and Mippipopolous are self-assured artists; and Jake we can admire, even as we sympathize with his bad luck and ineptness.

Second, as critics have noted, both novels involve frustrated patterns of initiation. The rich in *The Great Gatsby* are a select group, "a rather distinguished secret society" (*GG*, p.

18), to which Gatsby and Carraway seek to belong. Gatsby has money; Carraway has better family, better education, better connections, and could be a member fairly easily. But Gatsby is repeatedly denied admittance to this group by Tom Buchanan. Coincident with Gatsby's death, Nick finally realizes that the moral price of admission is too high to pay, so he breaks off with Jordan and with his pursuit of wealth in the East. Cohn seeks admission to the fraternity that Brett designates as "one of us" (*SAR*, p. 32). He, too, is barred, largely through his own actions, but through those actions, distinct as they are from Romero's, but both like and unlike Jake's, Cohn helps us to see Jake more clearly. Jake, like Cohn, has certain aspects of the steer to him, Jake has also played football and written a novel. Thus both novels are about their unreliable narrators as much, if not more, than they are about the individuals at whom the narrators direct our attention. Though Jake begins by telling us about Cohn, Cohn is obviously a foil for, and much less important than, Jake himself. Similarly Fitzgerald's book bears Gatsby's name, but, though less apparent, the novel also tells the story of Nick Carraway.

Which brings me to the final point of similarity I wish to discuss. The climax of *The Great Gatsby*, for me, occurs when Nick shakes hands with Tom outside of a jeweler's shop on Fifth Avenue, just as Jake Barnes shakes hands with Robert Cohn after Cohn has hit him. At first Nick refuses to take Tom's hand, overtly implying unspoken condemnation and recognition of Tom as an accessory, before the fact, to Gatsby's murder. He makes this condemnation explicit in the narrative:

> I couldn't forgive him or like him. . . . They were careless people, Tom and Daisy—they smashed up things and creatures and then retreated back into their money or their vast carelessness, . . . and let other people clean up the mess they had made. . . . (pp. 180-181)

Then Nick, feeling silly at this unusual excess of moral sentiment on his own part, rejects the urge to tell Tom the truth that Daisy was driving the car that struck Myrtle, rejects it with the vain and foolish gallantry of Gatsby himself, and shakes hands with Tom, rationalizing his act by calling Tom a moral child. But is Tom the only child, the only careless person? When Nick first comes to the Buchanan house, the situation is such that his "own instinct was to telephone immediately for the police" (*GG*, p. 16), yet he does not, of course. He stays, he becomes involved with them, not only to the extent of voyeuristically participating in Tom's and Myrtle's affair, but even to arranging Daisy's and Gatsby's. Nowhere in the novel before the passage quoted above does he, even in his recorded thoughts, voice condemnation of the immorality around him. Even when he learns that Daisy was the driver of the hit-and-run car he remains silent, and that silence helps cause Gatsby's death. Thus the corruption of the East that repels him at the novel's end is a corruption he was part of, and I am not sure that Nick realizes this, any more than I am sure that most readers who accept Nick as their moral norm throughout the novel realize the significance of their own tacit approval of his silence, of his refusal to judge or condemn, and of his pandering. *The Great Gatsby* then, is a novel about our and Nick Carraway's complicity in the moral wasteland of America, which destroys such people as Jay Gatsby, and *The Sun Also Rises* is a novel about Jake Barnes' search for meaning and personal standards in a wasteland world where absolutes have been abolished and conventional standards destroyed. As Nick had with Tom, Jake at first refuses Cohn's hand because Cohn had called him a pimp for arranging Brett's and Romero's affair, as Nick had Gatsby's and Daisy's. Then, like Nick, Jake accepts the offer. In both cases, the narrators shake hands with moral children, but there are differences. In *The Great Gatsby*, three deaths result from the childishness, while in *The Sun Also Rises* pride and bodies are only injured, not killed. And in *The Great Gatsby*, Nick's admitted snobbishness in the opening pages and self-proclaimed honesty cover up a certain self-deception, making him a moral child, too, though a sensitive one. Although Jake may lie to Cohn about being through with worrying (*SAR*, p. 11) and to Bill about not caring any more for Brett (*SAR*, p. 124), at the end of the novel, with his "Isn't it pretty to think so?" (*SAR*, p. 247), he seems to have abandoned another remnant of romantic childishness and to have realized that he and Brett could never have had an idyllic relationship even if he had not been wounded, and to accept that fact, however bitterly.

Thus I think that the two novels have definite structural and situational similarities and that Hemingway, consciously or not, was influenced by Fitzgerald more than has been realized. Both authors used imagery and symbolism borrowed from T. S. Eliot to criticize the patterns of life they saw around them. Both used sports and unreliable narrators engaged in quests. But as befitted their temperaments at the time they wrote, Fitzgerald's novel is a criticism of society couched in lush prose that conveys his own romantic hope; while Hemingway's book transmutes Eliot's and Fitzgerald's material into a philosophical statement about a harsh universe, a statement expressed in a flatter, less lyric prose more attuned to the author's view of life's very limited possibilities.

Faith G. Norris

A MOVEABLE FEAST AND *REMEMBRANCE OF THINGS PAST:* TWO QUESTS FOR LOST TIME

IN THE SPRING OF 1964, when *A Moveable Feast* was published, it won a spectrum of judgment ranging from Lewis Galantiere's declaration in *The New York Times* that the book was a "true triumph of Hemingway's art"[1] to Geoffrey Wagner's pronunciamento in *Commonweal* that "for all the good it is likely to do Hemingway's reputation (it) could have stayed in Cuba permanently."[2] Whatever the critics' final assessment, they all seemed to agree that the book's strength, or its weakness, lay chiefly in Hemingway's descriptions of certain other writers and in the "light it threw on his own mode of writing and the way he went about perfecting his famous style."[3]

In all the thousands of words of praise and condemnation there was not a single sentence contrasting the author of *A Moveable Feast* with Marcel Proust. Perhaps naturally. At first sight it may seem that such a task is ridiculous. Whether people have actually read the French writer or merely heard of him, they tend to think of him as a shrunken individual with perverse sexual tastes who spent most of his last seventeen years shut up in a cork-lined room, doing little except writing long

---

[1] Lewis Galantiere, "A Moveable Feast," *New York Times Book Review,* May 11, 1964, p. 1.

[2] Geoffrey Wagner, "A Moveable Feast," *Commonweal,* May 29, 1964, p. 302.

[3] Granville Hicks, "A Moveable Feast," *Saturday Review,* May 9, 1964, p. 29.

paragraphs about Parisian aristocrats wandering from one salon to another between the 1890's and the 1920's. The very name "Hemingway" at once conjures up the sound of a prose stripped to its essentials plus the vision of a large, healthy outdoorsman kneeling beside some dead lion in Africa. As writer and as human being, who could be more different than the creator of the Baron de Charlus and the begetter of Nick Adams?

All the same, there are a number of illuminating parallels between *A Moveable Feast* and Proust's monumental *Remembrance of Things Past*. To Proust in the volume entitled *The Past Recaptured* "the only true paradise is always the paradise we have lost."[4] To Hemingway there is "never any ending to Paris" and though "Paris was always worth it,"[5] it is clear that the city which he knew when he was "very poor" and "very happy" was in 1957 a paradise which he had lost forever. One of the major themes of both works is identical—that time is an ever-flowing substance which, once gone, will never return. And both men state, or imply, that the only way one can stop the ravages effected by time is memory sought deliberately or called back by unconscious association.

In the case of the invalid Proust it is clear that the capital of his "lost paradise" was his childhood home, the hawthorn-hedged village of Combray. Though the village still stands, the people who gave it its charm are long gone or dead: his childhood sweetheart Gilberte, his parents, his mysterious neighbor M. Swann, and the Duchesse de Guermantes whom he never knew as a boy but whom he worshipped when he saw her at Mass in the Combray church.

---

[4] Marcel Proust, *Remembrance of Things Past*, trans. Scott Moncrief and Frederick Blossom (New York City: Random House, 1932-34), II, 1045, 1932.

Note: References in my text are given in terms of the original seven volumes. Citations are given in terms of the two-volume American translation.

[5] Ernest Hemingway, *A Moveable Feast* (New York: Charles Scribner's Sons, 1964), p. 8.

In the case of the dying Hemingway who wrote *A Move-able Feast* the capital of his lost "paradise" is some Parisian cafe which he visited often in the twenties but where he can drink no more. The first of his "sketches" describes one of his favorite cafes, the "Closerie des Lilas," which he found ideal as a place for writing, especially on cold, wet days. The final sketch, No End to Paris, implies an unfulfillable wish to see again not only the "Lilas" but also the "Dingo" and the "Dome." Of the twenty sketches comprising *A Moveable Feast* fourteen are laid in one of the three mentioned cafes.

In their dreams of the past both authors are deeply concerned with recalling the dramas they experienced in various places in Paris, especially events of the night hours. To the Frenchman, glamorous though certain of his Parisian experiences may have been, they form a wall hard to breach in his search to recapture his lost childhood world of Combray. To the American, return to the cafes as he once knew them is impossible not only because of his shattered physical and mental health but also because their other habitués are either dead or, thanks to quarrels, divorced from his company as he once knew them when he was no world-renowned figure but a struggling would-be writer. For both men, imagination, scrawled notes, and associative memories are their means of living again their past life. That their quest is not, cannot be, a complete success is the major factor in giving each work its poignant quality.

By bracketing Proust and Hemingway in respect to their search for the inaccessible, I am in no way suggesting that the two men were alike. My contention is just that the sick and emotionally depressed Hemingway who wrote *A Moveable Feast* was, as man and author, much like the creator of the nostalgic passages in the last hundred pages of *Remembrance of Things Past*. The two authors' ways with prose and life style prior to writing each work have served to blind us to the similarities between the two hundred and ten pages of *A Moveable Feast* and the twenty-three hundred pages of *Remembrance of Things Past*.

The *Times Literary Supplement*, like a number of other critics, praises *A Moveable Feast* for its "freshness" and "vigor" of style[6] but makes no reference to the fact that its author was a man as sick in mind and body as was Proust while revising the proofs of the last long chapter of his seven-volume novel. For, according to Mary Hemingway, her husband began work on the "Sketches" in Cuba in the fall of 1957 but did not make his final revisions until he moved to Ketchum, Idaho, in the autumn of 1960, less than seven months before his self-inflicted death. In 1957 he was a man sick in body as a result of enduring two plane crashes in two subsequent days. In the fall of 1960 he was even sicker in body but also sick in mind, a man soon to enter the Mayo Clinic under the fiction that he had high blood pressure but whose major problem was severe depression, the result of causes we shall never know. Nothing can testify more eloquently to the importance in both men's lives of their artistic work than their still making revisions during their last days on earth.

Although this point has not been stressed by either of Hemingway's biographers, A. E. Hotchner and Carlos Baker, it seems to me worth emphasizing inasmuch as the twenty "Sketches" written under the shadow of death were composed by means of the same technique described in Wallace Fowlie's *A Reading of Proust*, a book-length analysis of the French author's mode of working.[7]

That both men kept notebooks with entries about various moments in their youthful days we now know beyond question. According to A. E. Hotchner, Hemingway said to him one day in 1950, "I have always made things stick that I wanted to stick. I've never kept notes or a journal. I just push the recall button and there it is."[8] But when Hotchner comes to deal

---

6 "A Moveable Feast," *Times Literary Supplement*, May 12, 1964, p. 425.

7 Wallace Fowlie, *A Reading of Proust* (New York: Doubleday-Doran, 1964), pp. 3-18.

8 A. E. Hotchner, *Papa Hemingway* (New York: Random House, 1966), p. 39.

with the Hemingway of 1958 he proceeds to tell the same story recounted in Professor Carlos Baker's biography—of how during a brief stay in the Paris Ritz that year Hemingway discovered a long-abandoned trunk in the hotel's cellars, a piece of luggage that contained "notebooks in which he had written about those Paris days of the twenties."[9] Eight years earlier, in 1950, literary detectives had accidentally discovered a thousand pages of notes for what was to be *Remembrance of Things Past*. Both men, in short, had unacknowledged aids for their trips backward in time. Granted that for both writers their regular memories, plus their associative ones, did the major work of helping to recover the past, nonetheless the hundreds of pages of written notes must have given a powerful, if unemphasized, support. One still admires the two men's laboring to the end, but it must have been a somewhat lighter task because of the notes.

In another respect both men are alike in that they omit certain experiences discreditable to them. Because of Proust's Jewish heritage, which he wished to conceal from his aristocratic Catholic friends, he is distinctly ambiguous when he discusses the Dreyfus case. After several hundred pages the reader still is unsure where his sympathies lay—with his friends or with his adored Jewish mother who supported the persecuted captain from the start.

In omission of the discreditable, Hemingway employs the same technique of ambiguity. The last sketch, "There is Never any End to Paris," leaves us far from clear as to his feelings about having deserted Hadley for Pauline. He wanders away from Paris to a description of the mountains and vague maunderings about the coming of "the pilot fish" and "the rich," as if to imply that his change of wives was due solely to the machinations of Pauline and her wealthy friends.[10] He fails likewise to include a single word about his notorious boxing match with his young Canadian admirer Morley Callaghan, in

---

[9] Carlos Baker, *Ernest Hemingway: A Life Story* (New York: Charles Scribner's Sons, 1969), p. 459.

[10] Hemingway, p. 209.

which he was defeated badly but which he claimed not to have won only because of Fitzgerald's ineptitude as a time-keeper.[11]

Such omissions of personality weaknesses are common enough in works full of autobiographical detail, but it is the *nature* of the two men's omissions that is interesting. Ill though he was when Hemingway wrote *A Moveable Feast*, he must have deliberately employed a style so different from his normal clarity because he wished to conceal something. Perhaps he wished to protect the still-living Hadley and his three sons. Or maybe, despite his illness, he wished to preserve his self-created legend of the physical superman by making no reference to the much gossiped-about boxing defeat. As for Proust, he was often called, and apparently with reason, a snob. Yet the only woman he ever loved was his mother. Hence his dilemma over the Dreyfus case and his attempt to resolve it by being unclear as to his position.

But if both men are silent about certain of their own faults, they give us a God's plenty when dealing with the weaknesses of others. Especially women. From Madam Verdurin's first appearance in Volume I to our final glimpse of her in the last fifty pages of Volume VII, we see nothing to make us like the social-climbing bourgeoise. She is vulgar, over-talkative, disloyal, and intellectually dishonest. Albertine's first appearance in Volume II seems to be that of a charming chaste young girl. In Volume V we learn that she is a lesbian with sadistic tendencies. To mention only one more tenant in Proust's dream of ugly women, there is Odette, who shares Madam Verdurin's expertise in social climbing but achieves it through sexual wiles rather than by the aid of a dead husband's money.

Hemingway spends less time on unpleasant women than does Proust, perhaps because he knew fewer or perhaps because he was painting a smaller, less crowded canvas. But

---

[11] Andrew Turnbull, *Scott Fitzgerald* (Princeton, N. J.: Princeton Univ. Press, 1966), pp. 168-170.

about women he dislikes he is unsparing. And four out of
his twenty sketches he gives to them alone. First comes
Gertrude Stein. After admitting that she was most hospitable
to him and Hadley when they were new to Paris, he launches
his attacks. He faults her for her dislike of "the drudgery of
revision and the obligation to make her writing intelligible;"[12]
later he implies that her relationship with Alice B. Toklas was
lesbian, and he concludes his assault on her by saying that she
quarreled with everyone she knew.[13] Zelda Fitzgerald also
comes under his whiplash. As Hemingway depicts her, she was
the chief cause of Fitzgerald's crack-up. He accuses her of
being jealous of his writing talents and of saying that her
husband's penis was too small to make any woman happy.[14]
Even her famous beauty he denies her. In his memory she
looked and acted like an unsparing hawk.[15]

Hemingway calls his second wife a "pilot fish," but Hadley,
on the other hand, emerges as all that a woman should be.
Although I feel that Lewis Galantiere was being rather extreme in writing in *The New York Times Book Review* that
A Moveable Feast is "a chant of love addressed to his (Hemingway's) first wife,"[16] there is no denying that she is pictured
as ever pliant, always good-natured, and happy under the
most trying circumstances. Typical of his memory of her mode
of reacting and speaking is a brief episode in the fifth sketch,
"A False Spring." After husband and wife have spent some
time idly exploring Paris, Ernest asks:

> "Are you hungry again?" I said.
> "Of course, Tatie. Aren't you?"
> "Let's go to a wonderful place and have a truly grand
> dinner."
> "Where?"

---

[12] Hemingway, p. 12.
[13] Hemingway, pp. 118-119.
[14] Hemingway, p. 191.
[15] Hemingway, p. 180.
[16] Galantiere, p. 26.

"Michaud's?"

"That's perfect and it's so close."[17]

According to Professor Carlos Baker, the actual Hadley was far less docile. When Ernest had a chance to report on the Greco-Turkish war of 1922, Hadley did not want him to go and "They quarreled 'dreadfully' and she refused to speak to him for three days before he left."[18] The Hadley of his "remembrance of things past" is a different woman. Even in the last sketch when he is supposed to be dreadfully in love with that "pilot fish" Pauline, he still derives a thrill from the mere sight of Hadley's radiant beauty as she stands waiting for him at a small Austrian railroad station.[19]

In the more than two thousand pages that comprise all seven volumes of Proust's work there is no woman comparable to Hadley in personality and looks, but there are two females who remain untouched by the ravages of time. Francoise, the energetic maid in the kitchen of Combray in Volume I is to be found laboring just as hard in Volume VII, "The Past Recaptured." As for the ambitious courtesan Odette, she obsesses Swann with her looks in Volume I; and in the final chapter of Volume VII Proust stresses that her looks are very little changed despite the passage of the years. On the last occasion on which he sees her, he comments that she "looked like a sterilized rose."[20]

As for the portraits of men in the two works, it is ironic that the two males most acidly depicted are attacked primarily for weaknesses that their creators possessed. In the ninth sketch in A Moveable Feast, "Ford Madox Ford and the Devil's Disciple," Hemingway attacks Ford for being a liar and "ignoble,"[21] two traits which Carlos Baker repeatedly assigns to Hemingway. On one occasion, for instance, Baker refers to the

---

[17] Hemingway, p. 56.

[18] Baker, p. 431.

[19] Hemingway, p. 210.

[20] Proust, Vol. II, p. 1053.

[21] Hemingway, p. 86.

"preposterous lies" Ernest began telling his friends in 1943, though the biographer adds that his friends did not know that "truth stretching had been among his leading avocations since boyhood."[22]

In *Remembrance of Things Past* the man made to seem most despicable is the Baron de Charlus who is attacked for his relations with two men, Morel and Jupien.[23] To take just one instance, Proust has the Baron complain that "Everywhere the most famous whores can look at nobody but Morel and this fact is becoming a nuisance."[24] According to gossip such was Proust's own attitude during his homosexual relationship with his chauffeur Agostinelli.[25]

Because the Baron de Charles has a number of other traits, notably pro-German inclinations during World War I, it is critical commonplace to praise Proust for the complexity of this deviant's characterization as well as for his characterization in general. He is also acclaimed for the ingenuity of his structure in making Volume VII, "The Past Recaptured," a summary of all the book's major themes as well as an explanation of certain obscurities in his preceding six volumes. But Hemingway has not won plaudits for either his characterization or his structure in *A Moveable Feast*. Although his portraits of Fitzgerald when drunk may not be kind, the three sketches, "Scott Fitzgerald," "Hawks Do Not Share," and "A Matter of Measurements" do leave us with the feeling that to know the author of *The Great Gatsby* must have been a liberal education and that hours spent with him must always have been interesting, at times even exciting, despite his idiosyncrasies.

I have mentioned the Fitzgerald portrait not only because it is the most fully drawn but also because it immediately precedes the final sketch, "There is Never Any End to Paris." On a first reading *A Moveable Feast* seems to have no struc-

---

[22] Baker, p. 381.

[23] Mostly in Vol. IV, "Cities of the Plain," but also in Vol. VII, "The Past Recaptured."

[24] Proust, Vol. I, p. 531.

[25] Fowlie, p. 25.

ture at all: "sketch" seems to follow "sketch" for no visible reason; one feels that Hemingway has left us at a total chronological loss, just as one sometimes feels with Proust. In both works, though, the authors do give us clues to orient us in time and to make us feel that we are being shown pictures of events from a succession of years. Sometimes the order is determined by simple, commonplace chronology; sometimes by associative memories of long dead years. Proust, for example, lets us know where we are in past time in Volume II, "Within a Budding Grove," because certain events take place during the Dreyfus case; in Volume VII we know where we are in the past because of Charlus' behavior during World War I and because other episodes occur after the war.

Hemingway orients us in time by his references to certain events or places which have been described by other writers. Others, for example, have depicted his first home in Paris and described the break-up of his first marriage. The references to "the pilot fish" and the "rich" in the last section make clear why he places the three Fitzgerald sketches immediately before them: it was not too long before the break with Hadley that he came to know the Fitzgeralds and their rich friends, the Murphys. Explicit time references by either writer would destroy a major thesis which each develops—that events in the past may live again in memory with great clarity but not necessarily in any exact order, or even in the right sequence. As Proust words it in his final seventh volume.:

> Thus does the form of the things of this world change; thus the center of empires . . . all that seemed definitely fixed is being continually made over and the eyes of a man can during a lifetime contemplate change in the very quarters where it had seemed to him the most impossible.[26]

For both men what counts is the clarity of personality and the ambience of the episode, not the month or year when such and such an event took place. To make the past come back in all its beauty or all its squalor is what counts; the precise

---

[26] Proust, Vol. II, p. 1102.

date is of little import. Reflection suggests that they are correct. In our own moments of retrospection certain episodes emerge three-dimensionally as to where and how they occurred, but the months and year elude us unless we are keepers of diaries. I have previously indicated that both writers did have diaries to guide them, but their failure to use the diaries in any strict chronological fashion is a key to their personalities. To both men the recapturing of the full flavor of time lost suggests their confusion on the matter. And, as I have suggested, since we ordinary mortals experience the same bafflement in putting in order our own time lost, the vagueness as to date brings them closer to us.

And both authors repeatedly use the same structural technique to bring back events long gone. They introduce us to a particular episode with a paragraph, or sometimes a whole page, describing its site and a few comments on the personalities of the characters involved. That done, they give us an exchange of dialogue and then terminate the event with a brief auctorial comment.

Frequently it is this comment which leads by some associative or unconscious process into the next sketch, we receive no mention of the year, though often of the season, to let us know if episode X or episode Y came first. Conventional logic would seem to suggest that Y came after X, but when we are dealing with our own remembrances of things past we realize that the search for lost time in our own lives is often a process devoid of logic.

The utilization of this trait is more obvious in Hemingway than in Proust because the American writer's style is bare; the Frenchman's florid. But both writers use the identical method at times, as we all must do in attempts to quarry out our own pasts. For some reason most of us find it easier to recall quite complex details of the "where" of some long-dead event than the simple fact of the "when."

Paradoxically it is at this very point where the two works approach most closely in method that is also where they most differ. Although there is no denying that in Proust's pages many of the episodes are thinly disguised representations of actual fact, that certain characters in the book bear the name they carried in real life—notably the servant Francoise, and, of course, Dreyfus—one also feels that all seven long volumes owe as great a debt to their creator's imagination as to his memory. Despite scholarly attempts to find the "real" Baron de Charlus, Swann, and the Duchesse de Guermantes, no one has ever suggested that Proust's master work is anything but a novel. A *Moveable Feast,* on the other hand, has won from certain critics the verdict that it is part of what might have become a full-scale autobiography.[27] Yet in the penultimate sentence of his Preface, Hemingway says: "If the reader prefers, this book may be regarded as fiction." Since a biographer as scholarly as Carlos Baker several times declares flatly that Hemingway is a liar[28]—a view also hinted at by the less trustworthy A. E. Hotchner—one is faced with a logical dilemma. If the author himself says that the reader is free not to believe some or all of the pages he is about to read, just where in the twenty "sections" is one to grant him credibility? The testimony of his friends and biographers leads one to rely on the honesty of his remarks about his writing methods but to regard much else as well-wrought fiction. But where?

Proust never asks for acceptance as anything but a novelist even though he includes a number of characters whom scholars have detected as barely disguised pictures of people he did know. In both works, clearly, there is an inextricable melange of fact and fiction. As source for a biography of Proust, *Remembrance of Things Past* seems far from reliable.[29] The same conclusion seems valid in connection with A *Moveable Feast.*

But if it seems ridiculous to regard either work as a reliable aid to a biographer, can one legitimately classify both

---

[27] Notably Frank Kermode, *New York Review of Books,* June 11, 1964, p. 4; also Richard Ellmann, *New Statesman,* May 22, 1964, p. 809.

[28] Baker, pp. 12, 207, 274, and 483.

[29] Scholars have generally agreed that all evidence suggests that Albertine was no female beloved but Proust's chauffeur Agostinelli.

as a novel of manners? I would submit that one can. For what each has to offer is a highly subjective and imaginative account of a social world that did objectively exist.

In the years of the Dreyfus case and of World War I, the French aristocracy did become interpenetrated by the wealthy bourgeoisie and did lose much of its power and exclusiveness. How this social phenomenon occurred Marcel Proust does show us in detail.

In the years 1921 to 1929 a number of American painters, writers, and would-be artists did go to live in Paris. How Hemingway was affected by this phenomenon he wants us to see in his terms. And for him the five years of his first marriage did form in Paris a "moveable feast." Some kind of festival was always observed each year, but the date and nature of the feasting changed each spring.

If we accept both works as a series of impressionistic paintings of Paris and not fault them for failure to be photographs of an era, we are being just. And what more can any writer hope for than justice?

To alter by a pronoun the seemingly nonsensical question which *New Yorker* writer Lillian Ross represents Hemingway as repeating several times during her interview of him, "How do you like them (it) now, gentlemen?"[30]

---

[30] Baker, p. 463.

Robert W. Lewis

HEMINGWAY'S SENSE OF PLACE

I

How does Hemingway come at us? Is it first the image of the man and the good portraits by Karsh and Capa, Man Ray and Malmberg, the countless photos in books and magazines? And then the books read and reread, taught and written about until the cream rises and is skimmed off in books and articles, bars, and classes. Hemingway's good books remain inviolate, untouched by what we say. It is with some considerable if veiled pride and arrogance that we think of "getting at" a book or its author, but we do, even if only as the blind men circling an elephant and trying to describe it.

Certainly we can identify the body of the elephant (and the work) and maybe the analogy would work as far as describing its head and tail and legs. *The Old Man and the Sea* was described as Hemingway's *coda* novel, and *coda* originally meant *tail*. Would *The Sun Also Rises* be the head, masterpieces being *chef d'oeuvres* or head-works, and would the non-fiction be appendages? The epidermis would be the overall texture, the seemingly tough, thick-skinned Hemingway we know for a superficial, a skin-deep Hemingway, who is soft and bleeding underneath.

Let this increasingly absurd analogy continue a step further as we turn from blind men into anatomists, murdering to dissect, getting at what is beneath, ignoring codas and bodies and heads and trying to discover, if only to caress with our scalpels, the tendons that hold the body together.

Continuity and design can obliterate meaning, and at this point in time in Hemingway criticism, perhaps we have said enough about his heroes, about love and death themes, a style and a writer with certain continuities and designs that now seem so obviously to be the bulk of the elephant.

As anatomists, let us consider Hemingway as a fiction writer and start out with something simple. Fiction is prose narrative with characters, plot, and setting, and the setting of fiction is made of time and place. From his first book Hemingway's emphasis of "time" and its ravages seems central. His very titles seem to give him away: *In Our Time, The Torrents of Spring, The Sun Also Rises, A Farewell to Arms, Death in the Afternoon, For Whom the Bell Tolls.* These book titles seem to point to a nearly obsessive concern with the theme of mutability, and the matter of the books is supportive. Even the discursive non-fiction book, *Death in the Afternoon,* almost nostalgically sees bullfighting in primitive, Golden Age, and decadent stages. Elsewhere, and notably in the Nick Adams' stories, we see the theme of initiation developed from childhood through adolescence and even maturity (as in "The Short Happy Life of Francis Macomber"). And even unto his last work, discovery, change, and death loom large in *Across the River and into the Trees, The Old Man and the Sea, A Moveable Feast,* and *Islands in the Stream.*

The other side of the coin of setting is "place," but it has not concerned us as thoroughly, and for some good reasons. Just as the lover discovered by the husband in the bedroom closet said, "Everybody has to be someplace," but our concern, like the betrayed husband's, has not so much been with places as with people. The scene is "The English camp at Agincourt" or "Another part of the forest," and that has usually been enough. Even when settings in modern fiction have been explicit, they have generally been instrumental rather than objective. From Aristotle on, our critical vocabulary is significantly simple in dealing with setting. A dramatic rule prescribed unity of time and place, and then a later age broke the rule. Good writers manipulated time and shifted place. Critics noted what was done, but the absorbing interest continued mainly to be focused on characters in action and, inductively, meaning. Place might be an extension of character, a larger significant like the conventional descriptions of physiognomy and clothing. A character "wore" a place (drawing room or heath) as he or she wore clothing. Henry James made us see his characters better when he showed us their quarters and their tours through galleries and their views of the Colosseum. Conrad showed us that the heart of darkness was not so much a political state as a state of mind (or "heart," if you will). And when Willa Cather called for a new novel *démeublé* she was asking for the removal of settings that were extraneous and did not contribute organically to the writer's meaning. E. M. Forster's heuristic book *Aspects of the Novel* devotes nary a word to setting, and his neglect does no damage to our usual view. While setting may be useful to mimesis, it is contributory and tributary to character, action, and meaning.

Our overall title here is "Hemingway in Our Time," and perhaps nothing would be more contemporary than to make of Hemingway a literary ecologist, a writer who perceives the places of his settings in a literarily unconventional manner, and basic to that perception is the achievement of a tolerant sympathy with and understanding of the common peoples indigenous to those places. In fact, these two not obviously related and usually minor fictive elements of place setting and minor native characters might combine in an insight to the anatomy of the elephant.

As man perceives himself and achieves his identity through an ethos and an ethnic "set" that he feels even if he does not recognize them or intellectualize them, so Hemingway the artist sought himself, hunted himself in peoples who seemed to belong to themselves and to a place. Before he went to Paris after the war, Hemingway was already an expatriate, as were, in a mythic sense, most sophisticated European Americans. Were the Hemingways *natives* of Oak Park, Illinois? They migrated annually, not following the buffalo or the ripening wild rice, but perhaps following a yearn for a place, a place for roots and self-knowledge.

In that incredible book *Studies in Classic American Literature*, D. H. Lawrence, a wanderer and an expatriate like Hemingway, gives us something to go on: Before truly feeling a new place, the old inhabitants (like Indians) must be "dead or absorbed" (or "vanished"?) and "the Spirit of Place" must be "atoned for," the "demons . . . placated." "As yet, there is too much menace in the American landscape."[1] The factories must fall down again before the American becomes other than a motherless child a long way from home, alienated not only from his cultural roots and his people, but also from a place to enspirit and nurture him.

Can Hemingway be seen as an executor of Lawrence's program or call to literary action? Does Hemingway also reject perfectability and the fat dream and opt for passion and freedom? And does he seek a sense of place and spirits of actual landscapes, even though he seems the ill-fated wanderer even more than most of us?

Another *auslander*, V. S. Pritchett, has also noted the American sense of place: "As in pretty well all intelligent American novels," he writes, "the sense of America as an effluence of bizarre locality is strong."[2]

Stephen Vincent Benet fell in love with American places, or at least their names, and ended his poem "American Names" with a line that rings ironically different today: "Bury my heart at Wounded Knee."

Archibald MacLeish in "American Letter" wrote with envy of the realized sense of place that Europeans may have, and then came "home" ready if not eager to accept his American role, living on the wild edge of the world, bewildered in wilderness America.

Another British writer, Lawrence Durrell, like Hemingway was also a D. P., a product of troubles in our time; and he more than most writers, unlike certainly most American

---

[1] New York: Viking Press, 1964, pp. 35, 51.

[2] "Clowns," *The New York Review of Books*, July 1, 1971, p. 15. Pritchett is writing about Walker Percy's *Love in the Ruins*.

authors, is able to write discursively about place. For Durrell, landscape is "a collective noun encompassing ambience, atmosphere, essence, a way of life, all the innumerable forces impinging on the writer during his stay in a given place, as well as all his imaginatively felt and reconstructed reactions to them."[3] For Durrell, character is merely background for place and not the other way around. (Especially in *The Quartet* the city of Alexandria dominates.) Theme and motif emerge from the relationship of character and place. To be loving and creative, the character must be "at home" with his place, though not dominated by it nor enraptured by it. And finally, he says, place may be the central metaphor for the story of the growing and searching individual who is looking for a spiritual and artistic integrity—a "home" in another sense.[4]

What is to be got at here is similar to the religious concept of holy ground. The very same passion that led to the Crusades and pilgrimages to the Holy Land (to free it from the infidel or to free the inner man from the outer man) and has led historians to gauge the fervor of Christianity on the basis of

---

[3] Alan Warren Friedman, *Lawrence Durrell and "The Alexandria Quartet,"* Norman: University of Oklahoma Press, 1970, p. xiv.

[4] Lawrence Durrell, *Spirit of Place*, New York: E. P. Dutton, 1969, pp. 187-190, 160, 162, 163. For examples of Durrell's own power to evoke landscape, see his travel books and essays, *The Alexandria Quartet*, and, as an epitome, the lovely and poignant "A Landscape Gone." In "Landscape and Character" he writes that landscape or place changes character: ". . . writers each seem to have a personal landscape of the heart which beckons them"; that is, one has to find his own right place to be turned on to art and life. Similar people and institutions (like the Catholic Church) are different from one country to the next simply because their landscapes are different, and man has problems when he is not attuned to his place. Durrell advises "tuning in" to new landscapes, opening the inner eye through the outer sense, repressing "too much factual information." Furthermore, the truly good "big" books are tuned in to their settings. Even ordinary novels that are "well and truly anchored in nature . . . usually become classics," and he cites *Huckleberry Finn*, *The Grapes of Wrath*, and *Typee* as books pervaded by "senses of place." "You could not transplant them without totally damaging their ambience and mood."

Christians' concern for the Holy Land is the passion in which we localize our emotions. Banal examples further along on the same continuum with that of the Holy Land are the lake cottage, the dream home, the retirement ranchette. Chekhov's "Gooseberries" is a beautiful version of Everyman's dream of place come true. The minor official sacrifices everything, including his long-suffering wife, for retirement on a little piece of heaven, and he doesn't even know that his triumphantly served gooseberries are sour.

In this sense, it is difficult to know what most Americans feel about place, but we may wonder about such recent reports as one of Italian-Americans returning to their Italian home towns upon retirement; and the nomadism of Americans is well documented and felt, even leading one state recently to try officially to discourage newcomers. And when our writers and critics react to a felt shallowness of American life, as in Hawthorne's and James' laments and in the demonstrations of the wandering, alienated characters like Melville's Ishmael and Bartleby, Dreiser's Clyde Griffiths and Sister Carrie, Fitzgerald's Gatsby and Dick Diver, who fill our literature with their painful placelessness, they show us the drifting. The anchorages of characters, the homesteadings and the homecomings, are usually present only in the background, among minor characters, or like marriages and deaths, appropriate as convenient if artificial endings.

Even our novels of the soil seem generally to lack the sense of spirit of place that characterizes Hemingway's descriptions of the fishing trip to Burquete in *The Sun Also Rises* and some of the Michigan, Italian, African, and Caribbean settings, to mention important recurring ones. Even where our writers dwell on the beauties, charms, or strengths of places, they often see the place as a thing apart from and alien to the characters. Thus, in writers like Willa Cather and O. E. Rölvaag, the wilderness may be personified and invoked as a place of strange power and beauty, but it is indifferent to man and must be subdued and converted to a "garden." For some writers, men and women are forged in the conflict with nature, but with the advance of civilization, nature is corrupted, and we long nostalgically for the good old days of the pioneers and frozen hands and feet, cholera epidemics, drouth, grasshopper plagues, at the very least brutally hard labor and the like enspiriting conditions that made for heroes. A strange circle, if not a vicious one.

We have, in extenuation of our flagrant expropriation of American Indian land, explained our action as "manifest destiny" and also—and more importantly for our present interest—the displacement of a nomadic unfounded culture by a stable, place-oriented people. It is a Big Lie. Not even many of our farmers any more, our people of the soil, seem to have any love of it or stability. The movement from the farm to the village to the city still continues. The fat dream includes winters in Florida or California, vacations in Tahiti or Acapulco, and a retirement home in Tucson or Coral Gables. It is the white American who continues to be the nomad, and the red American is drawn or held even to the sterility of a reservation if that is home. He points to the four directions, to the sky above and the earth below, and he realizes that he is at the center of the universe. Speaking in another context about his quest for place in *The Way to Rainy Mountain*, the Kiowa N. Scott Momaday said, "I am interested in the way that a man looks at a given landscape and takes possession of it in his blood and brain."[5] Through an act of the imagination we must see and understand the world around us.

When we are strong, we know where we are, even though we may be, as Hemingway often was, in a foreign land, "in another country."

II

There are frequent references by other writers to Hemingway's "sense of place"; some of them include Malcolm

---

[5] N. Scott Momaday, *Indian Voices*, San Francisco: The Indian Historian Press, 1970, p. 53.

Cowley's recognition of "exact evocations of landscapes"; Carlos Baker's analysis of symbolic geographical description in *A Farewell to Arms* and E. M. Halliday's response to it; Leo Gurko's mention of Hemingway's non-fiction as "rhapsodies of place;" Emilio Cecchi's writing that "more than a chronology, the art of Hemingway has a topography"; Charles A. Fenton's observation that Hemingway had a deeply felt "personal typography": "You need local knowledge," Hemingway had written to Fenton; Philip Young's noting that Jake in *The Sun Also Rises* moves through places (Paris and Spain) with the awareness of a professional soldier reconnoitering new terrain. The action is always foremost, but it is supported by real country and real city; Baker's recognition of Hemingway's love of earth and sense of place and Baker's giving "sense of place" (with sense of fact and sense of scene) primacy as Hemingway's "three esthetic instruments." Hemingway once told George Antheil, " 'Unless you have geography, background, . . . you have nothing.' . . . Few writers have been more place-conscious."[6]

And what Richard Bridgman sees as a stylistic device, Hemingway's use of prepositions, can also be seen as a meaningful descriptive device: the artist aware of landscape, place, and terrain renders action and fact through the use of the tactician's most essential kind of word, the preposition. Delbert Wylder sees this view of place very well in the contrast of Spain and France in *The Sun Also Rises*. And although she is approaching the elephant through her and Hemingway's special interest in the arts, Emily Watts writes instructively and at length about his landscapes and seascapes, particularly as they are perceived panoramically.[7]

    [6] Carlos Baker, *Hemingway: The Writer as Artist*, 4th edition, Princeton: Princeton University Press, 1972, pp. 48-51, 54.

    [7] Emily Stipes Watts, *Ernest Hemingway and the Arts*, Urbana: University of Illinois Press, 1971. The only disparaging remarks about Hemingway's descriptions of settings that I found were on the subject of the presentation of nature in literature in a Mary McCarthy essay. It is interesting, but rather too impressionistic and superficial, covering a

In addition to these repeated observations of Hemingway's keen awareness of and sensitivity to "place," there is one other interesting notion of terrain that others have given us to start with, and that is of terrain as metaphor. But it seems to me basically inept, or at least hostile to my sense of how Hemingway used and presented terrain. Jonathan Baumbach has written about some post-Hemingway writers in a book called *The Landscape of Nightmare,* and both Norman Mailer and Richard Hovey write about Hemingway's *inner* landscape or terrain, the dark reaches of his soul, as *places* of nightmare.[8] The metaphor is fine except that it so harshly contrasts to the literal and symbolic ways Hemingway usually presented physical landscape. True enough, there are scenes of horror and nightmare in Hemingway, but very often they do not occur in fully visualized landscapes where natural rather than human details dominate. The traumatic and dispiriting experiences for the heroes tend to occur in man-made environments (bars, homes, hotels, bullrings, hospitals, "developed" areas like towns and cities), and therapeutic or enspiriting experiences tend to be set where the marks of humanity are minimal. And when we do find more or less "natural" landscapes of nightmare in Hemingway, they are heavily invaded by men bent on "unnatural" missions, as in war and as in the wounding episodes in *A Farewell to Arms, For Whom the Bell Tolls,* and *Across the River and into the Trees.* And more importantly, we find few detailed descriptions of "bad" places, important exceptions being the nightmarish evocations of the places where Frederic Henry and Nick Adams are wounded. In the many places where Nick Adams is hurt and twisted, description gives way to action and dialogue as setting subsides. Almost every Hem-

---

mighty range of works and ideas with short shrift: Mary McCarthy, "One Touch of Nature," *The Writing on the Wall and Other Literary Essays,* New York: Harcourt, Brace and World, 1970.

[8] Norman Mailer, *Cannibals and Christians,* New York: The Dial Press, 1966, p. 159. Richard Hovey, *Hemingway: The Inner Terrain,* Seattle: University of Washington Press, 1968, p. 196.

ingway novel has its memorable place, but they are generally the good places, not the bad. And could we not almost say that whenever the Hemingway protagonist knows where he is, he is in a good place, and when he is disoriented he is in trouble? Even in the perilous chase of *Islands in the Stream,* Thomas Hudson's keen perception of terrain, landscape, and seascape somehow seems to reassure us of his strength. Among the familiar islands, even in danger, he is on his home "ground."

Hemingway's first novel may be, as he has said, not about the lost generation, but the "abiding earth."[9] Yet the abiding earth is not a character, and the limited number of words devoted to the relatively uncorrupted earth and sea suggest that indeed the novel is about people (lost or otherwise), though we know something very important about them because of their relationship to the earth.

The Spanish Earth is one Hemingway work we don't pay much attention to, but at least its title and theme are very apt here. When Hemingway and Dos Passos were working on the film together, "Dos Passos wanted to stress the predicament of the common people in the midst of civil war. Ernest was far more interested in the military aspects," and after the battle at Guadalajara and Brihuega, he rushed to the scene "to examine the terrain before the burial squads had completed their work."[10] Later, in writing "Night Before Battle" and "Under the Ridge," he would explicitly incorporate what he had seen and demonstrate his literal sensitivity to terrain.[11]

Hemingway seems to have had an unusual grasp of terrain, a ready apprehension of where he was physically in regard to terrain features like hills and directions. Both fellow writers like Dos Passos and non-writers like his hunting friends

---

[9] Baker, *Writer,* p. 81.

[10] Carlos Baker, "Hemingway: Living, Loving, Dying," *The Atlantic Monthly,* (January 1969), pp. 49-50.

[11] *The Fifth Column and Four Stories of the Spanish Civil War,* New York: Charles Scribner's Sons, 1969, see especially pp. 116 and 138.

noted it in his life.[12] And he himself used terrain both literally and figuratively in his writing, and on one occasion he spoke of the "country of his work."[13] But it is in the writing itself that what we are after emerges. It is there where the "inner terrain" meets the objective world that he himself writes of in "Mitraigliatrice [sic]":

> "Ugly short infantry of the mind,
> Advancing over difficult terrain
> Make this Corona
> Their mitrailleuse."[14]

The terrain of the mind is metaphysical. By and through real terrain we discover form, and through form, idea. The ordinary tourist is after the same thing, perhaps, but the eye is not trained and he usually does not write about his touring. He does not usually get beyond sensations to sense.

" 'Sense' in 'sense of place' means both receptivity by sense organs and awareness. Narrowly speaking, the input from sense organs excites and directs consciousness; but the structure and activity of the central nervous system are inherent. The distinction of inside awareness from outside stimulus is only a convention. As Alan Watts says, inside and outside are often banal expressions of our general mode of thinking . . ."[15]

---

[12] See, for example, Dos Passos' comment that Hemingway would have been a first-rate guerrilla chief because he was a leader and he had "the sense of topography that military tacticians have. He knew what the country in the next valley [in Montana] would be like before his horse scrambled up over the rimrock." *The Best Times*, New York: Signet Books, 1968, p. 226. See also Lloyd R. Arnold, *High on the Wild with Hemingway*, Caldwell, Idaho: The Caxton Printers, Ltd., 1968, p. 25.

[13] George Plimpton, "An Interview with Ernest Hemingway," reprinted in *Hemingway and His Critics*, ed. Carlos Baker, New York: Hill and Wang, 1961, p. 30.

[14] *The Collected Poems of Ernest Hemingway*, Pirated Edition, San Francisco, 1960, p. 18. The conventional spelling of the title word is *mitragliatrice*.

[15] Paul Shepard, *Man in the Landscape: A Historic View of the Esthetics of Nature*, New York: Ballantine Books, 1972, p. 27.

Hemingway was very explicit about such an attempt to merge inner and outer terrains in his foreword to *Green Hills of Africa:* in trying to make a historical account have the quality of a work of the imagination, he would render "the shape of a country."[16] He had already done pretty well in rendering the shape of the Spanish high plateau country Jake Barnes visits in *The Sun Also Rises,* but elsewhere in that novel are many less intense feelings for locations. The motif of place begins on the purely physical (or "outer") plane in Paris with repeated references to place names as the characters (and Jake especially) seek to *orient* themselves, to *find* themselves in an urban landscape of charm if not beauty or sublimity. It is interesting to note that even when the characters (Jake, Brett, and the Count) drive to the Bois de Boulogue, they seem not to look upon it but are only egotistically interested in themselves. By contrast, the Paris reminiscences of "The Snows of Kilimanjaro," that veritable Baedeker of a story, suggest Harry's longing for a landscape that he was "at home" in, and it seems to me there is a very important difference in that Harry was then poor and very close to the natives of Paris; he was living in, not on, the landscape, urban though it was, not as an expatriate but like a native. Similarly, the autobiographical *A Moveable Feast* is full of the warm sense of knowing Paris and belonging to it as he and his first wife lived like the poor people of Paris, knew them intimately, and shared their lives. Mary Hemingway reported that she returned to Paris before the posthumous book was published, and she found that his place names and directions and distances were uncannily accurate.[17]

Jake Barnes also knows Paris well and describes it vividly (as at the beginnings of Chapters III, IV, and V), but Hemingway portrays him as a man out of joint with his time and place,

---

[16] New York: Charles Scribner's Sons, 1935, p. iii. Hereafter, GHOA.

[17] "The Making of the Book: A Chronicle and a Memoir," *New York Times Review,* May 10, 1964, pp. 26-27.

though not, certainly, as out of place as Cohn who finds all of
Paris physically boring and "dead and dull."[18] Nonetheless the
carefully observant Jake is not in his native land, in several
senses. The one time in Paris when *Cohn* is "at home" is in the
artificial though comforting environment of a bar: "This is a
good place," he tells Jake, who laconically agrees, "There's a
lot of liquor," (*SAR*, p. 11). Then when Cohn tries to persuade
Jake to go with him to South America, Jake erupts. He had
found Cohn's preoccupation with W. H. Hudson's *The Purple
Land*, "a very sinister book" set in "an intensely romantic land"
(*SAR*, p. 9), incredibly naive. Cohn's concepts of place were
strictly literary, and Jake tells him that he cannot "get away
from [himself] by moving from one place to another. . . . Why
don't you start living your life in Paris?" he asks him (*SAR*,
p. 11), but Cohn has no feel for Paris where, on wandering
its streets alone at night, he only gets stopped by a bicycle
cop as a suspicious person (*SAR*, p. 12).

Of course, there is a lot of what Jake dislikes in Cohn in
Jake himself.

In "suspended" time (a holiday) and "in another country"
(Spain), Jake finds himself, at least momentarily. In one terrain, that of the bullring, he tries to help others find their way,
but they are not at home there, as Jake is, and he too is out-
cast (by other *aficionados* like Montoya) when he betrays the
holy ground to the unbelievers who do not convert. (Note, in
passing, that in both Spanish and English the bullfight is partly
understood in terms of the different *terrains* of the participants,
including most importantly the bulls.[19] Between times, the
place settings of Pamplona are spiritually indistinguishable
from those of Paris, and they are often international (which
is to say nation-less and place-less) hotels and bars. The ex-

---

[18] *The Sun Also Rises*, New York: Charles Scribner's Sons, 1926
(1954), pp. 41-42. Hereafter, *SAR*.

[19] See especially the Glossary entry *terreno* and Chapter 14 in *Death
in the Afternoon* and references in "The Capital of the World" (p. 46)
and "The Undefeated" (p. 249). *The Short Stories of Ernest Hemingway*,
New York: Charles Scribner's Sons, 1953. Hereafter, *Stories*.

cursion to the cathedral, "where the show started" (SAR, p. 208), is a failure for Brett if not Jake. The carefree holiday ends in cares, including the violation of the *place* as Montoya and Jake had previously conceived it.

The one "good place" that is more or less saved from the antics of the expatriates is the high country around Burguete where Jake and Bill go for the trout fishing (an activity that also looms importantly in the Michigan stories), but as soon as Jake leaves Paris, a "pestilential city" (SAR, p. 74), he begins to find some inner peace. In Bayonne, he not only drinks but drinks in the heat, the smells, the sea breeze, and the colors; in the drive through the Basque country, there is a minimum of action and dialogue as Jake soaks in the "very rich and green" land (SAR, p. 91). As Bill, Cohn, and Jake ascend the mountains into the "real" Spain, Bill and Jake perceive and appreciate the landscape while Cohn sleeps (SAR, p. 93). (The description could provide an illustrator or cartographer a good beginning in his art.) Cohn also misses the fishing trip, as do Mike and Brett, so the good place is not spoiled by those who would not understand it.

Bill and Jake leave on the bus and ride like and with the Basque peasants, sharing their food and wine and good humor as they share their landscape. Although they are not natives, they are accepted by the people, and they in turn accept their land. Later, Bill says, "This is country," (SAR, p. 117), and in the midst of his detailed description, Jake thinks that "the country was very fine" (SAR, p. 118).

When they return to the city of the plain, the expatriates explode with the fiesta, and the narrative seems dominated by dialogue and action rather than description, though certainly we again get nearly visual images of Pamplona. But the place is not holy. The religious aspect of the fiesta is lost upon the other *auslanders* and is nearly unavailable to Jake. Interestingly, one drunken night he retires to read Turgenev's *A Sportsman's Sketches*, and it is the perception of the "country" in one of them that loosens his head: "The country became very clear," he notes, and it was a perception that he would never lose

(*SAR*, pp. 147, 149).[20] Even in literature, Hemingway seems to be saying, the sense of place may be created in the midst of chaos.

Throughout Hemingway's first novel and setting a pattern for all his fiction, there are continual references to place names as Jake defines himself and seeks to orient himself, finding himself as man in a landscape. He is alternately cleansed and sullied[21] as he moves about in varied terrain with his various friends, and the novel ends in another pair of symbolic settings: in San Sebastian where the martyred hero ritually bathes in the sea in solitude, and in a bar in Madrid where he administers the rite of the sharing of the gin and the vermouth. It is a stereotyped Hemingway bar, a clean, well-lighted place, an artificial refuge like a zoo that cages while it protects, and a place where the "natives"—the efficient and discreet bartenders who belong to a higher order of men—do not live but are merely on duty, serving. The bars and the drinks offer an illusory steadiness in a temporary refuge. Brett and Jake must finally leave just as the old man is driven out of his clean, well-lighted place which held off the *nada*.

As some critics have aptly observed, Hemingway was not content to stick with a winning formula and image.[22] Although he may have confused some reviewers who anticipated continuity and wanted to fit new novels into old Procrustean beds, if the fingerprints of his concern with place and the natives in it were not lopped off, that concern might have proved that the

---

[20] The specific Turgenev sketch is unmentioned, but the collection is permeated with landscapes perceived *with* Russian serfs, if not *through* their eyes. Hemingway is also probably referring to one of Turgenev's stories from *A Sportsman's Sketches* in *Green Hills of Africa* (p. 108) where he says that it was through reading Turgenev that he had learned to see the prairie and woods he knew in the United States.

[21] In *Hemingway on Love*, Austin: University of Texas Press, 1965, pp. 31-32, I have commented on the frequent references to bathing.

[22] Recently and in some detail, Jackson J. Benson in *Hemingway: The Writer's Art of Self Defense*, Minneapolis: University of Minnesota Press, 1969, and Delbert Wylder, *Hemingway's Heroes*, Albuquerque: University of New Mexico Press, 1969.

author of his later works was the same as the one who wrote *The Sun Also Rises* and the early stories. Even a brief survey of some memorable landscapes may suggest the continuity.

A *Farewell to Arms* is set mainly in Italy, one of the countries Hemingway loved best (including Spain, East Africa, the islands of the Caribbean, and northern Michigan). It opens with a memorable descriptive chapter that foreshadows the entire novel, and among a number of vividly described and thematically functional settings is one of a good place that is never visited: the Abruzzi homeland of the good priest who wanted Frederic Henry to take his leave there in a highland of good hunting and good peasants.[23] In regret that he did not take the priest's advice and invitation, Henry later recalls the missed opportunity. And then when Henry and Catherine escape to a promised idyll in the mountains of Switzerland, it seems to me that their joys are tainted; they do not belong there in that "fine country."[24] They are not part of the landscape but are rather in suspended animation waiting to descend to "real" life again. And note the artificial isolation from natives. They hardly know their hosts the Guttingens who also have a wine parlor downstairs. Nor do they know anyone at the inn where they walk or in Montreux except for Catherine's hairdresser (*FTA*, p. 292). "Isn't it grand how we never see any one? You don't want to see people do you, darling?" Catherine asks defensively or insecurely, and what can Henry say but "No" (*FTA*, p. 303). Catherine wants to be alone in the "fine country" with her true love (see also *FTA*, p. 307), but if Frederic Henry is of a piece with or at least related to other Hemingway protagonists, one does not have access to the sacrality of the good places except after long intimacy and with or through the natives of the place. Otherwise one is

---

[23] For a possible source of the idea of the Abruzzi as a "good" place, see "A North of Italy Christmas," *By-Line: Ernest Hemingway*, New York: Charles Scribner's Sons, 1967, pp. 128-129.

[24] *A Farewell to Arms*, New York: Charles Scribner's Sons (Scribner Library), 1957, p. 303. Hereafter, *FTA*.

merely a pilgrim (like those mocked in *The Sun Also Rises*[25]) or a tourist (as is Frederic Henry on his whore-chasing leave).[26] The one time when he begins to approach an ambience, to sense a place, is at Stresa where he has visited before and where he does know some friendly "natives"—Emilio the barman who tends a clean, well-lighted place and who also likes fishing, and Count Greffi with whom he plays billiards and talks. But he is driven off from this one landscape that promises harmony.

Similarly is Robert Jordan in *For Whom the Bells Tolls* at home in the Spanish mountains but prevented the ultimate correspondence with them because of the artificial intrusions of war. What he does come to know and understand of his place, Jordan's last stand, he owes to the indirect instruction of the rude Spanish natives Anselmo, Pilar, Pablo, and the others. The mind-blasted Maria is also reoriented, chiefly by the witchery and kindness of Pilar, and the older woman's prescription is an act of love to which the Spanish earth itself responds by moving under the lovers.[27]

More explicitly than in any other work, Hemingway presents his feelings about "country" and the relations of natives to it in *Green Hills of Africa*. Both the time and the place of setting are crucially important and deliberately chosen, as his foreword notes. The time of the action covers the entire safari by means of summary and flashbacks, but the present action is of the last several days of the hunt for the last trophy, the kudu, before the seasonal rains arrive to end the hunting and drive them "home." Again, there is the theme of time's winged chariots, and here, besides the competition of the various hunts, the conflict may be seen as between time and place. Time is running out in the vast spaces of this new happy hunt-

---

[25] Pp. 86-88.

[26] See also the tourists and the federal agents and the fate of the uprooted veterans in *To Have and Have Not* as contrasted with the native wisdom of the conchs who stuck together and thoroughly know their islands and coastal waters.

[27] *For Whom the Bell Tolls*, New York: Charles Scribner's Sons, 1940, p. 159. Hereafter, *FWBT*.

ing ground, and Hemingway has not yet found himself. Africa is not his. He has suffered from amoebic dysentery, his unsuccessful rivalry with the moody Karl, distrust of and anger with some of the native gun bearers and trackers, and an undercurrent of the rivalry of a territorial (and latently sexual) imperative with his guide Pop whom he admires but who nonetheless belongs and gets along and is "at home" as Hemingway is not. While many exciting and pleasurable events have occurred on the safari, Hemingway has well arranged the sequence of events to create a fine climax. Will pursuit be happiness before the rains come, or will the safari end in frustration and self-hatred and alienation from the land and the people he is with?

As if to show that self-knowledge through the sense of place can only come without a Mentor, Pop leaves Hemingway to run off on what looks like a wild goose chase rather than a kudu and sable hunt, and with the rains closing in, Hemingway travels fast and light with a dubious native guide and several of the safari natives into a new country, a pocket of green hills no whites have hunted before. While Hemingway had said that he loved the other Africa, at the end of the book and the safari, he enters a Shangri-la and is transformed. When he returns to the others several days later, the competitiveness and hostility are gone. "I'm all right again," he says, and Pop reveals that the thumb-pulling with his native companions at the end of the hunt was a form of blood brotherhood (GHOA, p. 293). In a good place, instructed and led by unsophisticated natives, Hemingway had achieved the enlightened harmony of the man who knows where he is, who perceives without pride that he is at the center of life.

The change may be seen as a humanizing of a "good place." Jake alone in Burguete would not have the ambience that he achieves with Bill, the natives, and Wilson-Harris. Romero in the stylized terrain of the bullring must share his grace and sense of place with Brett and aficionados while he paradoxically performs well only for himself (SAR, p. 216). Robert Jordan wounded and as good as dead feels the pine needles under him as he performs one last unselfish act for his friends who escape. Santiago has dreams only of places now, as of the African beaches where the lions play, but it is for Manolin the young boy that he maintains his strength and dignity and performs well.[28] Without Frederic Henry's erstwhile military companions, the enlisted men who are one by one separated from him, he is adrift. And in *Green Hills of Africa,* Hemingway reaches his harmony with place only after acceptance of and by some others, some simple people who live close to and in the land. Toward the beginning of his narrative, Hemingway had announced a romantic view of place saying he was "homesick" for this Africa that he is now for the first time visiting, but the "home" is notably devoid of people, though there are a Pop and a Poor Old Mama so designated among his companions (*GHOA,* pp. 72-73). Not every part of the country is good. Some parts are hot, dirty, dusty, and infested with tsetse flies. One afternoon while he is reading, he reminisces about good places in Italy, another country he loved and "better than any book" (*GHOA,* p. 108), though good books, if they are works of art, may endure forever and outlast both people and places:

> A country, finally, erodes and the dust blows away, the people all die and none of them were of any importance permanently, except those who practised the arts, and these now wish to cease their work because it is too lonely, too hard to do, and is not fashionable. (*GHOA,* p. 109)

The safari moves into new country, fresher country, kudu country, but it is perceived not for what it is but as a version of another country, Spain:

"It's like Galicia," his wife says.

> "There's no bloody difference," I said. "Only the buildings. It was like Navarre in Droopy's country too. The limestone out-cropping in the same way, the way the land lies, the trees along the watercourses and the springs."

---

[28] *The Old Man and the Sea,* New York: Charles Scribner's Sons (Scribner Library), 1952, p. 25. Hereafter, *OMS.*

"It's damned strange how you can love a country," Pop said.
"You two are very profound fellows," P.O.M. said. "But
where are we going to camp?" (*GHOA*, p. 151)

With the self-deflating comment on "profundity," Hemingway
acknowledges that he is still seeing pretty much with the eyes
of a tourist, albeit a perceptive one, and romantically, that is,
as we have been taught to see nature by the Romantic poets
and with some confusion of sexual and esthetic emotions with
the emotions generated simply by a place itself.

Throughout the book, Hemingway tells us about the
natives: M'Cola who favors Poor Old Mama initially and whose
trust Hemingway has to win; Droopy and his good humor;
Garrick and his detested theatrics. With only two days left,
Hemingway and M'Cola finally are "hunting together . . .
with no feeling of superiority on either side any more, only
a shortness of time and our disquiet that we did not know the
country . . ." (*GHOA*, p. 176). That is, it seems to him that he
cannot put together into the complete perception and understanding what he has alternately had separately: either the
merely geographical and romantic perception of the country
or the harmony with the natives, but not both together.

But in the last several days, without the Virgilian guide
Pop, in the fresh green hills, with mutual understanding and
respect between him and the natives, Hemingway achieves a
new sense of place and at last is able to articulate it. Before
setting off by himself, he has an exchange with Pop on the
subject of foreign languages: If you want to get to know the
truth about a country, you must know its language.

> "You get your good dope always from the people and when
> you can't talk with people and can't overhear you don't get any-
> thing that's of anything but journalistic value."
> "You want to knuckle down on your Swahili then."
> "I'm trying to."
> "Even then you can't overhear because they're always talk-
> ing their own language."
> "But if I ever write anything about this it will just be land-
> scape painting until I know something about it. Your first seeing of
> a country is a very valuable one. Probably more valuable to

yourself than to any one else, is the hell of it. But you ought to always write it to try to get it stated. No matter what you do with it." (*GHOA*, p. 193)

Hemingway then has one setback in his growing friendship with M'Cola when the native neglects to clean a wet rifle, and the beginning of Hemingway's last hunt is ominous:

My exhilaration died with the stretching out of this plain, the typical poor game country, and it all began to seem very impossible and romantic and quite untrue. (*GHOA*, p. 216)

But the new native guide leads him on.

Then the plain was behind us and ahead there were big trees and we were entering a country the loveliest that I had seen in Africa. The grass was green and smooth, short as a meadow that has been mown and is newly grown, and the trees were big, high-trunked, and old with no undergrowth but only the smooth green of the turf like a deer park and we drove on through shade and patches of sunlight following a faint trail the Wanderobo pointed out. I could not believe we had suddenly come to any such wonderful country. It was a country to wake from, happy to have had the dream and, seeing if it would clown away, I reached up and touched the Wanderobo's ear. He jumped and Kamau snickered. M'Cola nudged me from the back seat . . .

This was the finest country I had seen but we went on, winding along through the big trees over the softly rolling grass. Then ahead and to the right we saw the high stockade of a Masai village. It was a very large village and out of it came running long-legged, brown, smooth-moving men. . . . They came up to the car and surrounded it, all laughing and smiling and talking. They all were tall, their teeth were white and good, and their hair was stained a red brown and arranged in a looped fringe on their foreheads. They carried spears and they were very handsome and extremely jolly, not sullen, nor contemptuous like the northern Masai, and they wanted to know what we were going to do. . . .

They were the tallest, best-built, handsomest people I had ever seen and the first truly light-hearted happy people I had seen in Africa. . . .

Seeing them running and so damned handsome and so happy made us all happy. I had never seen such quick disinterested friendliness, nor such fine looking people. (*GHOA*, pp. 217, 218, 221)

Only the theatrical Garrick seems frightened by the Masai, and Hemingway uses the word *place* to suggest an interesting metaphor of *place* as inner terrain:

> I believe these Masai frightened him [Garrick] in a very old place. They were our friends, not his. They certainly were our friends though. They had that attitude that makes brothers, that unexpressed but instant and complete acceptance that you must be Masai wherever it is you come from. . . . It is an ignorant attitude and the people who have it do not survive, but very few pleasanter things ever happen to you than the encountering of it. (*GHOA*, p. 221)

Then up in the hills as far as the car can go, they meet some even more exceptional natives unlike any Hemingway had seen before, tall and good-looking, resembling noble Romans and clad in togas. Hunting, he begins to universalize the act as creating a brotherhood of men in good country like this (*GHOA*, p. 249), and three times connects those green hills of Africa with his feelings for northern Michigan, the first country he had known well (*GHOA*, pp. 222, 282, 284).

Here at the end of the book, most of us remember the resolution of the hunt, the shooting of the kudu and sable and the bittersweet parting with the old guide. I had already tentatively formulated an hypothesis regarding Hemingway's feeling for place and the importance of natives to it when I re-read *Green Hills of Africa* and read as if for the first time, like Keats reading Chapman's Homer, this remarkable passage that begins with Hemingway's recollection of his amoebic dysentery:

> It is easier to keep well in a good country by taking simple precautions than to pretend that a country which is finished is still good.
>
> A continent ages quickly once we come. The natives live in harmony with it. But the foreigner destroys, cuts down the trees, drains the water, so that the water supply is altered and in a short time the soil, once the sod is turned under, is cropped out and, next, it starts to blow away as it has blown away in every old country and as I had seen it start to blow in Canada. The earth gets tired of being exploited. A country wears out quickly unless man puts back in it all his residue and that of all his beasts. When

he quits using beasts and uses machines, the earth defeats him quickly. The machine can't reproduce, nor does it fertilize the soil, and it eats what he cannot raise. A country was made to be as we found it. We are the intruders and after we are dead we may have ruined it but it will still be there and we don't know what the changes are. I suppose they all end up like Mongolia.

I would come back to Africa but not to make a living from it. I could do that with two pencils and a few hundred sheets of the cheapest paper. But I would come back to where it pleased me to live; to really live. Not just let my life pass. Our people went to America because that was the place to go then. It had been a good country and we had made a bloody mess of it and I would go, now, somewhere else as we had always had the right to go somewhere else and as we had always gone. You could always come back. Let the others come to America who did not know that they had come too late. Our people had seen it at its best and fought for it when it was well worth fighting for. Now I would go somewhere else. We always went in the old days and there were still good places to go. (*GHOA*, pp. 284-285)

The passage does not prove Hemingway was a generation or two ahead of his time; though ecology is only recently a popular topic, conservation is not. The point of greater interest is the recognition that "natives live in harmony with" the good places and may restore place and oneness with it to alienated man. And suddenly it seems a truth widely demonstrated in Hemingway's work from the head of *The Sun Also Rises* to the tail of *The Old Man and the Sea* where we wonder at the strange power of Santiago, a fisher among men, knowing the sex of the unseen marlin, knowing the creatures of the sea, the weather, everything of his place, simple and *native* as he is. The Hemingway hero, of the sort from Nick Adams to Thomas Hudson, of the sort of the *auslander* "in another country," full of *platzangst*, is by contrast dislocated, and all of his stories are most importantly tales of the longing for the sense of place.

III

Curiously, what we sometimes call the scenic technique in short story narration does not admit description—realistic, symbolic, or whatever. It approaches the technique of drama, and some of Hemingway's most famous stories and episodes in them and his novels follow this pattern. *Place* is virtually relegated to a stage direction. There is virtually no exposition in "The Killers," for instance, and in contrast to the extended description in the novels and non-fiction books, very little description in a good number of Hemingway's short stories. The difference is in part a matter of proportion, but it is also a matter of the limitation of the dramatic technique to shorter fictions.

Descriptions or the absences of them in the short stories, however, are closely related to the ideas of place and native peoples. The first collection with its red-herring title *In Our Time* is better read as a series of place-oriented rather than time-oriented stories. And most of the stories are of dislocations, displacements, landscapes of potential peace invaded by the forces of chaos and destruction. From "On the Quai at Smyrna" and "Indian Camp" to "L'Envoi," the stories are almost uniformly of good places being disturbed or destroyed. That is not to say that they have detailed descriptions in them. Usually they do not, for the landscape of nightmare is impressionistic and symbolic. On another level, the simple truth may be that Hemingway had little interest in the stultifying city or town, and, like all of us, he was insensitive to that which he had no taste for. But there are some neutral grounds that are vividly described or imagined, and they can be either good or bad places, or sometimes both at once.

The settings of the short stories fall into three groups, those of "dislocations," those where home is found, and those that are potentially good places where some human disharmony exists or where man brings into a good place his own bad spirit. Many of the Michigan stories (including those previously unpublished in Philip Young's edition of *The Nick Adams Stories*) are of this last sort.[29] For instance, Paco of "The Capital of the World" is removed from his country village and living in Madrid. It is no nightmare, but a fairyland where he futilely

---

[29] New York: Charles Scribner's Sons, 1972. Hereafter, *Adams*.

seeks his place in the sun. To him, Madrid is "an unbelievable place" (*Stories*, p. 38). Similarly, Macomber's Africa is not home but a new place where he and Margot seek a new life. In the Michigan stories "Summer People" and "The Last Good Country," good places are marred by interlopers, people like Odgar and "rich slobs" from the city and law officers who do not belong. Both of these stories have forest retreats, redoubts with religious or holy overtones (*Adams*, p. 90) where the Tristan-like Nick can escape law and order with a loved one.

The stories of dislocations, of protagonists lost in space are much the most common. Such dislocation can be seen in "Soldier's Home" and "The Killers" where the response of both young men at the end of the stories is to get out of town, out of the bad place.[30] Nick Adams on the bum in "The Battler" and "The Light of the World" is also driven out of even the temporary havens of the hobo jungle and the tough Michigan bar. The old refugee in "Old Man at the Bridge" had had his place, his home town of which he is proud (*Stories*, p. 78), but he was driven from it by the war, and now he is at a symbolic crossroads, "not a good place to stop," as the narrator tells him (*Stories*, p. 79).

"A Way You'll Never Be" opens with a thorough description of a battlefield presumably like the one where Nick was traumatized. In his disorientation his mind jumps from place to place, unable to "locate." In the companion story "Now I Lay Me," Nick seeks tranquility first through thinking about girls but then through recreating places, the good places of Michigan. "I could remember all the streams" (*Stories*, p. 153), he says, and they give him some peace of mind. Another postwounding story, "In Another Country," opens with a fine evocation of place (Milan) and time (fall), but Nick is in the wrong country as well as another country, and he is alienated from both the natives of the quarter where he walks and his fellow patients who discover he is only superficially one of them.

---

[30] See "Soldier's Home," p. 153, and "The Killers," p. 289, *Stories*.

A clear instance of the effect of time (bad) on place (good) is "The End of Something" which otherwise might seem less well unified than it is. It opens with a brief history of the end of a town that is abandoned when the lumbering ends. Nick is out of joint, and the cutting of the trees, the desertion of the sawmill and the town, foreshadow and complement Nick's loss of "love." Similarly does "Up in Michigan" include a detailed description of Liz's town from her point of view. After her seduction by Jim, the story closes with her walking away from the one human being who had made her place warm. The description at the end of the story is of dislocation and loss as "A cold mist comes up through the woods from the bay" (*Stories*, p. 86).

A subgroup of dislocation stories is about people on the run, whether as criminals or tourists. These strangers in strange lands include Ole Andreson of "The Killers" and the Hungarian boy of "The Revolutionist" who "had been in many towns," loved Italy and the Alps, and ends up in a Swiss jail (*Stories*, pp. 153-158). The stories include those of alienated couples, aliens to each other and their homelands. In "Mr. and Mrs. Elliot," "Cat in the Rain," "Out of Season," "Hills Like White Elephants," "A Canary for One," and "The Sea Change" couples drift through scenery without feeling landscape, and notably the natives are remote from them and are usually only servants or remote fellow travelers. Even bleaker are the wanderers who are alone, without even the physical presence of a hostile or indifferent mate. In "A Pursuit Race," the advance publicity agent for a burlesque show is in his own country but has been so continuously on the move to various places that finally, in the heart of the continent, Kansas City, he is no place, he is "spaced out," and he pulls the bedsheet over his head in a futile denial of his condition and as a pathetic gesture of longing for the original motherland, the womb.

A curious variation on the theme that was originally published as an article and is apparently a non-fiction narrative is "*Che Ti Dice la Patria?*"[31] *La patria* or the fatherland is Italy, one of the several countries that Hemingway had known well and had come to love, but when he and his friend Guy Hickok visit it in 1927, the Fascists are in power and their ten-day trip in the northern part of the country is marred by some of the changes wrought by Mussolini's regime. Since the narrative is historical and not fictive, one might at first think the descriptions of the landscapes and the people were fortuitous in supporting the theme that what the fatherland now tells him (and the *New Republic* readers in 1927) is sad: the totalitarian and demagogic rule of the Fascists had converted the country from a land of warmth and spontaneity to one of all the evils of bureaucracy with worse threatening. But of course we are not so innocent as to think that the historian or the journalist is "objective" while the fiction writer is imaginative, symbolical, and worse. Both select, and Hemingway in this story (historical or not) wrote with the same goals of thematic unity and coherence as he would in a purely imagined story like "The Short Happy Life of Francis Macomber." Thus, the descriptions are "organic," and we see a country covered with dust, "coarse and thick" grape vines, "stained" houses (*Stories*, p. 290), and a restaurant that doubles as a brothel. In the restaurant, the narrator, trapped into conversation with one of the whores, ironically says that Spezia is "a lovely place."

" 'It is my country,' she said. 'Spezia is my home and Italy is my country.'

" 'She says that Italy is her country.'

" 'Tell her it looks like her country,' Guy said" (*Stories*, p. 295). Italy is whoring to false gods. Its manners have become thinly veiled insults, and it is a country of infection and corruption. When it rains the dust turns to mud, and the brown water of the river in Genoa discolors even the sea. The natives are unsettled, like the young Fascist who is "used to travelling" and the sad couple who seem to be on the run (*Stories*, pp. 291,

---

[31] See Audre Hanneman, *Ernest Hemingway: A Comprehensive Bibliography*, Princeton: Princeton University Press, 1967, C 178.

299). The people they meet are suspicious or hostile. The narrator notes that "'they drowned Shelley somewhere along here'" (*Stories*, p. 297), and it is with considerable relief that they finish their Italian sojourn.

"'Do you remember what we came to this country for?'" Guy asks.

"'Yes,' I said, "'but we didn't get it'" (*Stories*, p. 298).

The unstated purpose of their trip was apparently an attempt to go home again, to recapture the past of a decade before when Italy was adventure and warmth.

On the road back to France they pass "a sign with a picture of an S-turn and Svolta Pericolosa" (*Stories*, p. 298). Italy too has reached a dangerous turning, and the landscape of dust and mud is complemented by a people of heavy revolvers and heavy hands and heavy hearts. With bitter irony, Hemingway concludes, "Naturally, in such a short trip, we had no opportunity to see how things were with the country or the people" (*Stories*, p. 299).

Thus are most of the short stories set in landscapes and among people alien or lost. Rarely is it given the Hemingway protagonist except nostalgically and retrospectively to be in the good place with the good people, the "other" who like him is native, at home. In "The Snows of Kilimanjaro," Harry recognizes the pleasantness of the African camp, but he is with a woman he does not love and he is dying and longing for the place of the leopard, the center of the universe, the mountain top where both man and leopard are "out of place." A story like "Cross-Country Snow" seems exceptional in that the protagonist has a good companion in good country, but they hear time's winged chariot; they are not living for the moment, which is to say, they are not living for place by ignoring time. They are rather juvenile, in fact, wishing for a life uncomplicated by responsibility (as for pregnant women and school), a life of fondly bumming together along good ski trails to pubs and to "swell places" (*Stories*, p. 186). In fact, they are aliens too, and George even wishes they were "natives," in this instance Swiss, for then, he naively believes, life would be perfect. *A Moveable Feast* treats the same idea from a mature point of view, but the result is the same: when we were young and in love, we identified with the common people of our good places.

In "Fathers and Sons" and two previously unpublished stories, "The Last Good Country" and "On Writing," the protagonist has no mature companion or is, as in "Big Two-Hearted River," alone. But these stories of the sense and spirit of place achieved or realized, even though nostalgically, are so remembered because of a past harmony of natives with the protagonist in the holy place. "Fathers and Sons" opens with a description of a small town and the trees "that are a part of your heart if it is your town . . . It was not his [Nick's] country . . . all of this country was good to drive through and to see . . . Nick noticed which corn fields had soy beans or peas in them, how the thickets and the cutover land lay, where the cabins and houses were in relation to the fields and the thickets, hunting the country in his mind as he went by, sizing up each clearing as to feed and cover and figuring where you would find a covey and which way they would fly" (*Stories*, p. 488).

Memories of hunting the country remind him of his father. "His father came back to him" in the places they shared on hunts (*Stories*, p. 496).

And Nick remembers that he learned of landscapes, both terrestrial and sexual, from the Ojibways.[32] Nick's young son seems to sense the importance of place too. The story concludes with their discussion of the holiest of places, the burying ground. They must find " 'some convenient place in America' " for a family graveyard, the son humorously says. "That's an idea," Nick laconically replies (*Stories*, p. 499).

In "Big Two-Hearted River," as in "Now I Lay Me," Nick goes back to a well-known place (but now actually rather than simply in his imagination) to recreate his torn psyche.

---

[32] In *Across the River and into the Trees*, Colonel Cantwell also thinks of Renata's body in terms of its terrain: pp. 152-154.

But there are no natives in this story. Nick is alone. He does not need a map to know his location (*Stories,* p. 211), and he knows his direction by the sun (*Stories,* p. 212); the phrase "he knew" recurs three times, and we know that Nick is very knowledgable about the fauna and flora and the geography and history of the countryside.

He makes camp, eats, and fishes all very carefully, insisting that he fit into the Place exactly, correctly. There must be no knobby roots where he will sleep, and he will have good long tent pegs that will not pull out.

His tent quickly and well erected, "Already there was something mysterious and homelike. Nick was happy . . . He was there, in the good place" (*Stories,* p. 215).

In "The Last Good Country," Nick is intimate with a place (northern Michigan again) in part because of the natives who have taught him and who help him. He in turn becomes a guide for his young, loved sister. "On Writing" contains a vivid recollection of Walloon Lake, and Hemingway goes on to say that it is hard to write when you love "the world and living in it and special people. It was hard when you loved so many places" (*Adams,* p. 238).

Nick wanted to write as Cezanne painted—without tricks— and "to write about country so it would be there like Cezanne has done it in painting . . . Nobody had ever written about country like that. He felt almost holy about it. It was deadly serious. You could do it if you would fight it out. If you'd lived right with your eyes.

"It was a thing you couldn't talk about. He was going to work on it until he got it" (*Adams,* p. 239).[33]

Did he get it? At first I think not. And then I think he did. Certainly he perceived the positive values accruing to "natives" (people born to place) or to those aliens who rejected the labyrinths in our time for the woods and the streams, the hills

---

[33] Obviously, the passage would relate well to Emily Watts' *Ernest Hemingway and the Arts, op. cit.,* but the story was published after her book.

and the fields—"real country." But the bulk of the message is negative. May we perceive the light because Hemingway wrote so well of the shadows? Was sense of place his "fifth dimension"?[34]

In *Across the River and into the Trees,* he had written, "We live by accidents of terrain, you know. And terrain is what remains in the dreaming part of your mind."[35] As in all his later works, *Across the River and into the Trees* is full of the fifth dimension, sense of place. It reads like a narrative geography. The artificial, willed sense of time is subdued. The winged chariot is at the gate, but it is the sense of place that matters, to the dying hour.

Place needs to be important. We are creatures of a land, plants who live only by tendrils that suck and frailly clutch the earth. Else we are ill.

Hemingway solely as the literalist, the super-realist, the way-it-was author exists only as one blind man perceives the elephant. Landscape and terrain were *terribly* important to him, not as setting for fiction, to make it seem real, but as *terra sancta* and landscape of nightmare, both places of memory and dream.

---

[34] See Frederic I. Carpenter and the essays he refers to: "Hemingway Achieves the Fifth Dimension," reprinted in *Hemingway and His Critics,* ed. Carlos Baker, New York: Hill and Wang, 1961.

[35] *Across the River and into the Trees,* New York: Charles Scribner's Sons, 1950, p. 123.

JOHN CLARK PRATT

A SOMETIMES GREAT NOTION:
ERNEST HEMINGWAY'S ROMAN CATHOLICISM

FOR A READER attuned to Ernest Hemingway's symbolic and allusive impulses, *Islands in the Stream* begins appropriately. On the largest of the islands lives a man named Hudson, who owns a great house built not upon the sand but rather "into the island as though it were a part of it."[1] The houseboy's name is Joseph, and soon there appear Hudson's sons who possess the Biblical names of Thomas, David, and Andrew. When David, the youngest (who has never even been given a slingshot), fails to subdue his personal Goliaths first in the form of a shark, next as a giant marlin, one begins to wonder if the religious allusions which appear so tantalizingly in *For Whom the Bell Tolls* and *The Old Man and the Sea* are once again to pervade this posthumous work. However, they do not. Hudson is no Jordan (I think the name puns in both novels are intentional), and despite occasional comments on the Second Coming, and end of the world, Christmas, prayer, and relations with the Diety, this aging and somewhat pathetic artist-hero who has come to resemble a reincarnated Harry Morgan loses his climactic struggle with hardly a glint of the Christian glory shown by Hemingway's greatest fisherman.

I do not mean to imply that there is not much that is good about *Islands in the Stream,* but like Hawthorne's posthumous works, *Septimius Felton, Dr. Grimshaw's Secret,* and *The Dolliver Romance,* Hemingway's *Islands in the Stream* is a

---

[1] *Islands in the Stream* (New York: Bantam, 1972) p. 4. Subsequent references in the text.

first-draft novel which has primary interest more for what it shows us of Hemingway at work than for what it actually is as fiction.

A favorite subject that Hemingway might have developed during revision is his often noted concern with Christian prayer. In *Islands in the Stream,* the boys (as were Hemingway's own sons) are Roman Catholic, and at one point David says, "You don't know how I prayed for you, Roger," to which his father's friend replies, "I wish it would have done more good." "You can't tell," David continues. "You never know when it may. . . . I don't mean that Mr. Davis needs to be prayed for. I just mean about prayer technically" (p. 175). It is with this word, "technical," that one should properly approach Hemingway's Catholicism, for better than any other description, it defines his religious life, attitudes, and artistic method. That his works abound with Christian considerations and allusions has been discussed often but inconclusively, and I suspect that only by paying attention strictly to the essence of Roman Catholicism can one begin, and I mean begin, to understand what Philip Young has quite properly termed the "unresolved paradox" of Hemingway's religious life.

Hemingway definitely did not want "to be known as a Catholic writer," he told an inquiring priest in 1927[2] and Maxwell Perkins in 1939.[3] These dates are important, for they span not only the years which produced the elements of his most religious works, but also his marriage to Pauline Pfeiffer, a staunch Roman Catholic. During this period, Hemingway claimed to have "had 'so much faith' that he 'hated to examine into it,' but he was trying [at least in 1927] to lead a good life in the Church and was very happy."[4] One must take this and all other Hemingway statements about religion with care, for in the same year he published his snide "Neothomist Poem,"

---

[2] Carlos Baker, *Ernest Hemingway: A Life Story* (New York: Bantam, 1970), p. 239.

[3] Baker, p. 439.

[4] Baker, p. 238.

which stated simply: "The Lord is my shepherd, I shall not/ want him for long." Regardless, by 1927 Hemingway had been technically a Roman Catholic for nine years. As he explained it, he had been baptized immediately after being wounded in Italy,[5] an event which Sylvia Beach also describes. At their first meeting in Paris, Hemingway told her the following story:

> In the hospital, they thought he was done for; there was even some question of administering the last sacraments. But this was changed, with his feeble consent, to baptism—"just in case they were right."[6]

Sounding much like Count Greffi in *A Farewell to Arms*, the comment to Miss Beach typifies Hemingway's conditional Catholicism. Although he attended Mass frequently, he never seemed to become more than what Jake Barnes so aptly defines in *The Sun Also Rises* as "technically" a Catholic. "What does that mean," Bill Gorton asks. "I don't know," answers Jake.[7]

This "technical" concept pervades Hemingway's characters, the men who observe the forms and perhaps the spirit of religion, but cannot embrace it with body, mind, and soul. "It is in defeat that we become Christian," Frederic Henry says in *A Farewell to Arms*. "I don't mean technically Christian. I mean like Our Lord."[8] Despite his divorces, as late as 1959 Hemingway was still using the same term. He said in a letter,

> Technically for your information the last time I went to Mass was last Sunday at Bayonne. There was a twenty-minute sermon which would have bored you too.[9]

Later, in *Islands in the Stream*, young David prefaces his comment about "prayer technically" with the assertion that he

---

[5] Baker, p. 727.

[6] Sylvia Beach, *Shakespeare and Company* (New York: Harcourt-Brace, 1956), p. 78.

[7] *The Sun Also Rises* (New York: Charles Scribner's Sons, 1926, 1954), p. 124. Noted below as *SAR*.

[8] *A Farewell to Arms* (New York: Charles Scribner's Sons, 1929, 1957), p. 178. Noted below as *AFTA*.

[9] To John Clark Pratt, August 21, 1959, p. 2.

"used to do First Fridays for mother to give her the grace of a happy death" (p. 175). And the oldest of Hemingway's technical Catholics, Santiago, says, "I am not religious, . . . But I will say ten Our Fathers and ten Hail Marys that I should catch this fish, and I promise to make a pilgrimage to the Virgen de Cobre if I catch him."[10] As for the man himself, Ernest Hemingway was buried by a Roman Catholic rite with a priest officiating, no doubt technically absolved of the mortal sin of despair by the fact that his suicide could be considered the actions of an insane person.

Hemingway's often overlooked lengthy and direct association with Roman Catholicism can well serve as a basis for defining a religious attitude, and I do not agree at all with Leo Hertzel's overall view that for Hemingway, "members of the Catholic society emerge by contrast as human beings in a desirable state of spiritual security." Hertzel continues, "He seems to say that for those whom faith is an actuality life is a great deal more satisfying than it is for those who do not believe."[11] True, most of Hemingway's Roman Catholic characters are presented sympathetically, but there is more to the question than their orthodoxy. Many of Hemingway's Catholics are also seen to be foolish, limited in their awareness, or just plain stupid. His 1944 comment on then Archbishop Spellman, for instance, is a case in point:

> In the next war we shall bury the dead in cellophane
> The Host shall come packaged in every K ration
> Every man shall be provided with a small but perfect Archbishop
> Spellman, which shall be self-inflatable.[12]

In "Wine of Wyoming" (1930), he points out another problem. "En Amérique," says Madame Fontan, "il ne faut pas être catholique," a condition which leads the narrator later to be-

---

[10] *The Old Man and the Sea* (New York: Charles Scribner's Sons, 1952), p. 63. Noted below as *OMTS*.

[11] "Hemingway and The Problem of Belief," *Catholic World*, CLXXXIV (October, 1956), pp. 30, 31.

[12] "Second Poem to Mary," *The Atlantic*, 216 (August 1965), p. 97.

lieve that the Fontans will not have "good luck."[13] In addition, his bitterness toward one aspect of Catholicism (here the alliance between the Spanish Catholic Church and the Fascists) is quite obvious in his *Ken* article, "The Cardinal Picks a Winner,"[14] and what may very well have been a deep animosity becomes quite explicit in *For Whom the Bell Tolls*, when Anselmo, one of the paragons of the novel, is described simply as "a Christian. Something very rare in Catholic countries."[15]

As many critics have incorrectly ignored Hemingway's Roman Catholicism in their religious studies, so is it improper, I believe, to see only what some feel to have been his favorably disposed attitude toward the Church. Like Hawthorne, I suspect, whose wife's religious practices so affected his subjects and style, Hemingway's personal associations with Catholicism could not have helped but flavor the approach he would take in his art. If he did not want to be known as a Catholic writer, neither for obvious reasons did he want to be seen as an overtly anti-Catholic writer—and it may well be that his ambivalent feelings toward the Church produced the earlier mentioned "paradox." True, he practiced the outward forms, but he could not "feel" totally religious. Nowhere in his writings is there an indication that his "devout" characters are to provide any kind of a model for mankind; in fact, the emphasis is usually just the opposite: a rejection of the spirit (albeit genially) for the frailties of the flesh. His characters always live in the valleys or at the base of his symbolic mountains; although their Kiliminjaros and Abruzzis beckon, they never quite seem to be able to make the trip.

Nevertheless, Hemingway remained attracted to, even obsessed with Roman Catholicism, for what I think is basically a quite consistent reason. Above all other Christian beliefs, Roman Catholicism is a "code" religion, ritualistic in precisely

---

[13] *The Short Stories of Ernest Hemingway* (New York: Charles Scribner's Sons, n.d.), p. 457. Noted below as SS.

[14] *Ken* (May 5, 1938).

[15] *For Whom the Bell Tolls* (New York: Charles Scribner's Sons, 1940, 1968), p. 287. Noted below as *FWTBT*.

the manner Hemingway found so appealing in aspects of war, sport, and life itself. True, his sympathetically treated Roman Catholic characters practice and believe in their religion, but they also subscribe in a more general sense to what Philip Young has so aptly defined as the Hemingway code. In *Death in the Afternoon,* Hemingway provides an example:

> At the start of their careers all [matadors] are as devoutly ritual as altar boys serving a high mass and some always remain so. Others are as cynical as night club proprietors. The devout ones are killed more frequently. The cynical ones are the best companions. But the best of all are the cynical ones when they are still devout; or after; when having been devout, then cynical, they become devout again by cynicism.[16]

As altar boys go, so do matadors, and I think this statement provides an illuminating key to the presentation of all Hemingway's religious characters. Commenting elsewhere in *Death in the Afternoon* on the bullfight as ritualistic tragedy, he asserts that the matador should increase the danger *"within the rules provided for his protection. . . .* It is to his discredit if he runs danger through ignorance, through disregard of the fundamental rules, through physical or mental slowness, or through blind folly."[17] For a Roman Catholic, the rules have been traditionally explicit, thus providing at least one code to live by. Even though a man might never have the time to learn, as Frederic Henry says, one has no real choice, even though the inevitable result might be that "They threw you in and told you the rules and the first time they caught you off base they killed you."[18] Perhaps to Hemingway it was, after all, how you played the game that counted—and Roman Catholicism was the oldest and grandest game of all.

With his ambivalent attitude and desire not to be seen as an overtly religious writer, it is no wonder that Hemingway chose subtlety and irony as a technique to present some of his

---

[16] *Death in the Afternoon* (London: Jonathan Cape, 1932, 1956), p. 62. Noted below as *Death.*

[17] *Death,* p. 26.

[18] *AFTA,* p. 327.

views on Catholicism in his time. Although he rarely attacked the Church openly, he nevertheless began, after his marriage to Pauline, to incorporate more and more specific Roman Catholic references, allusions, puns, and veiled mockery of many of the Church's traditional beliefs. Catholic critics might have been expected to notice and respond, but they did not. Instead, almost to a man they reproached Hemingway for *failing* to consider spiritual subjects at all. One called him a "literary garbage collector,"[19] another felt that for Hemingway, "if God was still in His heaven, the outlines of Divinity were hidden behind some rather red clouds,"[20] and a third believed strongly that Hemingway had "spelled his doom . . . by omitting from his writings all concept of universal values."[21] As late as the 1950's, Roman Catholic reviewers still felt that Hemingway was a writer who lacked "the inspiration, the vision to uncover anything in life beyond an animal struggle for existence."[22] Interestingly, no mention was made in the reviews of the 1930's that Hemingway was then calling himself a Catholic and attending church.

What the doctrinaire reviewers missed was the fact that Hemingway's artistic method had changed during his close association with the Church. In his early novels and stories, religion appears thematically. In *The Sun Also Rises*, the religious theme is submerged as part of the entire view, as is the fact that each major character represents one religious attitude: Brett, the pagan; Bill, the Protestant; Robert Cohn, the Jewish; Romero, the devout Catholic; and Jake, the "technical" Catholic. Stories such as "Soldier's Home," interchapter VII of *In Our Time*, and the play "Today is Friday" do not

[19] Fr. John S. Kennedy, "Hemingway's Latest," *Sign*, XX (December, 1940), p. 289.

[20] H. Allen, "Dark Night of Ernest Hemingway," *Catholic World*, CL (February 1940), pp. 522-529.

[21] R. A. Klinefelter, "Estimate of Hemingway," *Catholic Mind*, LIII (November 1955), pp. 681-684.

[22] Clare Powers, review of *OMTS*, *Sign*, XXXII (November 1952), pp. 63-64.

show Hemingway seriously exploiting Catholicism in his art. Few of the stories in his first two collections carry religious overtones, but almost all of his later works show a careful consideration of Catholic elements, presented allusively as well as thematically. The change came after *A Farewell to Arms,* in which the subjects of love, God, and war form the tripartite thematic base of the novel. Having shown what happens to the truly devout, regardless of the object of their devotion, Hemingway began treating specific aspects of Roman Catholicism in both short and long fiction. Usually concerned with aspects of tradition and ritual, he used Catholic allusion, pun, and allegory in a much different manner than he had before.

Most of the time he was rather clumsy, a fact which many readers could or would not admit. In a story which he claimed "nobody else ever liked,"[23] he took the title "The Light of the World" from John 8:12 and created an extended pun on Christ's subsequent words, "He that followeth me shall not walk in darkness but shall have the light of life," and "Ye know neither me, nor my Father: if ye knew me, ye would know my Father also." Unable to determine even the correct name of their "God," the fighter who was killed by his father, the prostitutes provided no more satisfactory a model than does the homosexual cook. Rather than "follow" any of these "lights," the boys decide to go the other way. Similarly, in "God Rest You Merry, Gentlemen," the opening words "In those days" introduce a Christmas fable which shall unfortunately come to pass when the boy, obsessed with his consciousness of sin, is unable to understand even the Roman Catholic justification expressed by the Jewish doctor with the ironic name of Fischer. And in a later story, "The Capital of the World," a young man becomes overly devout in his pursuit of the simulated bull. Paco, who "had no father to forgive him, nor anything for the father to forgive" (a double pun), dies in a state of grace even though he does not have time to complete an act of contrition. As Hemingway says, "A severed femoral artery empties itself

---

[23] SS, p. v.

faster than you can believe."[24] Believe in what, we might ask. His life draining, Paco tries vainly to apologize to God for having offended him and dies "full of illusions. He had not had time in his life to lose any of them, nor even, at the end, to complete an act of contrition."[25] He is thus equated in his ignorance with the boy of the previous story who did not know what castrate meant, and the misdirected religious devotion of each is seen to have no real substance at all. Faith, Hemingway shows, is just another illusion.

Not unlike Melville, Hemingway should be seen in his later stories not only attempting to create many-faceted fiction but also beginning to use veiled irony as a means to achieve multivalent meaning. In "The Snows of Kiliminjaro," for instance, the significance of the epigraph to the story depends upon the reader's interpretation of one word. To the summit of Kiliminjaro has come a leopard, but no one, says the epigraph, "has explained what the leopard was *seeking* [italics mine] at that altitude." What he was seeking is the House of God and by association, God's attendant ways. Thus even a Harry who has wasted his talent and now believes in nothing may possibly reach the "square top of Kiliminjaro," described climactically as "wide as all the world, great, high, and unbelievably white."[26] To explain the House of God is impossible, the story says; but in all its unbelievable (a nice pun) whiteness, nevertheless like Mt. Everest it is there, despite all formalized attempts at definition.

Concerning subjects such as these—faith, sin, and redemption—I think Hemingway felt toward the Catholic Church's prescriptions much as Jake Barnes does in *The Sun Also Rises* toward what he thinks to be the Church's unacceptable attitude toward his wound. "The Catholic Church had an awfully good way of handling all that. Good advice, anyway. Not to think about it. Oh, it was swell advice. Try and take it some-

---

[24] SS, pp. 38, 50.
[25] SS, p. 51.
[26] SS, pp. 52, 76.

time. Try and take it."[27] Repeatedly, as the protagonists of "Now I Lay Me" and "A Clean, Well-Lighted Place" show, the best recourse is to accept the undefinable and sleep with the light on, just in case. About the only other alternative is to believe as much in the next world as does the nun in "The Gambler, the Nun, and the Radio," but her desire to become a saint takes on sad irony when one realizes that she will have to die first. Neither fate (the gambler) nor religion (the nun) is more than an opiate. At least man has some control over his own works (the radio). He can turn it off.

I am not trying to suggest that Hemingway's use of Christian allusion in his later works approaches the technical intensity of Melville, Faulkner, Steinbeck, or even Edward Albee. Unlike many other American writers, Hemingway did not seem to feel cheated. For him, there was not the overwhelming blackness sensed by the nineteenth century ex-Calvinists, for instance. His humanism was not exclusive; he could not totally reject, as did Twain, the whole damned race of human believers. Instead, he preferred to underline paradox —that of unrewarded prayer, slaughtered "devouts," and successfully disobeyed commandments. Man, he felt, was just unlucky, as he shows in one of his last stories, "The Old Man at the Bridge." Even when surrounded by war, the old man's peaceful doves will fly somewhere and cats will look after themselves. Even on Easter Sunday, that "was all the good luck that old man would ever have."[28]

In addition to using allusion and irony, Hemingway also experimented with allegory. I say "experimented" because I do not believe he was an allegorist in the manner of Golding, for instance, or Melville. To create conventional allegory, a writer must remain so fixed upon the concept behind the surface reality of his prose that it is the idea which shapes and controls the action. For Hemingway, the reverse was usually true, except for occasional attempts at parable such as "The

---

[27] SAR, p. 31.
[28] SS, p. 80.

Good Lion" and "Today is Friday." His desire to write from sensed experience caused him to excise where an allegorist would build, to pare down a symbol to its essence instead of stratifying meanings. Accordingly, he seems to have produced archetypal rather than allegorical works. For instance, even though *For Whom the Bell Tolls* parallels the Christ story, complete with an anti-Virgin Mother, a Mary Magdalene, disciples, and a Judas, it does not demonstrate the disciplined, intellectually oriented allegory of *East of Eden* or *Light in August*. His Spanish novel reads almost as if Hemingway could not see his characters simultaneously as human beings *and* types, a basic requirement for modern allegory. El Sordo's hilltop battle in *For Whom The Bell Tolls*, for instance, is a brilliant piece of writing and itself an allusion to Christ's death, but it just does not fit into an overall allegorical scheme.

Hemingway was trying, however, and in *The Old Man and The Sea* he put it all together. Refined and polished, the Christian allusions and puns, as well as the elements of Roman Catholic doctrine, are fused together with no detriment to the verisimilitude one expects in a Hemingway story. And nowhere else in his fiction does the paradox of Hemingway's technical Catholicism so completely control meaning, structure, and style. The novel delineates, in a sense, the unexplicable, intentionally failing to define that which is itself undefinable: the mystery of faith and transfiguration. In humanistic terms, *The Old Man and The Sea* depicts not only the essence of Christianity but the nature of all myth as well.

Commenting upon the Christian allegory in this novel, many critics have run afoul of Hemingway's iceberg by either attributing a strict one to one allegory (Santiago equals Christ *or* Manolin equals Christ) or by not recognizing from his earlier works that Hemingway was now willing artistically to go far out as his central character does in his fishing boat. Carlos Baker sees no allegory, as such, in the novel, but he is talking in traditional terms, and with this limitation, he is right. Santiago is not strictly a parallel to Jesus Christ; he also is a disciple (Saint James) of the marlin, who is another representation of Christ in agony and death, complete with a spear in his side. Santiago is also a God-figure, a surrogate father to the boy, Manolin (Little Emmanuel), himself also a Christ as he takes on his new allegiance at the end. What Hemingway has done, I think, is to show syncretically all elements of the Christian myth in each of the three main characters, and in so doing has underscored one of the greatest paradoxes (to a "technical Catholic") of the Roman Catholic faith—the mystery of the Trinity: God the Father, God the Son, and God the Holy Spirit. To those on the one hand not familiar with traditional Catholic thought, or to Roman Catholic theologians on the other, no paradox exists. The answer is faith. To "think about it," as Jake Barnes would have, is futile. But paradox it is to a "technical" Catholic, summed up in two apparently contradictory statements. To Santiago's comment that "a man may be destroyed but not defeated,"[29] one should add Frederic Henry's earlier explanation that "It is in defeat that we become Christian, . . . like Our Lord." Yet Santiago in fact is neither destroyed *nor* defeated. Instead, he triumphs, as Christ (who is God) did, in a manner denied every other major Hemingway character.

I cannot resolve this aspect of the paradox, and I do not think that Hemingway could either. As critics, we often seek resolutions where there in fact are none—and I think Hemingway has presented us in *The Old Man and The Sea* with questions which can of course be answered by many, but only from their own particular points of view. Like the tourists at the end of the novel, any attempt on our part to define just what the message of this novel really is may make us mistake a marlin for a shark—or vice versa. As a comment on the future, Hemingway ends the novel with one of his most ingenious religious puns. "What do you want done with the head?" asks little Emmanuel of his surrogate father. "Let Pedrico chop it up to use in fish traps," Santiago replies, adding later, "Don't forget to tell Pedrico the head is his."[30] To Peter goes the head

---

[29] *OMTS*, p. 103.
[30] *OMTS*, pp. 124, 126.

of this symbolic fish's body—and we have the feeling that the cycle of suffering and passion has not ended at all; rather, it has once again only begun.

What emerges as an overview of Hemingway's use of Roman Catholicism in his works may be more simplistic than many of us would like to admit. Unsatisfied by the intellectual basis of his accepted doctrine, neither could he sense, as Robert Jordan also could not, "the feeling you expected to have and did not have when you made your first communion."[31] At times he seems to be imitating what he saw as the technique of El Greco, the only one of his favorite painters, Hemingway thought, who "believed in Our Lord and took any interest in His crucifixion" and who

> liked to paint religious pictures because he was very evidently religious and because his incomparable art was not then limited to accurate reproducing of the faces of the noblemen who were his sitters for portraits, and he could go as far into his other world as he wanted, and, consciously or unconsciously, paint saints, apostles, Christs, and Virgins with the androgynous faces and forms that filled his imagination.[32]

So could Ernest Hemingway, but not always. Sometimes, Roman Catholicism provided him with quite a great literary notion indeed, but his view, as has been often noted, was essentially too romantic to allow him go as far into the religious world as he might have wished. If he did in fact become "devout again through cynicism," his approach seems more like that of Count Greffi, who asks his friends to pray for him just in case they are right.[33] In essence, the meaning of the game eluded him. Like Santiago, Catholicism no doubt left Hemingway "feeling much better, but suffering exactly as much, and perhaps a little more."[34] Nevertheless, for depicting this felt paradox in his art, one can conclude that at his best, Hemingway was pretty good in there indeed.

[31] *FWTBT*, p. 235.
[32] *Death*, pp. 193-194.
[33] *AFTA*, p. 263.
[34] *OMTS*, p. 64.

John Griffith

RECTITUDE IN HEMINGWAY'S FICTION:
HOW RITE MAKES RIGHT

SETTING OUT TO DISCUSS Hemingway's sense of rectitude is a little like walking a line through a battlefield; one is likely to be distracted by missiles from more than one side. By now the debate over Hemingway's value as a moralist has produced two rather sizable camps—the one that believes Hemingway's stern, honest, uncompromising standards of thinking and acting contain all that really matters about morality any more, and the other which dismisses Hemingway's ideas of right and wrong as crude, neurotic, and intellectually stunted. I see no realistic hope of settling this broad dispute here, nor even of adequately taking into account all the variations and modulations appearing on both sides. But I would like to clarify one philosophical issue which might at least shed some light on where the fundamental disagreement lies. Let me begin with a two-part thesis the separate premises of which are, I think, almost universally accepted among Hemingway students, but the implications of which frequently seem to be ignored in the discussion of his works: First, Hemingway's work shows that he cared deeply about right and wrong; second, he was fascinated with, practiced, and celebrated ritualistic behavior. My contention is that while ritual correctness and moral right are related concepts, they are distinguishable; and that the special Hemingway sense of doing things right consistently has more in common, philosophically and psychologically, with correct observance of ritual than it has with systematic morality.

Hemingway certainly never wanted to be called a moralist; the term had obnoxious connotations for him. "So far, about morals, I know only that what is moral is what you feel good after and what is immoral is what you feel bad after," he said in the famous passage in *Death in the Afternoon*,[1] and in a way that pronouncement has turned out to be final. His Jake Barnes, after coming up with a similar proposition in *The Sun Also Rises*, cuts the subject short with heartfelt vehemence: "What a lot of bilge I could think up at night. What rot. . . ."[2] Nonetheless, to many readers Hemingway has seemed to be a moralist, and understandably so. His writing has always had the careful, unlaughing, sometimes ironic tone one associates with moral austerity. In manner and sometimes in content it has conveyed the strong sense that its author recognizes a grim duty to do things right. When he despairs, his despair seems to come at least partly from his vision of a fallen world, a world without principle. Many years ago his Frederic Henry threw away the big glossy moral tags—words like "honor," "courage," "sacrifice"—because the war had spoiled them for him.[3] But the ideas and emotions those tags signified were never thrown away. Principle, or at least some dramatic correlative of principle, has always pervaded Hemingway's prose. "Truth," "honesty," "integrity" are key words for him, seldom analyzed in much detail perhaps, but pronounced with strong feeling. "In Spain, honor is a very real thing," he wrote. "Called pundonor, it means honor, probity, courage, self-respect and pride in one word."[4] One feels Hemingway adding, Would that the world were Spanish.

For all his preoccupation with what are often called moral stances, Hemingway was notably shy about explaining what

---

[1] *Death in the Afternoon* (New York: Charles Scribner's Sons, 1932), p. 4.

[2] *The Sun Also Rises*, Scribner Library Edition (New York: Charles Scribner's Sons, 1970), p. 149.

[3] *A Farewell to Arms* (New York: Charles Scribner's Sons, 1929), p. 191.

[4] *Death in the Afternoon*, p. 91.

they meant to him. He was suspicious of abstract reasoning and seldom indulged in it. Certainly he never publicly tried to rationalize his "morality," nor to trace it back to ultimate principles. He did apply it to a number of activities, however: the right way to hunt, to fish, to fight, to kill bulls, to write fiction; and some commentators have found in his applied principles the skeleton of a moral system. But there have always been problems in that pursuit. For one thing, Hemingway's imaginative energy has often been spent on peculiar matters that range from the exotic to the trivial. His advice on the correct methods of killing a bull or catching a fish or writing an honest story can be seen as morally crucial only if they can be made to serve as paradigms for life generally. And when we obligingly take them as such, and see that the principles Hemingway seems to teach are as simple, even crude, as they are, then we are subject to the embarrassment one naturally feels when he hears himself saying "Life is like a bullfight." Life may well be like a bullfight in important respects, but the moralist who depends too strongly on saying so risks neglecting some large areas of experience that have moral significance but nothing to do with bullfighting.

But the point is that Hemingway didn't really say that life was like a bullfight, or like a hunting trip, or even like a war; and that even if he had said so, he would not really have been proposing a moral idea. When we go against his expressed wish and call him a moralist, and take his rules of behavior as a moral system, we make a subtle mistake about the category of meaning to which his work most deeply belongs. We (as, I'm afraid, did Hemingway) confuse ritual with morality.

The distinction between ritual and moral rectitude is not in all cases an easy one to make, but it is nonetheless real and both philosophically and aesthetically important as applied to Hemingway's fiction. Rather than attempt a comprehensive definition of the two terms here, let me propose a few of the conspicuous qualities of each by way of calling to mind their fundamental dissimilarity.

A true moralist goes on the assumption that moral principles are objective and real and rooted in the world outside himself—that they define, however imperfectly, the unavoidable obligations placed upon him by God or the universe or mankind or one's country or one's family—obligations which are not arbitrary, but arise from the fundamental nature of God, mankind, family. This is not to say that morality must be absolutist; it does not necessarily swear by any sacred decalogue of inviolable, unchanging imperatives; but it *is* predicated on the belief that right conduct is affected by and affects reality in its broadest sense. Genuine morality is profoundly relational—that is, it is relentlessly concerned with the connections between conduct and everything touching on it— not only an act in itself, but the reasons why it is performed (the actor's motives and intentions) and its consequences as well. Thus moral action cannot be staged; to set up a situation specifically to demonstrate one's virtue is to obviate any moral significance in the demonstration.

To the strict moralist then, ritual tends to be "mere ritual," a set of gestures without substance. And in this, of course, the moralist is both right and wrong. It is true that from the strict moral point of view, ritual is artificial, contrived, even whimsical. It is more abstract, more patently symbolic, far less concerned with practical consequences than morality is. Ritual is a kind of game—a serious game, but a game nevertheless: it creates its own occasions, its own setting; it builds arenas and altars and stages on which to act. But this is hardly tantamount to saying that it has no value or meaning—only that its meaning is of an order different from morality's. Ritual is, in an important sense, art; it can frequently be judged in aesthetic terms, as ✦ when Hemingway observes that bullfighting is "degenerate" when the purity of line is lost. Ritual is fundamentally expressive rather than utilitarian—it dramatizes the beliefs of the ritualist rather than attempting any crudely pragmatic manipulation of the outside world. It is, as Suzanne Langer has called it, "a disciplined rehearsal of 'right attitudes,'" a prescribed series of gestures which mechanically symbolize one's feelings about ultimate things—life, fertility, growth, God, death.[5] One's public, official feelings, that is; the feelings one professes or even aspires to, not necessarily his most private and personal ones. The emphasis in ritual is on acting out a preconceived drama that has its own meaning in which the ritualist claims participation. Where morality attempts to adapt itself to every human circumstance, ritual refuses to alter its form; it rigidly repeats itself, for its meaning is in the action itself, not in its effect on the world.

Consider some of the implications this has for the student of Hemingway. Take, for example, its application to a characteristic Hemingway issue, the problem of how one ought to face death. It is possible to call this a moral problem; for Hemingway, at any rate, there is emphatically a right and a wrong way to do it. He seems usually to recommend something like a traditional stoic attitude of meeting death grimly but accepting it without flinching. The best men in Hemingway's stories are like his Harry Morgan: "At first he tried to brace himself against the roll with his hand. Then he lay quietly and took it."[6] This heroic attitude toward death, viewed quite independently of any questions about the ideals or causes or people one should be willing to die for, puts Hemingway in touch with a large tradition of ultimate valor, and lends his writing the emotional and philosophical weight that large traditions customarily do lend. We sense in the dying courage of Harry Morgan (or Robert Jordan or Manolo the bullfighter) something akin to that of Roland at Roncevalles or Leonidas at

---

[5] Suzanne Langer, *Philosophy in a New Key* (1942; rpt. New York: New American Library, 1951), p. 134. Miss Langer, along with many other scholars, dispels the notion that ritual in its pure form is "used" to make things happen—as in the popular notion of the dance that "makes it rain." That is magic, not ritual proper; Miss Langer calls it "the empty shell of a religious act." Certainly one gets little sense in Hemingway's work of ritual that makes things happen in the external world.

[6] *To Have and Have Not* (New York: Grosset and Dunlap, 1937), p. 175.

Thermopylae or even Christ in Gethsemane: "If it be possible, let this cup pass from me; nevertheless not as I will but as thou wilt." We sense a kinship; and we run the risk of attributing to the brave deaths in Hemingway a moral grandeur which actually derives from situations crucially different from the ones he portrays.

In *The Varieties of Religious Experience* William James describes the dramatic moral appeal heroic death has traditionally had.

> In heroism, we feel, life's supreme mystery is hidden. We tolerate no one who has no capacity whatever for it in any direction. On the other hand, no matter what a man's frailties otherwise may be, if he be willing to risk death, and still more if he suffer it heroically, in the service he has chosen, the fact consecrates him forever. Inferior to ourselves in this way or that, if yet we cling to life, and he is able to 'fling it away like a flower' as caring nothing for it, we account him in the deepest way our born superior. Each of us in his own person feels that a high-hearted indifference to life would expiate all his shortcomings.[7]

James is not a completely impartial commentator, of course. He was himself something of a spiritual he-man who sometimes said that war or "its moral equivalent" was necessary to realizing the highest and best aspects of character. Perhaps he exaggerates when he supposes that everyone admires the man who is fearless of death even to the point of forgiving all his shortcomings. But still James does speak for a tradition which is easy enough to recognize even if we don't entirely subscribe to it. We know what he means when he speaks of "a high-hearted indifference to life" which allows one to sacrifice himself "in the service he has chosen." In part, his concept is appropriate to Hemingway's sense of the heroic; but only in part.

Death, in the old heroic tradition, is a thing to be overcome in a higher excitement; the hero is exalted by some grand design to the point where preserving his own life becomes immaterial to him, and he dies. Hemingway's Robert Jordan

---

[7] *The Varieties of Religious Experience* (1902; rpt. New York: New American Library, 1958), pp. 281-82.

states the concept perfectly when he recalls what it was like to be a communist in the early days: "It gave you a part in something that you could believe in wholly and completely and in which you felt an absolute brotherhood with the others who were engaged in it. It was something that you had never known before but that you had experienced now and you gave such importance to it and the reasons for it that your own death seemed of complete unimportance; only a thing to be avoided because it would interfere with the performance of your duty."[8]

But—and this is the key point in identifying the special Hemingway touch—for Jordan that old feeling goes away. His belief in the absolute validity of the communist cause dissolves under the ugly realities of war. By the time of the events of the novel, Jordan has no politics; he accepts communism only as a discipline, an arbitrary set of rules to play by. When he finally does come to face death, there is no longer any elevating feeling that, under the aspect of the brotherhood, death is unimportant. Hemingway specifically shows that Jordan's death is to be a waste, that it does not contribute substantially to the Cause because the attack of which it is a part is doomed to failure by bad communications. And Jordan is aware of the waste; he has clear evidence that the attack will be a failure and that by blowing up the bridge and sacrificing himself he will add nothing material to the Cause—will, in fact, renege on what he knows to be very real emotional bonds he has established with Maria and the others of the guerilla band. His courageous encounter with death, when it finally happens, has become almost wholly a ritual action. The thirtieth chapter of *For Whom the Bell Tolls* is a beautiful example of a man schooling himself in the strict attitude of ritual correctness. One by one Jordan considers the real-life consequences of his decision to blow up the bridge. One by one he excludes them from his deliberations. "You follow orders. Follow them and do not try to think beyond them."[9] As he has been doing throughout the novel, he tells him-

---

[8] *For Whom the Bell Tolls*, Scribner Library Edition (New York: Charles Scribner's Sons), p. 235.

[9] *For Whom the Bell Tolls*, p. 335.

self again to disconnect his personal, private feelings. He must not allow himself "the luxury of normal fear."[10] By the end of the chapter, the impending battle has become for him a kind of ceremony to be carried out precisely, dispassionately, without thought of its results. He comes to think of it as a festival, and "he was sure now the festival would not be cancelled."[11]

The prominence of other rituals involving death in Hemingway's fiction hardly needs mentioning. Malcolm Cowley pointed out their existence many years ago in an essay on "Nightmare and Ritual in Hemingway" which says in brief something of what I would emphasize here. In this matter of capturing the peculiar essence of Hemingway's notion of right and wrong, it is instructive to ponder the way his imagination goes repeatedly to those instances of "serious play" that most closely flirt with death, and where rigorous rules give shape and meaning to the event: the bullfight, the boxing match, the hunting trip, duels of various sorts. Even in those episodes where death is presented as something other than part of a formal ritual, many of the ritual impulses of stylization and decorous movement are often present. The complex human issues tend to be simplified, pared down, rarefied; there is often a pervasive stillness, too, an evocation of the encompassing silence appropriate to a sacred moment. "It doesn't do to talk too much about all this," as Wilson reminds Francis Macomber.[12] "You do not want music" on your clean, well-lighted stage. "Certainly you do not want music."[13] But you do want an audience, a knowledgeable, initiated audience—a Wilson or a Pilar, not the philistine tourists who mumble stupidly over Romero's "nervousness" in the ring, or the skeleton of Santiago's marlin. The audience plays up the aesthetic character of the performance, and also links up with the fact that primitive

---

[10] *For Whom the Bell Tolls*, p. 335.
[11] *For Whom the Bell Tolls*, p. 340.
[12] *The Short Stories of Ernest Hemingway* (New York: Charles Scribner's Sons, 1954), p. 33.
[13] *Short Stories*, p. 480.

ritual is almost always public and tribal, calling for some sense of community.

Hemingway's rituals seldom seem calculated to effect moral good; but they do serve a purpose of another kind. Cowley likened Hemingway's rituals to primitive rites of propitiation by which angry spirits are held at bay.

> Some of the forest-dwelling tribes believe that every rock or tree or animal has its own indwelling spirit. When they kill an animal or chop down a tree, they must beg its forgiveness, repeating a formula of propitiation; otherwise its spirit would haunt them. Living briefly in a world of hostile forces, they preserve themselves —so they believe—only by the exercise of magic lore. There is something of the same atmosphere in Hemingway's work. His heroes live in a world that is like a hostile forest, full of unseen dangers, not to mention the nightmares that haunt their sleep. Death spies on them from behind every tree. Their only chance of safety lies in the faithful observance of customs they invent for themselves.[14]

In at least one important respect Cowley is exactly right. Hemingway does reveal a deep, even superstitious fear of the more shapeless, unnameable evil forces of existence before which, or whom, the only appropriate attitude seems to be one of eternal defensive watchfulness and a kind of placating self-sacrifice or mortification. That he owned such superstitions in real life, his biographers attest; on several occasions he insisted that he could literally smell the coming of death, and his reliance on lucky pocket pieces and other little fetishes to ward off evil was well known. His fiction, too, sometimes dramatizes the same kind of fear. The narrator of the story "Now I Lay Me" perhaps puts the matter most plainly: "I do not remember a night on which you could not hear things," he says. "If I could have a light I was not afraid to sleep, because I knew my soul would only go out of me if it were dark."[15] The

---

[14] Malcolm Cowley, "Nightmare and Ritual in Hemingway," in *Hemingway: A Collection of Critical Essays*, ed. Robert P. Weeks (Englewood Cliffs, N. J.: Prentice-Hall, 1962), pp. 47-48.

[15] *Short Stories*, p. 367.

darkness may hide no gods for Hemingway, as John Killinger and others have said; but it hides something. There is something out there against which we must be on guard. If we choose to call it Nothingness or the Abyss, we must not forget it is a nothingness with a character, an abyss with a predisposition toward our destruction that feels, from the human point of view, a good deal like hatred. One scholar of ancient Greek cults uses language that might apply to Hemingway: "The formula of that religion was not *do ut des* 'I give so that you may give,' but *do ut abeas* 'I give that you may go, and keep away.' The beings worshipped were not rational, human, law-abiding *gods*, but vague, irrational, mainly malevolent . . . spirit-things, ghosts and bogeys and the like, not yet formulated into god-head."[16]

But this talk of rituals of placation and self-defense only takes us part way into the analysis of Hemingway's use of ritual. True, there is clearly a motive of self-defense in many of the Hemingway rites. Frequently his characters use their rituals to avoid thinking about the terror that lurks just beyond their consciousness. The narrator of "Now I Lay Me" recalls or makes up fishing trips to occupy his mind while he holds back the nullity of sleep. "I would think of a trout stream I had fished along when I was a boy and fish its whole length very carefully in my mind; fishing very carefully under all the logs, all the turns of the bank, the deep holes and the clear shallow stretches, sometimes catching trout and sometimes losing them."[17] From this it is a short step to the meticulous behavior of Nick Adams in "Big Two-Hearted River," who likewise wants to "keep his mind from working," and the careful, fastidious drinking sessions of the old man in "A Clean, Well-Lighted Place" and the systematic radio-listening of Mr. Frazier in "The Gambler, the Nun and the Radio."

---

[16] Jane Ellen Harrison, *Prolegomena to the Study of Greek Religion* (Cambridge: Cambridge Univ. Press, 1903), p. 7.

[17] *Short Stories*, p. 363.

It is apparently a much longer step, though, from these pathetic little rituals of self-control to the full-scale rites of death. One cannot so readily say that Manolo fights bulls to keep from thinking about death—or that Robert Jordan blows up bridges to keep from thinking about it, or that Jack Brennan goes into the boxing ring or Santiago goes to the far reaches of the sea to keep from thinking about it. In at least the obvious sense, a man does not confront death in order to avoid the thought of it.

Yet all that really needs correcting, in order to make the connection between the large and the small rituals apparent, is the superficial explanation of how those lesser rituals work. In fact all these ceremonies, large and small, are attempts to make the gestures which will symbolize one's power to overcome his fear of evil. They all have the same basic elements. There is first of all the ascetic purity; even the ceremonies of sex and drinking are austere, bare and abstract—anything but riotous and libertine. There is the element of absolute clarity and conscious attention to detail—every particular etched and meticulously considered. There is the presence of death in one of its literal or figurative forms—the actual physical death of the ritualist or his adversary, or a kind of totemic death of a fish or animal with which he sometimes identifies ("I have killed this fish which is my brother," says Santiago;[18] "the bulls are my best friends," says Pedro Romero[19]), the sexual death of orgasm, the psychic death of nervous collapse, or a brutal beating, or drunken oblivion, or merely sleep. And there is some clearly established, even conventional method for dealing with death: the refined techniques of cape, or rifle, or fishing tackle, or one's fists, or even brandy-drinking or radio-listening.

Hemingway never implies that the ritual staves off death. In fact it frequently gets the ritualist killed. Its power ulti-

---

[18] *The Old Man and the Sea* (New York: Charles Scribner's Sons, 1952), p. 95.
[19] *The Sun Also Rises*, p. 186.

mately is not in what it can do to manipulate the external forces arrayed against a man, as Cowley's description perhaps suggests; its power is that it expresses the hero's firm, unflinching feelings about death, and puts into visible, tangible form his desire or his resolution to resist the menace. Psychologically the great desideratum is to lose one's private, frightened self in the bravery of the impersonal, mechanical gestures of the rite. When the ritual does its full work in Hemingway, it has a quality of radical spiritual breakthrough that is very nearly mystical. Santiago sees "a great strangeness" when he kills the marlin;[20] Francis Macomber feels "a wild unreasonable happiness that he had never known before" when he masters the ceremony of the hunt.[21] Even Nick Adams on the Big Two-Hearted River makes a version of the same breakthrough just by setting up his camp correctly. "Already there was something mysterious and homelike. Nick was happy as he crawled inside the tent. He had not been unhappy all day. This was different though. Now things were done. There had been this to do. Now it was done. . . . Nothing could touch him."[22]

This feeling of the ritual well acted is the touchstone, the ultimate standard in Hemingway's theory of rectitude. Probably it is the same "good feeling" he had in mind when he said that "what is moral is what you feel good after"—a remark which in context referred, of course, to the effect of watching a bullfight. Hemingway himself does not seem to have distinguished clearly between ritual and morality; he may well have thought Nick had done a *good* thing rather than only a *correct* thing in laying out his camp, just as he seems to picture Robert Jordan as doing good in accepting his martyrdom, or Jake Barnes as doing good every time he resists "getting messy." But the rest of us have no trouble, I hope, in seeing the profound difference between this kind of ritual observance and

---

[20] *The Old Man and the Sea*, p. 98.
[21] *Short Stories*, p. 32.
[22] *Short Stories*, p. 215.

genuine moral achievement. Psychologically, perhaps, the loss of self in the ritual parallels that loss of self felt by the hero who serves the Cause, but there is always that crucial difference. It is the difference between a closed, self-contained gesture which has great subjective value but little objective consequence, and an act intended to do tangible good to the world or some considerable part of it. In practice, it can boil down to the difference between seeking a cause, any legitimate cause, in which to prove one's manhood, and accepting one's duty because natural circumstance demands it.

Ultimately there is not much profit and potentially a good deal of injustice in treating Hemingway as a moralist. I do not mean to say that his sense of right is devoid of moral implications; of course it is not. His ideas of honesty, courage, integrity, do have moral value, and can serve many purposes in the endlessly complicated sphere of moral right and wrong as well as the conceptually simplified one of ritual correctness. And I do not mean to say that Hemingway's fiction deals in exclusively ritual situations that are somehow divorced from moral issues. For Hemingway to remind us, as his best writing so sharply does, of the hard facts of the human condition—of cruelty, violence, terror, hypocrisy, outworn and dishonest ways of thinking, the bitter jokes of fate, death, and the way the human psyche in extremity tends to react to all these—is surely to contribute something to our moral potency, since it makes us more fully conscious of the contexts in which moral action must take place. But I am arguing that the positive sense of *right* which Hemingway does project in his works—that spirit common to all his best-known dicta: exhibit grace under pressure, refuse to "get messy," survive and do one's work, be true to one's craft, "write one true sentence"—has its most crucial roots in the soil of ritual, not morality.

The reason there is potentially much injustice in forcing Hemingway to play the moralist is that this implicitly denies that the ritual sense of principle has a philosophical validity of its own. Those who have most frequently emphasized the prevalence of ritual in Hemingway have tended to link it with certain neurotic, compulsive traits of his own personality, and the effect has in part been to dismiss it from serious consideration philosophically. I am not denying a connection between Hemingway's personality and the ritualism of his fiction; I am only asking that we resist letting any (perhaps quite valid) psychological thesis about the author overshadow the real merits of what he wrote. Likewise, to call ritual "primitive" because it is conspicuous among tribes and cultures over which we assume some superiority, and thereby to dismiss it, is to presume a great deal in this problematic matter of the life of the spirit. Ritual meaning has a long and honorable place in the spiritual traditions of the human race. We must not be too hasty to discount ritual as valid spiritual achievement.

And that is what we do, I think, when we read Hemingway as if he were fundamentally a moralist. We rob him of his legitimate artistic value by making him seem unintelligent. To approach a characteristic Hemingway story like, say, "The Killers," or even an uncharacteristic one like *The Old Man and the Sea,* with the assumption that it demonstrates important moral principles and the way to act on them, is to diminish the story's value terribly. Going out further than other fishermen and keeping one's lines straight in the water do not really make a man good; and there is little moral profundity in Nick Adams' seeing that the murder of Ole Andreson is "an awful thing." That the murder is morally wrong and that Santiago is a good man are, or course, true; but merely to recognize this is to do little to appreciate the real importance, the specialness, of the stories they figure in. The power and fascination of "The Killers" and *The Old Man and the Sea* lie in their presentation of the cruel, inhumanly beautiful rigor of "the code," the ordered ritual by which both Ole and the fish must die. Their deaths are, indeed, an "awful" thing; they touch one's sense of awe.

Hemingway's was an imagination in search of the ceremony which overcomes the fear of annihilation by making death one of the structural possibilities or even necessities in a stylized, choreographed dance. The dignity of his vision is not the high seriousness which invests the shapeless networks of principle and emotion and intuition that make up realistic morality, but the high seriousness of the structured games of ritual, art, and sacrament.

Michael Friedberg

HEMINGWAY AND THE MODERN
METAPHYSICAL TRADITION

IN ONE OF HIS EARLY NOVELS of the 1920's Aldous Huxley sums up the climate of intellectual doubt, spiritual loss, and moral confusion of the post-war period:

> I persist that you made a mistake in so timing your entry into this world that the period of your youth coincided with the war and your early maturity with this horribly insecure and unprosperous peace. How imcomparably better I managed my existence! I made my entry in the fifties—almost a twin to *The Origin of Species* . . . I was brought up in the simple faith of nineteenth-century materialism. . . . We were all wonderfully optimistic then; believed in progress and the ultimate explicability of everything in terms of physics and chemistry, believed in Mr. Gladstone and our moral and intellectual superiority over every other age.[1]

The world inherited by the generation here addressed is a world cast adrift from the basic assumptions which propped up the old order. The First World War and the Russian Revolution swept the nineteenth century forever into the past and exploded the modern age upon the historical stage. By the twenties, in the midst of a "horribly insecure and unprosperous peace," gone was the moral order of the Christian universe, fallen victim to the long siege of science which began with Copernicus, Galileo, and Bacon. Gone was the rational, positi-

---

[1] Aldous Huxley, *Those Barren Leaves* (New York: Doran, 1925), p. 43.

vistic order of the human mind, suddenly found to contain unpredictable subterranean dimensions by Freud, Jung, and Frazer. Gone too, finally, with Planck's discovery of the uncertainty principle, the belief in the ultimate truth of scientific knowledge. The war, in its unprecedented technological carnage and prolonged, stupid brutality seemed to reflect the moral and spiritual degradation of the new age. No wonder that bitter disenchantment, disgust, and disillusionment should be the predominant attitudes conveyed in the works of the major writers of the period.

When Jake Barnes alludes to his war wound he is answered by the French prostitute that "Everybody's sick. I'm sick, too." While this sickness might refer to the nausea and disillusionment of those who lived through the war experience, it is no doubt also a reference to the state of the world itself. This pessimism is a theme which runs through the works of Huxley (*Crome Yellow, Those Barren Leaves*), Waugh (*Vile Bodies*), Lawrence (*Women in Love*), and Eliot (*The Waste Land*) in roughly the same years. Modern man is characterized in these works as a petty, too proud and too utterly profane king in a vast and indifferent kingdom. While he has successfully extended his dominion over the material world, he has neglected to develop his spirituality and has become alienated from himself.

The pessimism in these works derives from the individual visions of their authors. Thus Eliot can ultimately see a reason for optimism in the Hindu formula: "Datta. Dayadhvam. Damyata./Shantih shantih shantih" (Give, sympathize, control), and Lawrence envisions the self-destruction of physical man (Gerald walking out into the snow) and the chance of survival given to the spiritual, spontaneous, creative, procreative man. Whether the man of the new spiritual age will survive physically is not yet known, but that his chances for spiritual survival are being enormously increased is strongly suggested. The trend which runs through the works of these writers is one of pessimism and negation seen in the present human condition and optimism and affirmation in a future spiritual condition. In many ways we can call these writers mystics.[2] Hemingway belongs in the same tradition.

Having served as an ambulance driver with the Italian army, Hemingway began his apprenticeship in Paris after the war. At this time he came under the intellectual and artistic tutelage of Gertrude Stein and Ezra Pound. He studied the art of the good modern painters, particularly Cézanne's landscapes.[3] He was also a member of an international society of expatriates whose shared experience of the war united them in a desperate search for a new moral and spiritual order. In *The Sun Also Rises* Hemingway responded to Miss Stein's remark that his generation was lost by depicting this set of expatriates from his own vantage point as member and participant.

Hemingway's learning experience in Europe, in the war and after, was, therefore, broad enough and deep enough to afford him a direct knowledge of the essential experience of his time.[4] It was then merely a question of temperament and style which would finally give shape to his personal vision and its expression. Unlike Huxley, Hemingway was not an intellectual; unlike Lawrence he was not a Dionysian lover; and unlike Eliot he was not an erudite philosopher. Yet, as these writers' interpretations had caught different aspects of the new

---

[2] Huxley offers his most complete account of his mystical philosophy in *The Perennial Philosophy* (New York: Harper, 1945); Lawrence took interest in Madame Blavatsky's Theosophical Society and later studied American Indian mythology; Yeats, in the previous generation, created his own elaborate mythology based on the *Kabbala* and other ancient mystical writings.

[3] Hemingway wrote of the influence of Cézanne on his early stylistic efforts: "I was learning something from the painting of Cézanne that made writing simple true sentences far from enough to make the stories have the dimensions that I was trying to put in them. I was learning very much from him . . ." *A Moveable Feast* (New York: Bantam Books, 1965), p. 13.

[4] It has become a commonly accepted view, in fact, that Hemingway was a spokesman for an entire generation.

reality, so would Hemingway add to the new metaphysical vision a metaphysic of style.

A man's style is his character. In Hemingway's fiction, as in his life, style is the basic mark of the man. And it is his style which truly distinguishes Hemingway as a writer. If it is too much to call Hemingway's style a metaphysical style, we could, at least, posit that Hemingway's style is basically the language of the new metaphysical ideology of twentieth-century fiction. Hemingway presented to the new age a style of fiction which could communicate the new experience. He went a step beyond Joyce's accomplishment of combining Flaubert's external realism with the psychological realism of myth, symbol, and stream of consciousness when he added a metaphysical realism. In *Death in the Afternoon* he describes the process of literary evolution:

> Every novel which is truly written contributes to the total of knowledge which is there at the disposal of the next writer who comes, but the next writer must pay, always, a certain nominal percentage in experience to be able to understand and assimilate what is available as his birthright and what he must, in turn, take his departure from.[5]

Hemingway's development as a stylist can shed some light on our description of his narrative technique in terms of the new metaphysical reality. What is significant here is that Hemingway deliberately studied to develop a new technique, taking his lessons eagerly from the different writers that were available to him. The first significant influence came from his early mentors on the *Kansas City Star* who taught him to write simple, declarative sentences containing few words and fewer personal reflections. He later learned from Miss Stein a technique resembling indirect discourse which was distinguished by its repetition, colloquialism, and rhythm (at times slow and

---

[5] *Death in the Afternoon* (New York: Charles Scribner's Sons, 1960), p. 192.

monotonous, at others rapid and intense).[6] He also picked up from Pound a predilection for the *mot juste*.[7]

At this early stage Hemingway also showed interest in the study of languages and dialects. In the *Torrents of Spring* (1925) he took advantage of his twelve years' study of the dialects of Northern Michigan Indians in his characterization of two Indian war veterans. In *In Our Time* the prefatory piece, "On the Quai at Smyrna," and two interchapters describing the "potting" of Germans employ a type of speech characteristic of the British officer caste.

In *Death in the Afternoon* Hemingway describes his early efforts to develop a style which would be "true":

> I was trying to write then and I found the greatest difficulty, aside from knowing truly what you really felt, rather than what you were supposed to feel and had been taught to feel, was to put down what really happened in action . . . the real thing, the sequence of motion and fact which made the emotion and which would be as valid in a year or in ten years or, with luck and if you stated it purely enough always, was beyond me and I was working very hard to try to get it (*Death in the Afternoon*, p. 2).

Hemingway's development as a stylist can be seen largely as an attempt to imply subjective states by presenting an illusion of objective reality. In his narrative technique Hemingway presents a dialectic between a surface style which mirrors a concrete and orderly objective reality and an underlying current which constantly asserts the chaotic and complex nature of subjective reality. It is this disparity between appearance and reality, between conventional expectation and

---

[6] See, for example, the assessment of Miss Stein's influence on Hemingway's development as a stylist in Earl Rovit's *Ernest Hemingway* (New Haven: Twayne Publishers, 1963), pp. 45-46.

[7] Hemingway wrote that he was greatly influenced by Pound in the early days in Paris. Pound was "the man I liked and trusted the most as a critic then, the man who believed in the *mot juste*—the one and only correct word to use—the man who had taught me to distrust adjectives as I would later learn to distrust certain people in certain situations . . ." *A Moveable Feast*, p. 132.

unconventional conclusion that stylistically marks Hemingway's fiction.

In "Ernest Hemingway, Literary Critic," Daniel Fuchs discusses Hemingway's little-known story "A Natural History of the Dead" and makes the observation that the story shows "the mind of the writer engaged in the typical modernist stripping away of forms." Mr. Fuchs goes on to say that Hemingway's work can be seen as "an attempt to redefine the actuality . . . abstractions might have."[8] This has always been part of the métier of the artist. In *A Farewell to Arms* Frederic Henry makes the now-famous remark that such abstractions as honor, glory, courage, and hallow are obscenely meaningless when compared to the names of villages, numbers of roads, names of rivers, and numbers of regiments. Krebs, who prefigures Henry, finds that he must lie to get people to listen to him: "His town had heard too many atrocity stories to be thrilled by actualities." What Hemingway is suggesting is that the old language does not agree with the new experience. The war has ushered a new age into the world. The generation of this new era, if it is to avoid the frustrations of Krebs, must have its own language. The failure of the old language to comprehend the new age is a theme developed in *The Sun Also Rises*.

It is characteristic of Hemingway's heroes to be wary of language. They are particularly distrustful of the spoken word. This attitude is best summed up by Wilson, the white hunter, in "The Short Happy Life of Francis Macomber": "There's that. Doesn't do to talk too much about all this. Talk the whole thing away. No pleasure in anything if you mouth it up too much."[9] The characters in *The Sun Also Rises* have adopted an unsentimental, rough, laconic form of speech as part of their code. Robert Cohn, who, as Brett asserts, is "not one of us,"

---

[8] Daniel Fuchs, "Ernest Hemingway, Literary Critic," *American Literature*, XXXVI (Jan. 1965), p. 437.

[9] *The Hemingway Reader*, ed., Charles Poore (New York: Charles Scribner's Sons, 1953), p. 569.

gives himself away by his elaborate, sentimental speech. Unlike the others, he does not discern the strict limitations of the spoken word.

The dialogue in *The Sun Also Rises*, stripped of all inessentials, is sinewy, at times even stark. The implicit rejection of the spoken word as a means to convey nuances of thought or feeling is made explicit in a conversation between Jake and Brett:

> "Couldn't we live together, Brett? Couldn't we just live together?"
> "I don't think so. I'd just *tromper* you with everybody. You couldn't stand it."
> "I stand it now."
> "That would be different. It's my fault, Jake. It's the way I'm made."
> "Couldn't we go off in the country for a while?"
> "It wouldn't be any good. I'll go if you like. But I couldn't live quietly in the country. Not with my own true love."
> "I know."
> "Isn't it rotten. There isn't any use my telling you I love you."
> "You know I love you."
> "Let's not talk. Talking's all bilge. I'm going away from you, and then Michael's coming back (*Reader*, p. 131).

There is too much experience here for conventional language. For Jake to talk about his condition in terms of pain, anguish, futility, anger, love, or fate would somehow devalue and falsify the experience. To be totally honest one cannot use the old forms of language.

The discrepancy between language and experience is generally the condition of irony, and it is the ironic effect Hemingway achieves in his treatment of language which sets the tone of the novel. Hemingway recognizes the demise of the old language and makes it a source of black humor. Black humor, or gallows humor, is one step more ironic than irony. It is, for example, a gallows humor which Hemingway effects in "On the Quai at Smyrna," the *In Our Time* interchapters, and *The Sun Also Rises* through the British officer dialect. Underneath the surface levity made about such old forms as the British upper

class language (it "must have fewer words than the Eskimo"),
and the pious language of nineteenth-century Protestant
America, there is a strain of nihilism and despair which is the
sine qua non of gallows humor. At Burguete Bill and Jake
celebrate the death of the old world with a mock populist
political-revival meeting over a few bottles of wine:

> "Utilize a little, brother," he handed me the bottle. "Let us
> not pry into the holy mysteries of the hencoop with simian fingers.
> Let us accept on faith and simply say,—I want you to join with
> me in saying—What shall we say, brother?" He pointed the drum-
> stick at me and went on. "Let me tell you. We will say, and I for
> one am proud to say—and I want you to say with me, on your
> knees, brother. Let no man be ashamed to kneel here in the great
> out-of-doors. Remember the woods were God's first temples.
> Let us kneel and say: 'Don't eat that, Lady—that's Mencken.'"
> "Here," I said. "Utilize a little of this" (*Reader*, p. 184).

When one considers that this celebration has a purely negative
motive, that its mockery triumphs through sheer destructive
energy and delights in meaninglessness, one cannot fail to see
the nihilism and gallows humor of the passage.

The nihilistic use of language is most clearly illustrated in
the leveling of all adjectives and adverbs. One encounters all
too often such words as "good," "nice," "wonderful," "splendid,"
"marvelous," "damn," "bloody," and "rotten." At times the
effect is simply understatement: "It was a nice hotel and the
people at the desk were very cheerful, and we each had a
good small room;" "It felt good to be warm and in bed." At other
times, especially when combined with the adverbs "really,"
"awfully," "damned," or "very" the effect approaches travesty:
"It was really an awfully clean hotel;" " 'He's so damned nice
and he's so awful. He's my sort of thing.'" In the latter passage
even nouns are leveled ("my sort of thing").

Thus Lieutenant Henry's rejection of the old abstractions
and his insistence on the need for new forms in language
indicates the need for a new language to replace that of the
old order which has passed with the war. When Nick Adams
returns home from the war in "Big Two-Hearted River," he

brings back the new language in its crudest form. Of course, he is not conscious of the fact that he employs a new language. But his experience in the war had forever changed his mode of perception. Under the immediate aftereffects of shell shock in "A Way You'll Never Be" he sees the chaos which threatens when one's perception does not match the processing apparatus of the mind:

> That house meant more than anything and every night he had it. That was what he needed but it frightened him especially when the boat lay there quietly in the willows on the canal, but the banks weren't like this river. It was all lower, as it was at Portogrande, where they had seen them come wallowing across the flooded ground holding the rifles high until they fell with them in the water. Who ordered that one? If it didn't get so damned mixed up he could follow it all right. That was why he noticed everything in such detail to keep it all straight so he would know just where he was, but suddenly it confused without reason as now, he lying in a bunk at battalion headquarters, with Para commanding a battalion and he in a bloody American uniform. He sat up and looked around; they all watching him. Para was gone out. He lay down again. (*Reader,* p. 397).

The world threatens to overwhelm man in its complexity and its chaos. Therefore, man must adjust his perceptions of the world and fashion a suitable processing system. This is precisely the *raison d'etre* of Hemingway's narrative technique.

The experience of the Hemingway hero is primarily outer-directed. Unlike Leopold Bloom, Jake Barnes tries not to think. Cerebration ultimately leads to the complicated state that Krebs and Nick Adams have both learned to avoid. What is needed, above all, is order and the light of reason. The preoccupation with light in Hemingway's fiction (the hero's fear of the dark in "A Clean, Well-Lighted Place,") is emblematic of the need for reason and clarity. In a world devoid of a sense of cosmic order, where the bond of shared values among men no longer exists, the individual is thrown back upon himself to solve the puzzle of existence. The need of the Hemingway hero to control his immediate surroundings, i.e., the preoccupation with expertise, reflects the individual's search for meaning in a chaotic and destructive world. With every instance of control over an objective process man asserts his freedom and claims a temporary token of meaning in life.

Life has meaning only insofar as man can transcend the chaos and the destruction of the post-Christian universe. In his code Hemingway formulated a set of directives for individual conduct in the new metaphysical order. Earl Rovit has pointed out the significance of the game metaphor in Hemingway's metaphysic and its relation to the code:

> . . . life is imaged consistently in terms of a game for Hemingway, but the game is like none that was ever played for sport. The rules are very simple: man the player is born; life the game will kill him. The code which does concern Hemingway and his tyros is the process of learning how to make one's passive vulnerability (to the dangers and unpredictabilities of life) into a strong rather than a weak position, and how to exact the maximum amount of reward ("honor," "dignity") out of these encounters.[10]

The conditions of the game of life are beyond man's control, and if he would play it well he must abide by certain rules. First among these rules is that he does not admit the ultimate futility of life. Only while the intimations of death and chaos can be kept out of life can life have any meaning.

As has already been pointed out, Hemingway's earliest studies in the art of narrative technique centered on the simple declarative sentence, stripped of all unnecessary adjectives and adverbs, with minimal dependence on reflective observation. The perception of reality reflected in this style can be compared to the perception which French impressionist painting sought to render.[11] There is emphasis placed on direct experience of the objective world. The inessential details, the distorting preconceptions, the cluttering individual meditations, have all been found to falsify the experience and have been extirpated. To

---

[10] Rovit, *Ernest Hemingway*, p. 109.

[11] Hemingway studied the impressionists in Paris at the Musee du Luxembourg: "I went there nearly every day for the Cézannes and to see the Manets and the other Impressionists that I had first come to know about in the Art Institute at Chicago." *A Moveable Feast*, p. 13.

the Hemingway hero, the clear, sharply focused perception is as much an article of faith as a credible guide to pragmatic action. In *The Sun Also Rises*, Jake's preciseness about his financial situation, as well as his tendency to size up his physical surroundings, reflect the underlying need for objective markers of reality.

The relationship between the hero's careful perception of reality and the author's style can be seen in the following representative passage:

> I looked back and saw her standing on the steps. She waved and I kissed my hand and held it out. She waved again and then I was out of the driveway and climbing up into the seat of the ambulance and we started. The Saint Anthony was in a little metal capsule. I opened the capsule and spilled him out into my hand.[12]

The succession of statements is made in a flat, objective manner. The effect is almost stark, a result of the simplicity and repeated regularity of the syntax, and the bareness of description. The only adjective in the entire passage is "little," and the only two adverbs are "back" and "again." The effect, however, is to evoke a most poignant sense of reality. There is a rhythm in the narrative flow which is almost hypnotic in its approximation of the rhythm of the mental processes of the protagonist. There is also a sinewy, muscular sense which derives from the concreteness and exactness of description. There are no wasted motions, no wasted elaborations. Furthermore the experience is designed to suggest an orderly, logical world. The action is ordered in terms of conventional logic. The effect of the chronological and causal organization of the passage is to reinforce the authority of the protagonist's impressions. Armed with this perception of reality, Hemingway's hero plays the game of life to the best of his ability. He cannot, however, ever win the game.

The first chapter of *A Farewell to Arms* ends with the following paragraph:

---

[12] *A Farewell to Arms* (New York: Charles Scribner's Sons, 1929), p. 45.

> At the start of the winter came the permanent rain and with
> the rain came the cholera. But it was checked and in the end only
> seven thousand died of it in the army (*A Farewell to Arms*, p. 2).

The simplicity and clarity of perception, the controlled, undramatic tone, and the logical consistency are here jarringly juxtaposed with the observation that seven thousand men died of cholera. The ironic effect derives from the disparity between the experience and the perception as refracted in the style. The ironic mode, originating in a fundamental stoicism and fed by a benevolent strain of cynicism, is the ultimate response of the Hemingway hero to his alien universe.

Logic and order do not inform this universe in which a man is unceremoniously blasted by an artillery explosion while sharing spaghetti and cheese with friends; in which a man is killed by the frightened rear guard of his own army; in which a decorated officer is accused of being an enemy spy and immediately executed or, in which a man's love, the most valuable part of his life, can be abruptly removed from him while others continue life as usual. Despite the hero's courage, his cold perspicuity, and his occasional passions, he is a prisoner of fate whose ineluctable process ends in the nothingness of death. Man is as helpless as the colony of ants Lieutenant Henry recalls having once carelessly destroyed over a camp fire. Finally, Lieutenant Henry ruminates:

> That was what you did. You died. You did not know what it was
> about. You never had time to learn. They threw you in and told
> you the rules and the first time they caught you off base they
> killed you gratuitously like Aymo. Or gave you the syphilis like
> Rinaldi. But they killed you in the end. You could count on that.
> Stay around and they would kill you (*Farewell*, p. 327).

As Hemingway's style reflects his ironic vision in the simultaneous treatment of cosmic and objective reality, it ultimately seeks to define a new reality—a reality of transcendence. In this new mode of experience the cosmic, infinite, and spiritual merge with the objective, finite, and material. The material-objective world may be seen as prefiguring a spiritual-subjective world. With his new language, his new perception (i.e., his style) Hemingway attempted to comprehend the inchoate metaphysical experience of modern man.

As already noted, the most significant feature of Hemingway's style is the evocation of a poignant sense of objective reality. At the same time the style imparts to the narrative a feeling of immediacy which interpenetrates the perception of the hero with that of the reader. The simple syntax, the bare description, and the unreflective mode are at once unobtrusive and potent. The reader is not only placed closer to the experience by being given only essential, undistracting details, but is, in fact, also forced to assume the viewpoint of the protagonist. Hemingway's practice of leaving out certain information which he hoped would "strengthen the story and make people feel something more than they understand,"[13] essentially draws the reader further out of his world into the world of the novel. The effect is often cinematic. The continuous, simultaneous perception of the protagonist can be likened to a camera's:

> He pulled back the blanket from the Indian's head. His hand came away wet. He mounted on the edge of the lower bunk with the lamp in one hand and looked in. The Indian lay with his face toward the wall. His throat had been cut from ear to ear. The blood had flowed down into a pool where his body sagged the bunk. His head rested on his left arm. The open razor lay, edge up, in the blankets.[14]

William Gifford cites the identification of points of view in Hemingway's style and observes that because it "overbears unbelief" it "produces the mood of heroic narrative."[15]

In the chaotic and destructive universe death is the only certainty. Horological time, death's agent, propels man toward nothingness. Only by going outside of horological time, by transcending conventional notions of time and space, can man attain immortality. In the objective-material world a quasi-

---

[13] *A Moveable Feast*, p. 75.

[14] *In Our Time* (New York: Charles Scribner's Sons, 1925), p. 20.

[15] William Gifford, "Ernest Hemingway: The Monsters and the Critics," *Modern Fiction Studies*, XIV (Autumn 1968), p. 262.

immortality is to be found in certain moments of special illumination. It is for these moments of grace that the Hemingway hero lives. In his preoccupation with courage, expertise, and freedom he tries to wrest control of his life from the twin specters of chaos and death. The fear of death enslaves man to horological time and the objective-material world. Only when he transcends the fear of death can man transcend his mortality.

Earl Rovit has written of the extraordinary moments of illumination in Hemingway's aesthetic.

> Revelation or illumination can be understood as an experience of *Gestalt* perception in which all disconnected fragments of experience (conscious and subliminal) cohere with a suddenness and completeness that is involuntary, compelling, and frequently termed "ecstatic." The experience has often been described in terms of mystical transport and transcendental elevation . . . and has traditionally been associated with the intense emotion that aesthetic contemplation is able to offer under unique and rare circumstances . . .[16]

Hemingway's narrative technique aims to impart to the prose the deep texture and brilliant glow of the true aesthetic experience. The singular achievement of this style is that it presents at once a sense of immediacy and permanence. When one reads such lines as "I looked back and saw her standing on the steps. She waved and I kissed my hand and held it out. She waved again and then I was out of the driveway . . .," or "Brett came over with her wrap on. She kissed the count and put her hand on his shoulder to keep him from standing up. As we went out the door I looked back and there were three girls at his table" (*Reader*, p. 139) one feels as if something extraordinary has just happened to him. The impressions are etched in the mind as with a hot needle and for a short breath the reader is transported out of horological time into the abiding aesthetic world of the narrative. Thus Hemingway's style ultimately merges the perceptions of the reader and protagonist

---

[16] Rovit, p. 134.

and places them both, while the experience lasts, in a state of metaphysical grace.

I have tried in this paper to describe certain aspects of Hemingway's style and to illustrate how that style locates Hemingway in the tradition of modern metaphysical writers. Hemingway's stylistic efforts were aimed from the beginning at the creation of a new language in fiction. The old order passed away with the war and the new age required its own expression. In his rejection of abstractions, his dogged pursuit of a simple, limpid description of objective reality, Hemingway broke the barriers of the old conventions and coined a new language. That language, as Gifford observed, created a heroic mood which accompanied the struggle of the Hemingway hero for freedom and meaning in a nihilistic cosmic order. At its best, Hemingway's style captured the state of grace that occurs when, leaving the realms of time and space, man glimpses a vision of the infinite goodness of God.

Richard Lehan

HEMINGWAY AMONG THE MODERNS

I mean my title literally. I am concerned with the way Hemingway is a modern writer—or more specifically how he can be related to his immediate contemporaries. Let me begin by suggesting that something was happening in the early part of the twentieth century that led to a shared sense of consciousness which is inextricably connected with the idea of the modern. I think of Henry Adams at the turn of the century differentiating between the Virgin and the dynamo, between a centripetal and centrifugal universe, between the ordered and the fragmented self. Adams believed that the imagination was the source of cultural order. He did not believe literally in the Virgin Mary but saw her instead as a historical extension of the pagan goddess, all related biologically to the idea of the queen bee, a subject he was reading about when he wrote his famous chapter on the Virgin in the *Education*. Adams maintained that it was the *idea* of the Virgin which gave unity to the twelfth century, which brought religion and political order, and which allowed the individual a frame of ordering reference outside himself. According to Adams, modern man had lost a synthesizing mythology and no longer had the means to shore his fragments against ruin. The dynamo had replaced the Virgin, the city (Boston) the town (Quincy), the money manipulators (State Street) the landed gentry (the class to which he believed he and his distinguished ancestors belonged). Moreover, the Virgin was a product of the imagination while the machine existed outside the mind and fed on natural resources for its fuel and was thus doubly capable of destroying modern man—first, by changing the structure of society

191

from agrarian to industrial; second, by exhausting natural resources, leaving man the entropic victim of a wasteland. Adams located the high point of western culture in the twelfth century. Like Adams, Ezra Pound also saw the ideal in the distant past, in his case fifteenth-century Italy with its city-states that encouraged both the great artists and the craftsmen. Venice was his ideal city; like Aphrodite it had emerged from the sea and embodied, in its design and architecture, a historical moment of heightened awareness and consummate skill. The Quincy of John and John Quincy Adams was also on Pound's list of ideal places in the tableau of history because it represented a turning away from the then corrupted cities of Europe and marked a new beginning in a new world. However, this dream was also corrupted by the usurers, a point which finds Pound and Henry Adams in complete agreement, and which explains why the Adams family plays such an important part in the *Cantos*. Pound firmly believed that the values of the past could be both isolated and perpetuated, and the *Cantos* are his attempt to write a redeeming history: to drive out the villains (Hamilton and Roosevelt, for example) and to extol the heroes (Jefferson and Mussolini).

While T. S. Eliot never went as politically far as Pound, Eliot also believed in a redeeming tradition, that (in the spirit of Matthew Arnold) we could recognize what was best thought and said in the past and perpetuate it in the present. *The Waste Land* is an attempt to contrast an idealized past with the burnt-out present, an attempt to shore the fragments of the self against ruin. Eliot reached the dead end of his doubt in "The Hollow Men," and then turned from Frazer and the possibility of a redeeming myth to the Church, not simply to the myth of the Virgin, but to the institution that preserved the myth, an unusual step for a modern writer.

William Carlos Williams had little respect for the poet Eliot. He felt that both Eliot and Pound had contaminated modern poetry by aligning it with not just the tradition of a past poetry, but of a European past. Williams did not object to the idea of mythology, but he was concerned that it be an American myth. In his introduction to "Kora in Hell," he called Pound a traitor to American poetry; and in his *Autobiography*, he refers to *The Waste Land* as "the great catastrophe of our letters." He continued: "Critically Eliot returned us to the classroom just at the moment when I felt that we were on the point of an escape to matters much closer to the essence of a new art form itself—rooted in the locality which gave it fruit." *In the American Grain* was Williams' attempt to define a usable American tradition, and *Paterson* was the poem in which his ideas were applied. He depicted the land betrayed, the river polluted, all in the name of commerce and industry. Language had also become polluted: speech fails the inhabitants. Man must turn inward, toward the land, and allow the imagination to recreate reality, to penetrate to the meaning of things and lift them up from the polluted world.

In Pound, Eliot, and Williams, we have three modern writers trying to find a substitute for Henry Adams' Virgin—Pound in the meaning of the fifteenth century, Eliot in a classical tradition, and Williams in a return to American roots. The common denominator is the attempt to pick up the pieces, to restore the fragments shattered by the crisis of lost faith in the era following the war of political disillusionment. We know that Hemingway admired Pound as a kind of literary maestro, even if the *Cantos* were an enigma to him. We also know that he had much less respect for Eliot, upsetting Ford Madox Ford by writing in the *transatlantic* that if he could bring Joseph Conrad back to life "by grinding Mr. Eliot into a fine dry powder and sprinkling that powder over Conrad's grave in Canterbury," he would "leave for London early tomorrow morning with a sausage-grinder." What Hemingway thought of Williams is more problematic. He certainly would be more sympathetic to him than toward Eliot, and probably Pound as well. For one, they shared a dislike of Eliot. Second, Williams did not want to locate a series of abstract ideals in a European literary past. Third, Williams wanted a mythology based on things; he believed in the need to move from objects to ideas ("no ideas but in things"), from experience to conceptualization, and he was thus suspect of universal and abiding truths. But Williams believed in a residual pattern of local experience, and here he would lose Hemingway. Hemingway rejected all traditions, literary and historical, in an attempt to return to fundamentals—to the essential cycle of life and death in its purest forms, such as one can experience on the big-game hunt or in the bullring. In *The Torrents of Spring,* Hemingway is especially hard on the idea that there is a romantic tradition of history which can vitalize the individual or that a literature of the land can substitute for the land itself. Ruth Suckow becomes the object of satire here, but Hemingway's scorn could also apply to Sherwood Anderson and William Carlos Williams:

> Workmen were coming home from the factory. Scripps's bird singing in its cage. Diana looking out of the open window. Diana watching for her Scripps to come up the street. Could she hold him? Could she hold him? If she couldn't hold him, would he leave her his bird? She had felt lately that she couldn't hold him. In the nights, now, when she touched Scripps he rolled away, not toward her. It was a little sign, but life was made up of little signs. She felt she couldn't hold him. As she looked out of the window, a copy of *The Century Magazine* dropped from her nerveless hand. *The Century* had a new editor. There were more woodcuts. Glenn Frank had gone to head some great university somewhere. There were more Van Dorens on the magazine. Diana felt that might turn the trick. Happily she had opened *The Century* and read all morning. Then the wind, the warm chinook wind, had started to blow, and she knew Scripps would soon be home. Men were coming down the street in increasing numbers. Was Scripps among them? She did not like to put on her spectacles to look. She wanted Scripps's first glimpse of her to be of her at her best. As she felt him drawing nearer, the confidence she had had in *The Century* grew fainter. She had so hoped that would give her the something which would hold him. She wasn't sure now.
>
> Scripps coming down the street with a crowd of excited workmen. Men stirred by the spring. Scripps swinging his lunch-bucket. Scripps waving good-by to the workmen, who trooped one by one into what had formerly been a saloon. Scripps not looking up at the window. Scripps coming up the stairs. Scripps coming nearer. Scripps coming nearer. Scripps here.

"Good afternoon, dear Scripps," she said. I've been reading a story by Ruth Suckow."

"Hello, Diana," Scripps answered. He set down his lunchpail. She looked worn and old. He could afford to be polite.

"What was the story about, Diana?" he asked.

"It was about a little girl in Iowa," Diana said. She moved toward him. "It was about people on the land. It reminded me a little of my own Lake Country."

"That so?" asked Scripps. In some ways the pump-factory had hardened him. His speech had become more clipped. More like these hardy Northern workers'. But his mind was the same.

"Would you like me to read a little of it out loud?" Diana asked. "They're some lovely woodcuts."

"How about going down to the beanery?" Scripps said.

Hemingway could reject Sherwood Anderson's vitalistic views because they sentimentalized modern man by connecting him with a kind of lost primitive racial energy (cf. especially *Dark Laughter*). The problem for Hemingway was more basic: man had become too far removed from the land and had put too many false myths between him and primal experience. In this context, Anderson's sentimental primitivism was just barely better than the stultifying puritanism which dried up the soul. We see this in the story "Soldier's Home" in the character of Krebs, who returns from the war to the spiritual death of a home he can no longer accept. Even the jockey in "My Old Man" is in Europe because "everything went on the bum" in the United States. America was not going to be saved by Anderson's mystical primitivism or by burned-out religions. The problem was physical, not metaphysical, and could not be separated from the history of the land.

In *Green Hills of Africa*, Hemingway expressed more clearly than he ever had before his theory about how a civilization decays when it moves too far away from the meaning of the land:

A continent ages quickly once we come. The natives live in harmony with it. But the foreigner destroys, cuts down the trees, drains the water, so that the water supply is altered and in a short time the soil, once the sod is turned under, is cropped out and, next, it starts to blow away as it has blown away in every old country and as I had seen it start to blow in Canada. The earth gets tired of being exploited. A country wears out quickly unless man puts back in it all his residue and that of all his beasts. When he quits using beasts and uses machines, the earth defeats him quickly. The machine can't reproduce, nor does it fertilize the soil, and it eats what he cannot raise. A country was made to be as we found it. We are the intruders and after we are dead we may have ruined it but it will still be there and we don't know what the next changes are. I suppose they all end up like Mongolia.

He then applies the general lesson to the condition of modern America:

Our people went to America because that was the place to go then. It had been a good country and we had made a bloody mess of it and I would go, now, somewhere else as we had always had the right to go somewhere else and as we had always gone. You could always come back. Let the others come to America who did not know that they had come too late. Our people had seen it at its best and fought for it when it was well worth fighting for. Now I would go somewhere else.

"Now I would go somewhere else." This was Hemingway's farewell to America, even though he did eventually return to the American West, which he thought of as different from the rest of the country. This is also Hemingway's farewell to the twentieth century, because the places which are left to go are places untouched by civilization. The search is for a kind of pre-time world, a journey back to the earth from which we came and to which we will return. Only the earth abides. In *The Sun Also Rises*, Hemingway let this biblical idea serve as an answer to Gertrude Stein's remark, "You are all a lost generation." Modern man is lost because he has lost contact with first things. Man is at the dead end of his culture because his being has no core. Along with Pound, Eliot, and Williams, he could accept the idea that the mythic imagination was dead. But unlike Pound and Eliot, he did not turn to the historical past of Europe for a prototype of lost values. And unlike Williams, he did not turn to American history for those lost values. Hemingway abandoned the idea of the romantic self and historical vitality and turned instead to an idea of pre-history— to a belief in residual, primitive values that are inextricable from the rhythms of life and death and the land. In his attack upon intellect, in his attempt to destroy the old literary myths, in his rejection of fixed social decorum, in his exaltation of the senses, in his simple restlessness and the desire for unencumbered experience, Hemingway anticipated today's cult of youth. In rejecting the literary frames of reference of Pound, Eliot, and Williams, Hemingway was also demythologizing modern literature. He was, to put this differently, rejecting all patterns of continuity—historical or literary—which took precedence over the self.

As I have suggested above, *The Sun Also Rises* addresses these questions directly. We begin with a world in fragments. The war has ended, and Europe is still in shock. We see the old aristocracy as dead with Lady Brett embodying the purposelessness and moral abandonment of that class. Mike Campbell, from a well-to-do bourgeoise family, represents the decline of that class both morally (he lives a parasitical life of almost complete abandonment) and financially (he has become soft, loses his business to a corrupt partner, and is literally bankrupt). Count Mippipopolous appears as a vital contrast between a heroic past and a shabby present. Even though he is of nobility, the Count was a man of his people, was wounded by arrow in Abyssinia, and has a sense of taste based on true experience. But the Count, who now owns a string of sweetshops in America, has lost contact with his land; his rootlessness makes him fit company for the expatriates. As Brett puts it, "he is one of us." Whatever was the source of the Count's vitality, it is now lost—and new sources seem totally lacking. "You haven't any values. You're dead, that's all," Brett tells the Count; and while this verdict is not confirmed, the novel does suggest that the wellspring of the Count's existence has been dried up and that a source of new vitality needs to be found.

This, without his really being able to articulate it, seems to be the mission Jake Barnes is bent upon. He is far from awed by the Count's and Brett's social credentials, sees Mike as pathetic, and is cut off by the wound from the routine of middle-class life, as illustrated by his experience with Woolsey and Krum, the two journalists with whom he rides in the taxi. While the novel does not discuss it at length, Jake is also cut off from a domesticized life in America, just as Krebs was in "Soldier's Home." I do not think that we need to make Jake into Frazer's Fisherking who has suffered an emasculating wound and who must die—or at least suffer—if the society is to be made whole. As I have already suggested, Hemingway does not turn to old myths for the answer but instead creates a new mythology out of the elemental. It is, I think, significant that the only moments Jake finds peace in the novel come when he is with a close friend and peasants, fishing the clear, cold streams of the Irati River in Spain; or when he has been washed clean of the fiesta by the sea of San Sebastian. These scenes stand in direct contrast to a disrupted Europe—to the neon-lit scenes in Paris; the drunken, frenetic activity at the Pamplona fiesta; even to the scene at the end with Brett in Madrid when Jake finally accepts his condition and seems capable of going on in the face of it. As Jake and Bill drive from Pamplona to Burguete, they see high in the mountains the castle Roncevaux, and suddenly we have two worlds superimposed on each other: the simplicity of peasant Spain and the elaborate romance of Roland, whose story is inextricably connected with the castle. So also the novel superimposes upon the jaded scenes in Paris and Pamplona the clean, simple activity of Burguete and San Sebastian. The first scenes seem to partake of death, the second of life; the first are connected with a dying order, the second with the elemental and primitive.

And the man who embodies the elemental and primitive in the novel is, of course, Pedro Romero. But he also participates in the dialectical between the primitive and the corrupt because he is vulnerable to the charms of Brett, who is kind of a modern Circe, an inversion of Adams' Virgin since she fragments rather than coalesces the group. Romero is a living link in a ritual that takes its origin from the earth's cycle of life and death. Hemingway once said that he became interested in bullfighting because it seemed to him the most elemental of acts. In *Death in the Afternoon*, he elaborated when he said that bullfighting gave him the "feeling of life and death that I was looking for." While the bullfight is going on, he continued, "I . . . have a feeling of life and death and mortality and immortality, and after it is over I feel very sad but very fine." Pedro Romero thus becomes the high priest in the most fundamental of rituals.

In contrast to Romero is, of course, Robert Cohn, who lives in terms of the old mythologies. He believes in courtly love (remember the Castle Roncevaux in the far distance) and "does battle for his lady fair." All his values are derivative, coming not from experience but from his reading. He wants to go to South America because he read W. H. Hudson's *The Purple Land*, and he dislikes Paris because he read Mencken. While Jake and Bill Gorton respond excitedly to the beautiful Spanish terrain, Cohn sleeps on the car trip from Bayonne to Pamplona. He has idealized Brett beyond reality and refuses to compromise his romantic conception of her.

Hemingway scorned the romantic vision in any form because it meant that one was living once removed from a direct sense of experience. This is why he was so fond of Huckleberry Finn, who had an elemental faith in the truths of experience, as opposed to Tom Sawyer, who got his ideas from books. If one could excise the ending of *Huckleberry Finn*—that is, the needless stratagems that Tom employs to satisfy his romantic conception of what Jim's rescue should be—then all modern American literature comes from *Huckleberry Finn,* or so Hemingway tells us in *Green Hills of Africa.* In accepting Huck and rejecting Tom, Hemingway turns to Sancho Panzo over Don Quixote, endorses the man of the earth over the man of imagination. It is for this reason that Hemingway can also scorn F. Scott Fitzgerald's Jay Gatsby, who really has much in common with Robert Cohn, since both have an uncompromising imaginative conception of a woman, one that is completely divorced from experience. While Fitzgerald portrayed the romantic dreamer as victim, he never condemned the dream, even as Hemingway chided him for exalting the rich and confusing growing old with growing up. But the differences between the two men were more profound—indeed, they were the differences of two totally opposed world views. Fitzgerald believed in a genteel tradition, believed in the old courtesies, as he called them, which could be handed down from generation to generation so long as there was a sense of honor and romance. Perhaps, like Robert Cohn, that is what Fitzgerald learned at Princeton. In any event, Hemingway would have none of it. In rejecting Cohn he rejected all men who live once removed from an elemental sense of experience—which is to say, a sense of life and death.

A Farewell to Arms makes use of the same ideas. The novel depicts the elemental rhythms of life—love, childbirth, and death. The novel expressly depicts what happens when these elemental matters are romanticized and endowed with a meaning that is not true to the self-contained nature of the cycle. To this extent, *A Farewell to Arms* is a study of two-fold disillusionment—Lt. Henry's disillusionment first with war, then with love.

Lt. Henry goes off to war as if it were a meaningful, romantic enterprise that can and will change the nature of the modern world. He thinks of his own part in the war as necessary and indispensable, until he returns from his first leave and is slightly shaken to find that all has gone well without him: "Evidently it did not matter whether I was there or not," he reluctantly concludes. His confidence in the romantic meaning of war is even more greatly shaken when he is wounded—not heroically, but while seemingly safely behind the lines as he eats a piece of cheese and drinks wine. This absurd wound defies rational understanding, forces Henry to accept his own vulnerability, and drives him to first causes. This frame of mind becomes intensified in the retreat from Caporetto when he is almost shot as a German infiltrator by the mindless battle police. Afer that he had "no more obligaticn" to other men's wars, only to himself and those values which he can test with his own sense of experience.

While Lt. Henry moves from a romantic to a cynical notion of war, he moves from a cynical to a romantic notion of love.

When he first meets Catherine Barkley he cannot take her seriously. She is beautiful, and he would rather have her than the prostitutes at the officer's club. "I knew I did not love Catherine Barkley nor had any idea of loving her," he tells us. "This was a game, like bridge." Such cynicism quickly gives way as Catherine nurses him in the hospital after his wounding. There she conceives his child. The absolutes of love are suddenly substituted for the absolutes of war. When Catherine dies at the end of the novel, Henry is thus deprived of all absolutes, and suddenly he is thrown back to an understanding of first things—that there is no escape from the rhythm of life and death: "They killed you in the end. You could count on that. Stay around and they would kill you."

There is no bullfighter or big-game hunter in this novel who turns this truth into ritual. We do have, however, a sense of place which serves the same purpose. The Abruzzi, for example, "where the roads were frozen and hard as iron, where it was clear cold and dry and the snow was dry and powdery and hare-tracks in the snow and the peasants took off their hats and called you Lord and there was good hunting." But Henry, to his regret, does not go to the Abuzzi because at this point in the novel he has been unable to differentiate between the real and the ersatz. What he is looking for, of course, is a moment in pre-history where he can be out of time in rhythm with the elemental. He and Catherine do find that moment in the mountains high above Montreux. There they spend the winter, before they come back to the big city, Lausanne, where Catherine dies in childbirth.

As in the fishing scene in *The Sun Also Rises*, the scene with Catherine in the mountains, with its simplicity of meaning, stands in stark contrast to the madness of the world outside. As Henry puts it, "It was lovely in bed with the air so cold and clear and the night outside the window. We slept well. . . . [and] the war seemed . . . far away."

The retreat to the mountains is for the Hemingway hero what the journey back to the classical past is for the personae of Pound and Eliot. But whereas Pound and Eliot wanted to return to classical values, Hemingway wanted to return to elemental values. In both cases, the writer is putting his land in order, is seeking a redeeming perspective. In *A Farewell to Arms*, as much as any novel Hemingway wrote, he rejects history for the primacy of the self, rejects what is extrinsic to personal experience. This is clearly shown in the exchange with Count Greffi, who tells Henry that he thought *Mr. Britling Sees Through It* "a very good study of the English middle-class soul." Henry responds, "I don't know about the soul," a word that must surely embarrass him as much as the other abstract words he hates, like "sacred," "glorious," "sacrifice," died not "in vain." "I had seen nothing sacred," he says, "and the things that were glorious had no glory and the sacrifices were like the stockyards at Chicago if nothing was done with the meat except bury it." Everything returns to the earth from which it sprang, and the earth—the rhythm of life and death—is the primal hero in Hemingway's fiction.

In *To Have and Have Not* Hemingway explicitly contrasts the elemental man with a sick society that destroys him, and this novel is Hemingway's most expressed attack on America and modern culture. The rhythms of life and death play an important part in *To Have and Have Not*. The novel begins in the spring and ends in winter; during that time the elemental man, Harry Morgan, has been destroyed in a world that reeks of sickness and death. At the beginning of the novel we see Harry in contrast to Mr. Johnson, who skips town owing Harry $825, including the cost of the fishing equipment he lost. In the middle of the novel we see Harry in contrast to Richard Gordon, a popular novelist whose ideas are always commercially fashionable. At the end of the novel we see Harry in contrast to the wealthy yacht owners who live off stocks and bonds or the interest of inherited money. What we see are people living at various levels of abstraction; those who live most abstractly—who can manipulate shares, trusts, holding companies, and subsidiary corporations—make the most money. But since they live the furthest from the elemental—the earth and the sea—they are also the weakest physically, like the unnamed millionaire who "was now lying in a pair of striped silk pajamas that covered his shrunken old man's chest, his bloated little belly, his now useless and disproportionately large equipment that had once been his pride, and his small flabby legs, lying on a bed unable to sleep because he finally had remorse." What makes this world so bleak is that there seems no possibility of changing it. The revolutionists who rob the band in order to get money for the cause also function at a level of contradictory abstraction, murdering a working man in order to get money to help the working class.

Harry Morgan, the last of the primitives, is as able to live in the modern world as is a fish out of water. One man alone has no chance, he tells us; and his death is as inevitable as the decline of the seasons against which the story is told. Hemingway does not even allow him momentary escape—into the mountains of Spain or Switzerland as he did Jake Barnes and Lt. Henry. Harry must confront life in the twentieth century head on; he does not escape history but succumbs to it. In *To Have and Have Not,* admittedly one of his poorest novels, Hemingway sacrificed his mythic hero and left him unredeemed. And the story of Harry Morgan cannot be separated from the stories of Francis Macomber and the writer Harry in "The Snows of Kilimanjaro." The pattern of Harry Morgan's story is, in fact, reversed in the story of Francis Macomber. When Francis Macomber went to Africa, he was as morally sick as the wealthy yacht owners in *To Have and Have Not.* He is the American boy-man, spoiled by the good life, dominated by women like Margo Macomber, "the hardest, the cruelest, the most predatory" of women, so that like other American men, he had "softened or gone to pieces nervously as they hardened." Moreover, a good many of Macomber's ideas have come from books, "many books, too many books." Macomber is indeed a slightly older version of Robert Cohn. But Hemingway reverses his fate, and he does so by exposing Macomber to the primitive, by allowing him to confront death in the form of the charging lion, at which point Macomber flees in terror. But the experience strips him of all illusions and gives him a new model of self that had previously been beyond his imaginative reckoning. Macomber's experience is a form of demythologizing, of shedding an old self for a new one. Like an upper-class Huck Finn, he intuits the falsity of his past values and rejects the corrupting influence of civilization for the primitive vitality of the big-game hunt with its life-and-death consequences. Once he has participated in this ritual, once he has substituted the meaning of Africa for the meaning of America, he will never be the same again, a fact that Margo Macomber intuits when she aims at the buffalo and blows her husband's brains out.

A similar kind of transformation befalls the writer Harry as he is dying of gangrene in "The Snows of Kilimanjaro." Like Richard Gordon in *To Have and Have Not*, Harry has pandered his talents as a writer. He has lived off his wife's wealth, and the many compelling stories about life and death he had to tell went unwritten. Unlike the leopard that was found near the top of Kilimanjaro, he lived safely and settled for being less than a man by refusing to admit that there was a realm of experience beyond the safe and conventional limits he had set for himself. His realization comes too late, accompanied as it is by the cry of the hyena, which becomes a call to death. Both of these Hemingway heroes are transformed by Africa itself, by contact with the elemental that forces them to see anew from the perspective of a lost past.

For Whom the Bell Tolls might appear to be the one novel that cannot be reconciled with my thesis that, as a primitivist, Hemingway rejected the modern world and reduced all values to those that could be reconciled with the elemental. Robert Jordan seems to address himself to the historical moment when he goes to Spain to fight the Royalists. But it is a mistake to interpret this in political terms. Jordan tells Maria that he is not a Communist but rather an anti-fascist. Hemingway is very clear about why he fights in Spain: "He fought now in this war because it had started in a country that he loved and he believed in the Republic and that if it were destroyed life would be unbearable for all those people who believed in it." He fights, that is, because he is committed to the Spanish land that he loves and to the peasants whose way of life is threatened. As Allen Guttmann has pointed out, Hemingway believed the Spanish Civil War came at a pivotal moment in history, that it was a conflict between two ways of life, and that the whole agrarian nature of Spain was being threatened by the machine. This is why the bombers are so menacingly described:

> But these, wide-finned in silver, roaring, the light mist of their propellors in the sun, these do not move like sharks. They move like no thing there has ever been. They move like mechanized doom.

Many of the Leftist critics did not think that Hemingway portrayed the Communist officers and their cause sympathetically enough, and they were right. Hemingway hated the Communist mentality and saw it as part of the problem, a fact that can be documented by the conversation between Jordan and General Golz who fights the war at the highest level of abstraction. Hemingway's real sympathy is with peasants, and the peasants of both sides, with whom the future of Spain must reside. His sympathy is with a character like Anselmo who will die for his love of the land; with Pilar whose motherly strength comes from the land; and even with Pablo who knows how to talk to the horses. All of these people live off the land—simply, cleanly, elementally; and their very existence is being threatened by the encroaching modern world with its machine guns, tanks, and bombers. The transition in their character is already under way, as we can observe from watching Pablo; and Hemingway seemed to know that both the land and the peasants would never be the same again. *For Whom the Bell Tolls* begins and ends with Robert Jordan lying on the brown, pine-needled floor of the Spanish mountains, his heart beating against the earth. The novel takes place within seventy hours, analogous to the seventy years of life the Bible gives us. Robert Jordan dies, and the earth endures. But will the values of the earth endure? In *Green Hills of Africa*, Hemingway told us that once a country's land was ruined he would go somewhere else. But he was running out of places to go, and the death of Robert Jordan marks for him the death of Spain. In a sense, Jordan's death is to Hemingway what the passing of the Virgin was to Henry Adams. In both instances a way of life vanishes and man is left facing mechanized doom.

Across the River and Into the Trees seems like a most drastic departure from Hemingway's earlier narrative pattern. Some critics feel that Hemingway wrote it to show off, to prove that he knew his art history and that he could order the very best wine. Perhaps they come to that interpretation because they cannot make much out of the novel. The plot is not complex. Colonel Cantwell revisits Venice where he shoots ducks in the marshes, eats and drinks in the Gritti Hotel, and makes love to the nineteen-year-old Contessa Renata. All the while he anticipates his own death, which comes on the last pages. Yet a closer look at the novel reveals that Hemingway was once again contrasting two kinds of worlds. It is important to remember that Hemingway was working on this novel concurrently with *The Old Man and the Sea*. As a city, Venice sprang from the sea. It is an elemental city that has been made into a monument of western civilization. The old Venice has participated in the cycles of life and death, victory and defeat, and it has the ability to endure in the face of the elements. The Colonel loves this city, which he connects with his wounding in battle, and the sense of completing a cycle of life brings the Colonel back to Venice. The almost holy nature of the experience is revealed at the hotel by the meeting of the Colonel and the Grand Master:

> the Colonel extended his own hand which had been shot through twice, and was slightly misshapen. Thus contact was made between two old inhabitants of the Veneto, both men, and brothers in their membership in the human race, the only club that either one paid dues to, and brothers, too, in their love of an old country, much fought over, and always triumphant in defeat, which they had both defended in their youth.

Across the River and Into the Trees is to Hemingway what the *Education* was to Henry Adams. The whole point of the story is to contrast the old with the new, a narrative plan easily accommodated since a fifty-one-year-old colonel spends much of his time reminiscing with the nineteen-year-old Contessa. What emerges from these pages is a sense of the old world that has been lost. But as great as Venice is as a monument, it is still inferior to the earth, which has its final claim on the Colonel. Before he arrives in Venice, the Colonel visits Fossalta, and there "relieved himself in the exact place where he had determined, by triangulation, that he had been badly wounded thirty years before." Before he leaves, the Colonel also buries a ten thousand lira note in the earth. Thus the Colonel, who has given to the earth his blood, now gives also a token of his body and his earthly goods. The earth is the real God in Hemingway's fiction, and in this scene we see a Hemingway character praying at its altar. No other scene in the Hemingway canon reveals so clearly the priority of the elemental. All things come from the earth and sea, including man and his monuments (which means the city of Venice itself), and to the earth and sea all will return. Hemingway shared his adoration of Venice with Ezra Pound, who saw the city as a lasting monument to the Renaissance of western culture. In contrasting Venice with its elemental origins, Hemingway reversed Pound's priorities and revealed the basic difference between their cultural views.

In all his novels Hemingway questioned the very meaning of civilization. His characters are cut off from the wellspring of life, except for an occasional moment when, like Jake Barnes, they are able to make contact with the elemental. But the moment is fleeting. The city calls—Paris and then Madrid in *The Sun Also Rises,* Lausanne in *A Farewell to Arms;* or the establishment intervenes, as in *To Have and Have Not;* or the hero becomes a victim of men of abstractions, as with Robert Jordan in *For Whom the Bell Tolls.* Only in *The Old Man and the Sea* does Hemingway allow a character the unmediated experience, and the old man becomes the apotheosis of the Hemingway hero: his story summarizes the essential meaning of the canon. Here Hemingway eloquently describes the vital relationship between man and nature: the sea as the source of both life and death, as alive and vital as well as malignant and violent. The secrets and power of the sea are the secrets and powers of creation; it gives and it takes away without logic or reason. Santiago called the sea *la mer* and thought of her as a woman, "as feminine and as something that gave or withheld favors, and if she did wild or wicked things it was because she could not help them. The moon affects her as it does a woman, he thought." The sea which gave Santiago the marlin also gave him the sharks to take it away, and this ritual takes place "beyond all people in the world." What we have is an essential moment, a moment before time and yet of all time, a ritual that embodies the very structure of existence. Santiago and the marlin are locked in a sacred death struggle, a holy union, fixed within the boundaries of human and animal endurance, a struggle that makes them "brothers" and binds them in a ritual as old as Cain and Abel. What we see is the grand cycle of life and death, or as Santiago puts it, "everything kills everything else in some way. Fishing kills me exactly as it keeps me alive." The understanding between man and the marlin is violated by the sharks which bring gratuitous destruction, as gratuitous as Lt. Henry's wounding or Aymo's death in *A Farewell to Arms*, or as gratuitous as Harry Morgan's losing his arm in *To Have and Have Not*.

Such gratuity is part of the ritual of life and death too. Man will triumph and be defeated. He can participate in the essential conflict with a sense of the ritual that binds Santiago and the marlin into holy brotherhood, or he can participate in the ritual with the glutinous abandonment of the sharks. It is significant that the tourists at the end of the novel confuse the marlin for a shark. Hemingway alone among modern writers based his novels on the architectonic assumption that the process by which life gives way to death can be ritualized. He is singular in trying not only to depict the contract that man has with death but how man can turn that contract into a way of life.

The Old Man and the Sea is a story of man alone with the sea, experiencing the architectonic moment, participating in the universal struggle, confronting death and inflicting it, refusing to give up when he is defeated, and triumphing in spirit over his surroundings. This is the primal triumph, and behind it is the urge which sent Santiago deep into the sea and the leopard high into the Kilimanjaro. It is the urge to stay in touch with first things and to test one's very being against its limits. This urge kept Hemingway in pursuit of the primitive landscape, where the ritual of life and death could be seen through the eyes of Santiago and not those of the tourists.

Contact with the elemental was important to Hemingway from the beginning to the end of his career because it brought a way of seeing, and this is a fundamental point in the understanding of his fiction. The way people see and mis-see in Hemingway's fiction is an essay in itself. Remember, for example, how Jake Barnes and Bill Gorton become so excited by what they see as they drive from Bayonne to Pamplona, while Robert Cohn sleeps. Cohn, as we have seen, is cut off from the elemental, has derived all his romantic ideas from books, is incapable of understanding the meaning of the bullfight, and moves about in a completely befuddled way. The well-to-do yacht owners in *To Have and Have Not* have lost the capacity for elemental vision, as has Richard Gorton who sees Harry's wife, Marie, and then misinterprets what he has seen. The tourists in *The Old Man and the Sea* see the marlin's skeleton and confuse it for a shark. And T/5 Jackson in *Across the River and Into the Trees* cannot see at all without the Colonel's help. He is the sad, tired American for whom St. Mark's Square and a MacDonald's hamburg stand are one and the same. While he shares his name with Stonewall Jackson, from whose saying Hemingway took the title of his book, he has nothing else in common with his namesake, and he reveals by contrast how diminished America has become in one hundred years.

The elemental experience also brings a kind of moral sight. Lt. Henry sees the absurdity of war after he has escaped from the battle police and is washed in the raging river. Harry Morgan sees the contradictions of the revolutionists who kill working men in the name of working men, as does Robert Jordan for those who live on the level of abstraction in *For Whom the Bell Tolls*. And Francis Macomber sees for a short and happy time after his African experience.

The Hemingway style was honed to portray a way of seeing. I mentioned above the passage in which Jake and Bill drive into Pamplona while Robert Cohn sleeps. It is a typical descriptive passage, abundant with predicate adjectives and participles which follow nouns:

> there was a big river off on the right shining in the sun from be-
> tween the lines of trees, and away off you could see the plateau
> of Pamplona rising out of the plain, and the walls of the city, and
> the great brown cathedral, and the broken skyline of the other
> churches. . . . We passed the bull ring, high and white and
> concrete-looking in the sun. . . . There was a crowd of kids
> watching the car, and the square was hot, and the trees were
> green, and the flags hung on their staffs, and it was good to get
> out of the sun and under the shade of the arcade that runs all the
> way around the square.

What we have here is the noun and then the response to the noun: "river . . . shining," "Pamplona . . . rising," "bull ring . . . high and white and concrete-looking," "square . . . hot," "trees . . . green," "flags . . . on their staffs." We have first the thing and then the response to the thing, usually in terms of its physical characteristic, but sometimes in terms of an emotion: "shade . . . good." It is impossible to think abstractly in this language; one is rooted to the concrete, to the elemental, to the here and now—a point of view that Hemingway's vision both encouraged and perpetuated. Hemingway's language is a way of seeing, and those who violate the strictures of the language—the Robert Cohns, the abstracted revolutionaries and generals, the sybaritic tourists—will mis-see and distort what is before them.

It would be comforting if I could conclude that Hemingway's elemental vision was the redeeming vision. Obviously it was not—neither for him nor for us. To be sure, the Hemingway hero who feels home close to nature has many noble attributes. He is a man of skill, whether it be in setting up a camp site or in fishing a trout stream; he gets tremendous satisfaction in doing a job well; he has a sense of fair play, a capacity to endure, an ability to go on in the face of defeat. But he loses as much as he gains. He lives in a loveless world, where the woman is a threat, trapping him as Catherine traps Lt. Henry, tormenting him as Lady Brett torments Jake, or dominating him the way Margo dominates Francis Macomber. The Hemingway hero is much happier with the boys, unless the woman happens to cut her hair short, wear men's clothes, and call everyone "chap." Love gives way to friendship—the almost sacred friendship that Jake and Bill seem to share in the mountains. But even this kind of relationship is tenuous, and the Hemingway hero ends up alone— like Jake, Lt. Henry, and Santiago; or dead—like Harry Morgan, Robert Jordan, and Colonel Cantwell. But even more distressing, the Hemingway hero is too often mindless. In his desire for the elemental, he lives on an intellectual plane not much beyond the animals. He is sensitive to good food and drink, appreciates the comforts of life, and takes great pride in his skills as hunter and fisherman; but he is intimidated by the city and by any kind of abstract system. He is a man out of time, in a world that will never be again. Whatever his virtues, they are not conducive to life in the twentieth century.

On final analysis, the primitive vision becomes a substitute for other kinds of equally arrogant stances, and the contradictions it allowed seems to prove the point. We have a Jake Barnes, for example, who dislikes the sentimentalism of a Robert Cohn who is restless and emotional; yet Jake himself is equally restless and emotional. Lt. Henry finds great fault with the way he is perfunctorily handled by the battle police, but does not think twice about perfunctorily killing the sergeant who will help him free his ambulance from the mud. Harry Morgan is rightfully scornful of Mr. Johnson, the inept sportsman, who cheats on his bill; but Harry thinks nothing of breaking Mr. Sing's neck and taking his money. The contradictions are completely summarized in the character of Thomas Hudson in the recently published *Islands in the Stream*. Hudson is arrogant and self-pitying, tough and sentimental, brave and anxious, disciplined and self-indulgent, confident and insecure, joyful and depressed, caught in the moment and capable of nostalgia, and confused about life's meaning and yet cruel to anyone who violates the laws of the self-styled code. To function on the level of the primitive may allow an unclouded vision of some things, but it does not save the Hemingway hero from fundamental contradictions that would make civilized life intolerable.

Albert Camus recognized this when he complained about the American "innocents" who live in a one-to-one way with nature. He saw this as a "degraded unity, a levelling off of human beings and of the world." Camus could and would not accept Hemingway's desire to escape from history. "Our task," he said, "is not to terminate [history] but to create it, in the image of what we henceforth know to be true." The vision must thus be compromised, as indeed must the very different visions of Hemingway's contemporaries. Hemingway was interested in a natural aristocracy outside of culture. He built a coherent fiction out of this notion—a fiction which can give us perspective on how far we have moved beyond and perhaps betrayed our primitive beginnings. If the Hemingway view cannot supply the answer, it does supply the question, and in that Hemingway does more for us than most of his contemporaries who also believed that we had need of a new beginning.

CONTRIBUTORS

BRENNER, GERRY. Associate Professor of English, University of Montana; published on Chaucer, Updike, Cooper, and Hemingway in such journals as *Twentieth Century Literature* and *Modern Fiction Studies*.

DeFALCO, JOSEPH M. Professor of English, Marquette University, author of *The Hero in Hemingway's Short Stories* (University of Pittsburgh Press, 1963); editor of the *Collected Poems of Christopher Pearse Cranch;* published on James, Frost, Whitman, Poe, and Thoreau in such journals as *Literature and Psychology* and *Studies in Short Fiction*.

FRIEDBERG, MICHAEL. Graduate student in English, University of Oregon; completing an M.A. with an emphasis in American Literature.

GRIFFITH, JOHN. Assistant Professor of English, University of Washington; published on Edwards, Franklin, Longfellow, James, MacLeish, and Malamud in such journals as *Texas Studies in Language and Literature, Arizona Quarterly,* and *The Journal of Narrative Technique*.

HAYS, PETER L. Associate Professor of English and Comparative Literature, University of California - Davis; author of *The Limping Hero* (New York University Press, 1971); published on Hemingway, Styron, Ellison, Melville, and Henry Miller in such journals as *Critique, Western Humanities Review,* and *Hemingway Notes*.

LEHAN, RICHARD. Professor and Chairman of the Department of English, University of California - Los Angeles; author of *F. Scott Fitzgerald and the Craft of Fiction* (1966), as well as books about Theodore Dreiser and French literary existentialism and the modern American novel; currently at work on a cultural history of modern American literature.

LEWIS, ROBERT W. Professor and Chairman of the Department of English, University of North Dakota; author of *Hemingway on Love* (University of Texas Press, 1965); published on Hemingway, Sinclair Lewis, and Cozzens in such journals as *The Texas Quarterly, College English,* and *Journal of Modern Literature*.

NORRIS, FAITH G. Professor of English, Oregon State University, author of children's stories on Japan and Korea; articles on Kipling, Brecht, and Feuchtwanger; co-editor of *Men in Exile,* an anthology of prison writings published by the Oregon State University Press in 1973.

PRATT, JOHN CLARK. Lt. Colonel and Professor of English, United States Air Force Academy; author of *The Meaning of Modern Poetry* (Doubleday, 1962), *John Steinbeck* (Eerdmans, 1970), The Viking Critical *One Flew Over the Cuckoo's Nest* (1973), and a novel entitled *The Laotian Fragments* to be published late in 1973 by the Viking Press.

WICKES, GEORGE. Professor of English and Comparative Literature, University of Oregon; Fulbright Lecturer and Visiting Professor at French universities; U.S.I.S. Lecturer, Europe; publications include *Americans in Paris* (Doubleday, 1969) and the *Durrell-Miller Correspondence* (Dutton, 1963); articles, interviews, and reviews have appeared in *Paris Review, New Republic,* and the *New York Times Book Review.*

WYLDER, DELBERT E. Professor and Chairman of the Department of English, Southwest Minnesota State College; author of *Hemingway's Heroes* (University of New Mexico Press, 1969), author of articles on William Eastlake, Edward Abbey, Emerson Hough, and Frederick Manfred in such journals as *South Dakota Review, Western Review,* and *New Mexico Quarterly.*

YOUNG, PHILIP. Research Professor of English and Fellow in the Institute for the Arts and Humanities, Pennsylvania State University; author of over 200 items on American writers; best known for works on Hemingway, Fulbright lecturer in France and Italy; frequent contributor to such journals as *The Kenyon Review, Sewanee Review,* and *Atlantic Monthly;* most recent book is *Three Bags Full: Essays in American Fiction* (Harcourt, 1972).

EDITORS

ASTRO, RICHARD. Associate Professor of English, Oregon State University; author of *John Steinbeck and Edward F. Ricketts: The Shaping of a Novelist* (University of Minnesota Press, 1973); co-editor of *Steinbeck: The Man and His Work* (Oregon State University Press, 1971); articles on Steinbeck, Hemingway, Norris, and Fitzgerald have appeared in such journals as *Modern Fiction Studies* and *Twentieth Century Literature.*

BENSON, JACKSON J. Associate Professor of English, California State University at San Diego; author of *Hemingway: The Writer's Art of Self-Defense* (University of Minnesota Press, 1969); published on Faulkner, Hemingway, and other figures in American literature in such journals as *Rendezvous* and *Twentieth Century Literature;* currently at work on a major biography of John Steinbeck.